AF531728

DEVELOPMENT, CARE AND EDUCATION OF PRE-SCHOOL CHILDREN

DEVELOPMENT, CARE AND EDUCATION OF PRE-SCHOOL CHILDREN

By

Aparajita Chowdhury
M.Sc., Ph.D, (Post-graduate)
Professor & Head
Department of Home Science
Berhampur University
Berhampur – 760 007
Odisha, (INDIA)

&

Rita Choudhury
M.A., Ph.D.
Head
Department of Home Science
Rama Devi Autonomous Women's College
Bhubaneswar – 751 022
Odisha, (INDIA)

D P H

DISCOVERY PUBLISHING HOUSE PVT. LTD.
NEW DELHI-110 002

Published by:

Namit Wasan

DISCOVERY PUBLISHING HOUSE PVT. LTD.

4383/4B, Ansari Road, Darya Ganj

New Delhi - 110 002 (India)

Phone : +91-11-23279245, 43596064-65

Fax : +91-11-23253475

E-mail : discoverypublishinghouse@gmail.com

namitwasan9@gmail.com

sales@discoverypublishinggroup.com

web : www.discoverypublishinggroup.com

***First Edition:* 2016**

ISBN: 978-93-5056-768-5

Development, Care and Education of Pre-school Children

Printed at:

Infinity Imaging Systems

Delhi

Preface

We are in the second decade of 21st century, with a vision for the children of the world: that every one of them – without exception – lives a full and healthy life, with rights secured and protected, free from poverty, violence and discrimination. With a commitment to spare no efforts in making sure that all infants start healthy, all young children are nurtured in caring environments, all children including the poorest and most disadvantaged, complete a basic education of good quality and all adolescents have the opportunity to develop fully and to participate in their societies. This is the call of the State of the World's Children 2000. In tune with the efforts for caring, protecting, and preserving the rights of children, this book is a humble attempt to help all children throughout the globe in making their dreams come true.

The book on 'Development, Care and Education of Pre-School Children' in this form was one of our desire to cater to the needs and requirements of all those who would like to educate and be educated in bringing healthy development in children. Both being academicians, researchers in the field of Human Development and Family Studies; mothers of two children each, our theoretical and practical knowledge, experiences and above all our special concern for young children – the most 'valuable human resource' and 'future citizens' of any country inspired us for this noble pursuit of academic manifestation in writing this book. It is highly essential to be more conscious, enlightened and competent enough as parents, teachers and or adults to understand the children, to provide them required guidance and support to face the later life successfully.

This book is the need of the time to reaffirm the significance of Early Childhood Years, its Development and Education.

Children are the most precious assets of any nation. A happy child is a symbol of the development of any society and the progress made by its mankind. The survival and development of children in a developing country like India is a great challenge. Hence, the future of any country depends on the attention that is provided at any given moment to its children. As it is rightly said that, "as the twig is bent, so will the tree grow". A happy and healthy childhood is the basis for a stable and strong adulthood. So apart from the right type of physical, emotional, social and mental care, proper guidance, assistance and opportunities are required for the wellbeing and development of children to their full potential. Hence, investing in children for their healthy growth and development has benefits for the children, for their parents, families and the society as a whole. Today's changing world has led to pressures of different nature that affect children's development. Increased urbanization, industrialization, women's education and employment pattern have all led to profound social changes in our family life in general and especially for the children in particular. Traditional Indian family structure and functions are changing as a result, often leaving women as the head of the households with dual responsibilities, such as:

- Bringing up their children without much familial or societal or Government support;
- Earning money to provide basic necessities for children and family.

All of these are set against a backdrop of global economic recession, uncertainty in every sphere of life that places an additional burden on parents and children already coping with various types of disadvantages. As individual families and communities search for creative and effective approaches to provide care and give attention to children's need, there are enough pressures on our government to introduce measures that will support these efforts. Early childhood and/or called preschool period are the time of opportunity for every individual in which even small positive changes can generate long-term benefit. Those benefits include: A healthier population that is better educated, better trained and equipped with, more able to obtain and keep productive employment. According to United Nations International Children's Emergency Fund (UNICEF), investing in early childhood programmes is one way of having impact on a wide range of social issues:

- Less wastage such as drop-out and repetition in the school system;
- Lower delinquency rates; and
- Lower expenditure on welfare and social services.

Considering these as the basis, this book has been written for the benefits of young parents, teachers, and child care workers, students of Home Science, Psychology, Social Work and Education disciplines, Nursery School teachers and for various voluntary organizations, policy planners and administrators, who are concerned and working for the development and welfare of young children. A key aspect of children's development is the right to be taken care and to get education on the basis of equal opportunity. The global community reaffirmed this right in 1990 at the World Conference on "Education for All" in Thailand. Since then not much has been done in India, for this most precious yet vulnerable section of the population. Understanding this particular group of children will not only be helpful to the parents, teachers and child care workers, but also be very much beneficial for the young would-be parents, policy makers and society in general. Hence, we hope that this book will achieve its goal and will serve the World of Children, with a vision of 'healthy and productive life' and with a commitment of 'development and progress........'

Authors

Acknowledgements

We would like to express our deep and heartfelt gratitude to God Almighty for HIS blessings bestowed on us to fulfill this work. Further, there are many more people in our lives without whose support and co-operation this book would never have seen the light of the day:

- Our friends, colleagues, well-wishers for their continued responsiveness to our needs and their positive feedback which have supported us in developing this simple presentation of such complex subject matter of great concern.
- To our family, who taught us to never give up.
- To Discovery Publishing House Pvt. Ltd., New Delhi for bringing this project for the second edition through to fruition.

Aparajita Chowdhury
Rita Choudhury

Contents

Contents

Pre-School Children

WHO ARE THE PRE-SCHOOLERS?

'So long as the little children are allowed to suffer, there is no true LOVE in this World'

Early childhood begins when the relative dependency of babyhood is over, and it extends from 2 to 6 years of age. Educators refer to early childhood years as the 'preschool age' to distinguish it from the time when children are considered old enough both physically and mentally, to cope with the work they will be expected to do when they begin their formal schooling. This period paves the way for effective learning and the child is prepared in all respects to profit from schooling.

To the psychologist, this age is considered as the 'Pre-gang age', the time when children are learning the foundations of social behaviour as a preparation for the more highly organised social life they will be required to adjust to when they enter the formal schooling. It is a time of rapid assimilation of new stimuli, experiences and ideas. It is the foundation for the child's personality development. Most parents consider these years (two to six years) as a 'problem age' or 'troublesome age', because behaviour problems become more frequent and more intense during this period. Children at this stage often becomes obstinate, stubborn, disobedient, negativistic, antagonistic in nature and have frequent temper – tantrums due to bad dreams at night, show irrational fears and suffer from jealousy. Because of these problems, early childhood seems a less appealing period and difficult to manage.

Having acquired a workable control of his own body during the first two years of life, the child is now ready to explore his environment. The major development occurring during early childhood years centres is on gaining control over the environment. Many psychologists refer these years as the 'exploratory age', a label which implies that children want to know what their environment is, how it works, how it feels, and how they can be a part of it. This includes people as well as inanimate objects present around. At no other time in the life span is imitation of speech and actions of others more pronounced than it is during early childhood years. For this reason it is also known as 'imitative age'. Children mostly imitate their same sex parents. Moreover, children show more creativity in their play during this period than at any other time in their lives. For this reason, psychologists also refer it as a 'creative age'. This is also termed as 'Period of Plasticity' as the impressions that are made on the child's mind at this point of time 2 lasts throughout his life and thus, influence his personality. As the rate of growth and development is fast, any stimulation along these lines will have its maximum effect during these years.

A preschool child is one who needs space to be vigorous, alone and/or part of an active group, for his happiness, concern and self-expression. He needs an understanding adult to help himself, to explore manually, verbally, and to learn the lessons of life from both people and objects around. The more experience the child receives at this stage, the richer will be the dividend. Different names given by the educationists, psychologists, and adults are as follows:

Common Names of Pre-School Years

- Early Childhood Years.
- Foundation Years.
- Imitative Age.
- Period of Plasticity.
- Period of Learning.
- Formative Years.
- Pre-Gang Years.
- Troublesome Years.
- Exploratory Age.

SIGNIFICANCE OF 1 YEARS

There is a world-wide consensus among the psychologists, sociologists and biologists, that pre-school age is the critical period in the life span of a child. It is during this period that foundation for all later development is laid. The child is highly receptive to all that prevails in his environment and his learning potentials are at their peak. Whatever is assimilated in this foundation period gradually stabilises later on. Once, the high level of stability is reached in the cognitive, affective and behavioural dimensions of the individual significant change are difficult to occur later on. Research has also indicated that if these early years are not supported by, or embedded in, a stimulating and enriching physical and psychosocial environment, the chances of the child's brain developing to its full potential are considerably, and often irreversibly, reduced. Damage or impoverishment suffered at this stage is likely to be irreparable. Bowlby believed that, "during this early critical period, beyond which no amount of the right kind of experiences is effective, if the child has been deprived before its end whatever occurs during this critical period will produce permanent effects".

This early childhood stage is also important as a foundation for the inculcation of social and personal habits and values that are known to last a lifetime. It is an ideal period for learning new skills. Speech skills are developed during this period and the child reaches the stage of extremely rapid development of spoken language. The child masters much of his native languages or the mother s tongue without much of formal instructions. During this period the child learns the fundamentals of social behaviour and acquires the preliminary training and experience required for being a member of a group. Moreover, the achievement of first six to seven years of life is very significant for cognitive development as well. By the age of six, for example, the child s brain has reached 90 per cent of its adult size. It is during this period that interests, habits, attitudes and values of the individual are learnt. Children are active learners. They construct their own knowledge and understanding of the world through repeated interactions with people and materials in their environment. The more stimulating their environment and the more opportunities they have to explore, to question, to experiment, to play and to symbolise, the better they are for later life. Therefore, all kinds of facilities should be provided to the child to explore, to enquire, to play and to interact with his peers for optimum development. The extent of ultimate development and achievement is practically fixed by the experience the child has already had undergone during this Pre-school years. Hence, pre-school years have been acknowledged as the most significant period in the life of an individual. The reasons behind this are as follows:

1. Research has shown that the first few years of life influence later behaviour to a large extent. Many of the ways of thinking and behaviours of adults can be traced from early childhood experiences.
2. The rate of development in all areas (physical, motor, cognitive, language, social and emotional) is the most rapid during these years. In this period it is possible to learn skills which become difficult and at time impossible, to acquire at a later age/stage.
3. Since, development is proceeding at a very fast rate, unfavourable experiences such as: lack of adequate food, nurturance and care, unhealthy living conditions, sickness, lack of interaction with adults or exploitative working conditions will hinder development to a considerable extent. In the same way, favourable experiences will foster development.

All these factors serve to determine the child's future relationship to school vis-à-vis school readiness, enrolment, retention and performance. This period also provides a golden opportunity for intervention, not just in the disability and difficulties of the individual, but also in the process of social change. 'A Happy child is the Nation's Pride'. Hence, every effort needs to be taken to make the child happy and healthy. The child s home is his immediate environment at the early years and then gradually the nursery school/preschool. If the prevailing atmosphere of the home and nursery/preschool is happy and conducive, the child will be able to overcome temporary unhappiness without distorting his outlook on life and continue to be happy. Dr. Rajendra Prasad, the first President of our country had rightly pointed out that, "If one s childhood is well spent, well regulated and well organised, the better will he take up the responsibilities of a full grown citizen". To add to it, Dr. Radhakrishnan proclaimed "Our nation s future, its prosperity or poverty, strength or weakness depends on the care with which we build-up the character and habits of our children". All these above statements rightly justify the significance of pre-school years.

NEEDS OF THE YOUNG CHILDREN

All children, normal or special, need certain basic provisions of life to grow up from the helplessness of infancy and childhood to become mature, independent adults. If they are not met, then normal social, emotional and cognitive developmental processes are put at risk. Therefore, a sound knowledge of the needs of children is essential for guiding them properly. Needs are permanent trends of human nature which underline human behaviour from birth to death under all circumstances and in all kinds of societies. Application of the knowledge of child psychology and development helps to understand the needs of children, and help them to develop to their full potential. Maslow s theory on human being s needs identifies five basic needs, such as:

1. Physiological Needs.
2. Safety Needs.
3. Belongingness.
4. Self-Esteem Needs.
5. Need for Self-actualisation.

In the hierarchy of needs, those needs at the base of the hierarchy are assumed to be more basic relative to the needs above them in the hierarchy. In the beginning years of individual s life five physiological needs are to be satisfied, and then safety needs and so on for the normal growth and development.

Further, it has been well realised by the researches that, for full and harmonious development of his/her personality, the child needs to grow up in a family in an atmosphere of happiness, love, and understanding. It is the social, legal, and moral responsibility of the adults of a society to meet the needs of the child and prepare him/her to live an independent, responsible, and useful life in the society. However, the primary responsibility for children s development lies with their parents and immediate family members. There are innumerable children in our country living in exceptionally difficult and disadvantaged conditions whose needs remain unsatisfied, thus preventing them from attaining harmonious and optimal growth and development. These children

Fig. 1.1: Maslow's Hierarchy of Needs

need special care, support and education for their welfare, and overall growth and development. There are certain basic and/or essential needs of the children, which need to be taken care of by the parents or care takers for normal growth and development. They can be broadly classified into the following categories.

Physical Needs

There are certain physical needs without which life itself cannot continue. There can be little disagreement about it due to the following basic essentials of life. This need is to be fulfilled for normal and natural development of children during early stage of life. Physical needs are such as:

(a) Fresh water, air, and sunlight.
(b) Shelter and protective care.
(c) Adequate and appropriate balanced diet.
(d) Clothing for warmth, protection, socialisation.
(e) Activity and rest – vigorous and quiet states.
(f) Prevention and treatment of illness and injury.
(g) Training in habits and skills necessary for maintenance and growth of life.

Psycho-Social Needs

There are certain psychosocial needs of the children without which a child cannot attain self-reliance, normal relationship with others around, and contentment in life. These psycho-social needs are as follows:

(a) *Need for Protection*: Children need to be protected from danger of any type, including the risk of sexual abuse or physical violence within and outside the family.

(b) *Need for Love, Affection and Respect*: Children need to have affectionate, respectful physical contact, to be comforted when in distress, to be held with tenderness; to be listened to; to be taken seriously. They need to be given opportunities for challenge, exploration and the growth of a sense of competence. Further, children are to be encouraged to share feelings, including those that express anger, bewilderment and hurt.

(c) *Need for Approval*: Children need to be wanted and recognised by their parents, elders, friends and others. Through approval, they feel accepted and secured enough to lead normal and comfortable life.

(d) *Need for Stimulation to Learn and Access to Schooling*: Children being very inquisitive in nature need to be stimulated to learn maximum during the pre-school years. Throughout these years, children need to explore their world at their own pace; to have stimulating materials, play equipment and books. Their questions need to be answered. Once at pre-school, the children need to have access to appropriate educational opportunities in the contexts where there is a concern to provide them with resources to help them learn and realise their potential. Educational 7 needs of children with specific learning problems/inadequacy require special attention. Children have learning problems because of factors inherent in themselves or in the learning environment. Such children may be categorised as follows and require appropriate attention to be taken care of.

- children with mild disabilities like lower level of intellectual functioning;
- children with visual impairment;
- children with hearing impairment;
- children with locomotive impairment;

(e) *Need for Security, Guidance, Support and Control*: Children need to have a sense of continuity of care and the expectation that the family unit will remain stable. Routine and predictable patterns of care, a reasonable set of rules and consistent monitoring facilitates this sense of security. They need to be in a context where there is consistent, firm guidance on acceptable social behaviour, and where parents and adults act as good enough 'role models' to follow.

(f) *Need for Autonomy and Responsibility*: Children need to gain the experience of taking responsibility for themselves and others in age – appropriate ways. They should be given enough time and opportunity for self-absorbing, imaginative and socialising play, so as to enable them to learn autonomy.

A child grows and develops holistically with his/her physical emotional and intellectual needs interrelated and interdependent.

If Children's Needs are not Satisfied

When the needs of children are not met or receive too little attention on the part of the parents/adult caretakers that leads to several behavioural manifestations, such as: anxiety, social maladjustment, psycho-neurotic disorders, and behavioural problems like: aggression, destruction, stubbornness, hostility and exaggerated egoism. In order to prevent and/or overcome these problems, there can be several ways in which adults can help children towards their need fulfilment, such as: follows:

- Accept and respect children as they are, for what they are.
- Love unconditionally and abundantly.
- Assure each child that he is loved and wanted at all times.
- Provide healthy, creative and enriched opportunities for the child to grow and develop at his/her own pace.
- Understand the dynamics of behaviour of each child.
- Let the child have some well-defined boundaries and limits within which he can act upon.
- Adults need, to help and support him/her in meeting his/her developmental tasks.
- Parents and other family members need to be emotionally stable and consistent in their directions to children.
- Never strive to realise the unfulfilled needs through the child.
- Children learn quickly the way they live – hence, be a good model and example to be followed.

Thus, fulfilling the basic needs of children are not only essential, but also the rights of each and every child. It is the responsibilities of the parents and child care takers to fulfil these needs of the children for normal and natural growth and development on the part of the children. Otherwise, children will likely develop the behaviours, which are unsocial or anti-social. These children will be engage in activities, which are destructive for them as well as for others, creating problems in very many ways for all.

STATUS OF CHILDREN IN INDIA

The development of human resources is a basic pre-requisite to the growth and development of an economy. Children constitute the most important base of our human resources endowment and accordingly child welfare and development has always occupied a special place in the task of '*Nation building*'. However, in spite of considerable expansion in the public health and medical facilities, India has been facing a serious problem of high infant mortality, morbidity and malnutrition. Moreover, the general status of our children is far from satisfactory in comparison to many other countries of the world.

There are an estimated 300 million children between 0 and 14 years of age in India today, representing a little over one-third of India s population. Most recent data from the census of India 1991 indicate that there were 150 million children between 0 and 6 years of age out of which about 73 million were girls and 77 million boys. Around 78 per cent of children resided in 'rural' areas. The opportunities and facilities that are required to be secured to facilitate and ensure development of children are so very inadequate that protecting the basic rights of children 9 only becomes a virtual phenomenon. Non-discrimination among children is an overriding principle of the convention of the rights of the child. However, in India, not all children are treated equally, and many millions face asymmetric opportunities for survival and development. Among the groups of the disadvantaged, for instance, are the girl child, street children, children of prostitutes, and children belonging to socially and economically backward communities.

Nutritional and Health Status of Children

In India today, millions of children live in conditions of acute deprivations with inadequate access to basic health care, nutrition and safe drinking water, which probably results in many more deaths than famine, flood or war. This also gives rise to various related social problems like: destitution, juvenile delinquency,

Status of India's Children

- ***Child Survival and Child Health:*** *2.5 million Children die in India every year, accounting for one in five deaths in the world, with girls being 50 per cent more likely to die. One out of 16 children die before they attain one year of age, and one out of 11 die before they attain five years of age. India accounts for 35 per cent of the developing world's low birth weight babies and 40 per cent of child malnutrition in developing countries, one of the highest levels in the world. Although India's neo-natal mortality rate declined from 34 per 1000 live births in 2009 to 29 per 1000 live births in 2012. The 2001 Census data and other studies illustrate the terrible impact of sex selection in India over the last few decades. The child sex ratio (0-6 years) declined from 927 girls to 1000 boys in 2001 to 919 in the 2011 Census. Around 80 per cent of the total 577 districts in the country registered a decline in the child sex ratio between 1991 and 2001. About 35 per cent of the districts registered child sex ratios below the national average of 927 females per 1000 males. In the 1991 Census, there was only one district with a sex ratio below 850, but in the 2001 Census, there were 49 such districts. India has the second highest national total of persons living with HIV/AIDS after the Republic of South Africa. According to National Aids Control Organization (NACO), there were an estimated 0.55 lakh HIV infected 0-14 year old children in India in 2003. UNAIDS, however, puts this figure at 0.16 million children. According to the 2001 Census report, amongst all persons living with disabilities, 35.9 per cent were children and young adults in the 0-19 age group. Three out of five children in the age group of 0-9 years have been reported to be visually impaired. Movement disability has the highest proportion (33.2%) in the age group of 10-19 years. This is largely true of mental disability also.*
- ***Child Development****: The population of children aged 0-6 years is 16.4 crores as per the 2001 Census. According to a UNESCO report, however, of the total child population, 2.07 crores (6%) are infants below one year; 4.17 crores (12%) are toddlers in the age group 1-2 years; 7.73 crores (22.2%) are pre-schoolers in the age group 3-5 years. The report highlights that only 29 per cent of pre-primary age children are enrolled in educational institutions in India. Services under the ICDS scheme covered only 3.41 crore children in the age group 0-6 years as in March 2004, which is around 22 per cent of the total children in that age group. Supplementary nutrition too was being provided to 3.4 crore children, as against 16 crore children. Of these, 53 per cent were reported to be under-nourished.*
- ***Child Protection:*** *While on the one hand girls are being killed even before they are born, on the other hand children who are born and survive*

suffer from a number of violations. The world's highest number of working children is in India. To add to this, India has the world's largest number of sexually abused children; with a child below 16 years raped every 155th minute, a child below 10 every 13th hour and one in every 10 children sexually abused at any point of time. The National Crime Records Bureau (NCRB) reported 14,975 cases of various crimes against children in 2005. Most subtle forms of violence against children such as: child marriage, economic exploitation, practices like: the 'Devadasi' tradition of dedicating young girls to gods and goddesses, genital mutilation in some parts of the country are often rationalized on grounds of culture and tradition. Physical and psychological punishments take place in the name of disciplining children and are culturally accepted. Forced evictions, displacement due to development projects, war and conflict, communal riots, natural disasters – all of these take their own toll on children. Children also stand worst affected by HIV/AIDS. Even those who have remained within the protective, net stand at the risk of falling out of it.

- ***Child Participation:*** *Children in most sections of Indian society are traditionally and conventionally not consulted about matters and decisions affecting their lives. In the family and household, the neighbourhood and wider community, in school or in work place, and across the settings of social and cultural life, children's views are mostly not given much importance. If they do speak out, they are not normally heard. The imposition of restrictive norms is especially true for girl children. This limits children's access to information and to choice, and often to the possibility of seeking help outside their immediate circle.*

Source: Ministry of Women and Child Development (2007): Working Group Report on Women and Children for the Eleventh Five-year Plan (2007-12).

drug abuse, beggary, immoral traffic among women etc. The problem of overcoming avoidable child deaths continues to plague several countries of the world. The fact that children die in this scientific advancement age when there are simple and cost-effective solutions to prevent escapable mortality is a matter of shame. The percentage of children under age five years who are underweight is almost 20 times as high in India as would be expected in a healthy, well-nourished population and is almost twice as high as the average percentage of underweight children in sub-Saharan African countries. Although poverty is an important factor in the poor nutrition situation, nutritional deficiencies are widespread even in households that are economically well off. Inadequate feeding practices for children make it difficult to achieve the needed improvements in children s nutritional status, and nutrition programmes have been unable to make much headway in dealing with these serious nutritional problems.

Nearly two out of three pre-school age children in India are malnourished. Growth is influenced by nutrition. Frequently attacks of infectious diseases affect their growth and increase the requirements of various nutrients. Incidence of Protein Energy Malnutrition (PEM) and vitamin A deficiency are very high in among this age group. Repeated illness, especially the common illnesses such as: diarrhoea, measles, whooping cough and other respiratory infections are the principal under laying causes of malnutrition. They take away appetite and so reduce food intake often, inhibit the absorption of the food that is eaten, drain the body of nutrients through diarrhoea and vomiting, they burn up calories in fever. The result is frequent weight loss. Along with it, different household factors affecting the state of children s nutrition are as follows:

- Socio-economic condition of the family.
- Mother s knowledge about child nutrition and exposure to child care.
- Food availability and intake.
- Poor sanitation and water supply.
- Mother s domestic work and responsibility.
- Poor living conditions and crowding.
- Food preparation and cooking methods used.
- Demands on mother s time.
- Frequency and duration of baby s feeds.
- Contamination of baby food.

The Convention of Rights of the Child places primary emphasis on the right of every child to avoid escapable mortality, and morbidity, and to lead a healthy life. Most recent estimates place India s infant mortality rate (IMR) at 79 and the under-five mortality rate at 124 per 1,000 live births. India has made progress in reducing its infant mortality rate from a level of 129 deaths per 1,000 live births in 1971 to 79 in 1992. Yet, of the 25 million children born every year in India, two million die before reaching the age of one. A majority of these deaths are due to avoidable infections and malnutrition. The country has made significant progress in assuring children their rights to survival. There have been major gains in reduction of deaths due to vaccine-preventable disease and the country is on its way to eradication of poliomyelitis, However, there are significant variations in the fulfilment of child s rights – across states, geographical regions, caste and gender, and also between urban and rural areas.

Around fifty three per cent of our children are malnourished and 67 per cent of deaths under five are due to malnourishment. India still ranks 45th, out of 193, on the basis of under five mortality rate in the world and two million children under the age of one die annually (Prasad, 1999). Malnutrition among children in India is the biggest contributing factor to the high infant mortality and morbidity. Moreover, vitamin - A, iron, folic acid and iodine deficiencies leading to keratomalacia, anaemia and goitre affect the children. Protein energy malnutrition is also widely prevalent. Due to problems of malnutrition, inadequate health care services, poverty and lack of sufficient knowledge, a large number of children are born or are worst hit with various types of disability like: blindness, hearing impairments, orthopaedic handicaps and mental deficiency or retardation. The incidence of disabilities is mostly because of Vitamin-A deficiency, crippling diseases like: polio, leprosy, industrial/agricultural/rural kitchen accidents, lack of pre and postnatal care, and malnutrition. Recent studies also point out those children in urban slums and poor neighbourhoods in urban areas live under particular vulnerable conditions of health and nutritional well being. The risk of a slum child receiving a calorie – deficient diet, for instance, is reported to be twice as high as compared to those of children from middle income and low income families.

Apart from malnutrition, children in India usually suffer from and sometimes face death due to ten specific diseases such as: asthma and bronchitis, heart attack, pneumonia, tuberculosis of lungs, cancer, anaemia, gastro-enteritis, typhoid, acute abdomen and vehicular accidents. Around 29 per cent of deaths occur due to pneumonia, 19 per cent due to anaemia and typhoid, and 34 per cent because of gastro-enteritis in the age group between one to 4 years. It is estimated that about 1.5 million deaths occur every year because of diarrhoea or diarrhoea related causes. Access to and utilisation of health and medical services by children have

UNDERSCORING INDIA'S NOT-SO-MINOR PROBLEM

7 of 1,000 newborns die

42% children are underweight

58% stunted by two years of age

8.1 mn of 190 mn go to school

112 is the country's rank on the CDI

- India scores least in CDI among China, Brazil, South Africa and Russia
- It saw the steepest fall over last 5 years
- India's under-5 mortality rate is over 60 out of 1,000

- Bangladesh, Sri Lanka placed better than India

Fig. 1.2: Nutritional Health Status of Indian Children

tended to vary across the country depending upon the costs, quality, and levels of public provisioning as well as upon the effectiveness of demand for such services. While not many studies have focussed on the relationship of costs and quality to access and utilisation, provisioning in urban areas is undoubtedly better than in rural areas. Studies on the health status of children in India have also repeatedly pointed to the importance of women s education and awareness, and that of mothers in particular.

Assuring the best of children throughout their lives depends on assuring them the best beginnings. The health and well-being of their mother are essential, as is the care and attention children receive during their earliest years, from birth to age six years of age.

Social Status of Children Living in Difficult Circumstances (Child Labour, Child Abuse and Street Children)

India has several million children living under especially difficult circumstances. These include: for instance, estimated five lakhs street children in cities of India. Destitute and orphaned children are another group about which very little is unknown. Similarly, there is very little information available about children of prostitutes, children in institution, children of construction workers, children of fisher folk, disabled children, children working in hazardous industries as beedi, fireworks and children affected by riots and natural disasters. There is also reportedly sale of such children because of acute poverty and girl trafficking across regional and even national borders. The social status of children in India is all the more magnified due to two important categories of children such as: child labour and child abuse, which give a very pathetic picture about the conditions of the children in India.

(a) Child Labour

The term *child labour* embraces a complex reality. Child working people are unequal in India. They are also called child labour. Any child out of school is a child labour .According to International Labour Organization (ILO); the term child labour *"is often defined as work that deprives children of their childhood their potential and their dignity and that is harmful to physical and mental development. It refers to work that is mentally, physically, socially or morally dangerous and harmful to children; and interferes with their schooling by depriving them of opportunity to attend school; obliging them to leave school prematurely; or requiring them to attempt to combine school attendance with excessively long and heavy work"*. Child labour is recognized as a serious and enormously complex social problem in India. Children, under age 14 are often forced to work for as many as 18 hours a day. They are subject to malnutrition, impaired vision, deformities from sitting long hours in cramped over crowded workplaces; they become easy preys to deadly diseases like: serious respiratory diseases, T.B., and Cancer. They are often forced to lead solitary lives away from their families, deprived of meaningful education and training opportunities that could prepare them for a better future. Child labour not only lead to a perpetual cycles of poverty for a family, it depresses the economy also.

In India, the children are engaged mostly in various low-key jobs of the unorganized sectors which are hazardous in situation. The Census found an increase in the number of child labourers from 11.28 million in 1991 to 12.66 million in 2001 and 21.39 million in 2011. In addition, nearly 85 per cent of child labourers in India are hard-to-reach, invisible and excluded, as they work largely in the unorganised sector, both rural and urban, within the family or in household-based units. Children s work needs to be seen as happening along a continuum, with destructive or exploitative work at one end and beneficial work – promoting or enhancing children s development without interfering with their schooling, recreation and rest – at the other. And in between these two poles are vast areas of work that need not negatively affect a child s development.

Destructive and Exploitative Work ←— — — — —→ Beneficial Work

Children's Work

According to UNICEF child labour is exploitative if it involves the following:

- Full-time work at too early an age.
- Too many hours spent working.
- Work that exerts undue physical, social or psychological stress.
- Work and life on the streets in bad conditions.
- Inadequate pay.
- Too much responsibility.
- Work that hampers access to education.
- Work that undermines children s dignity and self-esteem, such as: slavery or bonded labour and sexual exploitation.
- Work that is detrimental to full social and psychological development.

There are various aspects of child s development that can be endangered and/or affected by child s working in hazardous conditions, such as:

- *Physical Development*: Including overall health, co-ordination, strength, vision and hearing.
- *Cognitive Development:* Including literacy, numeracy and the question of knowledge necessary to normal life.
- *Emotional Life:* Including adequate self-esteem, family attachment, feelings of love and acceptance.
- *Social and Moral Development*: Including a sense of group identity, the ability to co-operate with others and the capacity to distinguish right from wrong.

Economic exploitation of Children in India is extensive and appears to have increased over the years. The census of India 1981 estimated that there were 13.17 million child workers engaged mostly in rural agricultural activities. The National Sample Survey in 1983 estimated that there were 17.36 million child workers in the age group of 5 to 15 years. The operation research group placed the figure at 44 million in 1983. Most of these children work under stressful conditions in agriculture, match and fireworks, glass works, chemical industries, beedi industries, hotel industries, diamond polishing, carpet industries and the like often hazardous. Some are 'bonded' and even sold into prostitution. The planning commission of India estimates that there would be around 20 million child workers by the year 2000.

Fig. 1.3: Different types of Child Labour in India

Working children are exposed to several occupational hazards. Apart from disease they face the hostile environment which an exposed life style entails.

- *Causes of Child Labour:* Children are pushed into work that is often damaging to their development by three key factors: *(i)* the exploitation of poverty; *(ii)* the absence of relevant education and *(iii)* the destruction of tradition.
  - *Poverty* drives children into hazardous labour. The parents of child labourers are often unemployed or underemployed, desperate for secure employment and income.
  - *Yet, it is their Children*: More powerless and paid less – who are offered the jobs. Moreover, children are employed because they are easier to be exploited. They work for their own survival and that of their families. Most of the working children in India belong to families that are extremely poor.
  - The prevalence of such high levels of child labour is attributable in good measure to the fact that primary *education* for children is not compulsory in India. Children who are out of school invariably perform work of some sort, either at home or outside, and at wages that are often exploitive, and under conditions that are clearly harmful. The school system in India is blighted by more than just a lack of resources. It is too often rigid and uninspiring in approach, with a curriculum that is irrelevant to and remote from children s lives. As a result, keeping children in school is proving to be even more difficult than enrolling them in the first place. Moreover, most of their parents are illiterate and do not understand the importance of education for their children. Hence, the cycle goes on:

Parental Illiteracy ←— — —→ Children's Illiteracy ←— —→ Parental Illiteracy and so on.

- *Tradition* and entrenched social patterns also play a part in propelling children into hazardous labour. The harder and more hazardous jobs become, the more likely they are to be considered the province of the poor and disadvantaged, the lower classes and ethnic minorities.
- *Schooling problems* also contribute to child labour. Many time children seek employment simply because there is no access to schools. When there is access, low quality often makes attendance a waste of time for the students. Schools in many developing areas suffer from problems such as: over-crowding, inadequate sanitation and apathetic teachers.

- *Types of Child Labour*: The many manifestations of child labour can be broken down into seven main types. These are: domestic service, forced and bonded labour, commercial sexual exploitation, industrial and plantation work, street work, work for family and girls work. The most vulnerable and exploited children of all – as well as the most difficult to protect – may well be those in domestic service. They are often poorly paid or not paid at all; their terms and conditions are entirely at the whim of their employers and take no account of their legal rights. They are deprived of schooling, play and social activity, not to mention emotional support from friends and family. Moreover, they are vulnerable to physical and sexual abuse. Apart from the above mentioned types of child labours existing in India, other major types of child labour are:

1. *Bonded child labour* occurs in India, where children, often only eight or nine years old, are pledged by their parents to land or factory owners or their agents in exchange for very small loans. Their lifelong servitude never succeeds in even reducing the debt. In India, this type of transaction is widespread in industries such as: beedi (cigarette) rolling, carpet making, match-stick making, slate and silk. The most notorious of these is the carpet industry of Mirzapur-Bhadohi-Varanasi in Uttar Pradesh State. A recent study of these children describes how they are often "kept in captivity, tortured and made to work for 20 hours a day without a break. Little children are made to crouch on their toes, from dawn to dusk every day, severely stunting their growth during formative years".

2. The underground nature of the multibillion-dollar illegal industry in the *commercial sexual exploitation* of children makes it difficult to gather reliable data. But NGOs in the field estimate that each year at least 1 million girls worldwide are lured or forced into this form of hazardous work, which can often verge on slavery. Boys are also often exploited. The physical and psychological damage inflicted by commercial sexual exploitation makes it one of the most hazardous forms of child labour. Children involved have to confront serious health risks every day, including respiratory diseases, HIV/AIDS and sexually transmitted diseases, unwanted pregnancies and drug addiction.

Practically, there is no industry in India, which does not employ child labour. Economic exploitation of children in the form of child labour is extensive and appears to have increased over the years. The Planning Commission estimates that there would be around 20 million child workers by year 2000. Unofficial sources place the figure at a much higher level of around 45 million. Child labour in India is a product of socio-economic and cultural conditions. Anti constitutional policies, inadequate legislative measures and lack of political will are also important factors responsible for the persistence of this unlawful social evil. Besides addressing socio-economic factors, a comprehensive legislation aimed at progressive eradication of child labour is the need of the hour. The existing Child Labour Act concentrates only on hazardous occupations and processes. The time has come to go beyond and to include other types of work 18 that children are engaged in. Child labour related offences should be made recognisable in nature. Above all, the enforcement machinery to ensure compliance with the law has to be made much more effective.

(b) Abused Children

Child Abuse and Neglect is the intentional, non-accidental injury/maltreatment of children by parents, caretakers or adults which may lead to temporary or permanent impairment of their physical, mental and psychological development, disability or death. In simple words, any kind of harm done to a chid whether physical, sexual or emotional maltreatment or neglect is child abuse. It can occur at homes, schools, orphanages, residential care, and street or in the workplace. Many children suffer and die every year as a result of the battered child syndrome. The body and the mind of the victims of this problem are irreparably mutilated. This contributes to the frequency of the cases of crippling and death and should be a considerable factor every time that child has a fracture, cerebral haemorrhage, a multiple wound or difficulties with typical growth. Child abuse in India is hidden phenomenon especially when it happens in the home or done by family members. Indian families have been known for their patriarchal joint families who take care of their children with utmost care and concern. Most of children in India are highly dependent on their parents and elders; they continue to have submissive and obedient towards their parents and care takers. Hence, parents, child care takers, adult family members or people known to the child when they behave, treat or conduct themselves in any abnormal way hampering the children physically/psychologically/sexually, which is unable to be identified at the beginning, as they are the protector of the children. Moreover, the child is unable to understand, and express to others regarding the abnormal treatment. The research indicates that in a majority of cases, the child s relatives, family, friends or someone known and trusted by the child involved in the abuse. Such abuse often takes place in child s home. According to a National level study conducted in the year 2007 by the Ministry of Women and Child Development, government of India, 69 per cent of children reported to have been physically abused. Out of these 55 per cent were boys and every second child reported facing emotional abuse.

- *Causes of Child Abuse:* Child abuse usually occur at any place, home school, neighbourhood, work place and residential care institution. The exact incidence of child abuse in India is difficult to estimate, since it does not always come to the notice of the authority. Many cases never get 19 exposed and reported because of social apathy and concerned towards children s plight. There is generally not a single factor that results in the abuse or neglect of a child; it is usually a combination of various factors. In addition, the duration (such as: the duration of an illness) or intensity (such as: the level of drug or alcohol abuse) can make it more or less likely that a child will be at risk for abuse. When trying to understand child abuse and neglect, we often look at possible contributing factors in the adult, factors based on something in society, and factors based on something about the child leading to child abuse in India.

1. *Possible Adult Contributing Factors:* Research tells us that there is no 'typical' abuser. People who abuse children may be male or female and the majority of child abuse is committed by someone who knows the child. In over 80 per cent of cases a parent is the identified perpetrator. The following are characteristics of some people who abuse children.
   - low self-esteem;
   - poor control over their emotions;
   - a history of being abused themselves;
   - stress;
   - financial problems;
   - social isolation;
   - relationship problems with a partner (may include domestic violence);
   - lack of parenting skills;
   - is abusing drugs or alcohol;
   - illness;
   - belief that too much praise or attention will spoil a child;
   - belief that fear and embarrassment are the way to make sure children obey;
   - doesn't understand children's needs or abilities and criticizes children who can't meet their high expectations;
   - belief that children should be quiet at all times;
   - inability to cope with life stressors;
   - focused on own troubles or things other than their children;
   - has been diagnosed or exhibits symptoms of depression.

The family and community in India have been insulated, authoritarian and patriarchal, with parent (s)/guardian and caretakers having full right over their children, to treat them in whichever way they deem fit. Child rearing practises allow for physical force/punishment as means of disciplining. Child battering, corporal punishment or maltreatment by the parents/ guardians or even teachers has not been considered or recognised as illegal because it is supposed to be in the 'interest of the child'. It is generally considered that whatever happens in the family is an internal affair to be sorted out in the family. Maltreatment and exploitation on the part of the parents or guardians towards children is not 'leaked out' to the outsiders. The child is traumatised and in a number of cases lives of low esteem or revolt and revolution against mankind as a whole.

2. *Possible Societal Contributing Factors:* There are many deeply rooted, complicated and interrelated societal factors that can contribute to child abuse and neglect. While we cannot list them all here, the following two factors are often identified as increasing the likelihood that child abuse and neglect will occur.
   - stresses of poverty;
   - community violence;

The other social factors constitute various forms of child abuse in India are poverty and low-socio-economic family status. The frequency of child abuse is higher in lower socio-economic classes. A review of research on child abuse indicates that several factors like: poverty, parental poor health, alcoholism, marital disharmony and higher numbers of children in the family contribute to the problem of child abuse. Child abuse in India is essentially a concomitant of poverty. Other factors like: malnutrition, large families, destitution and inadequate facilities for schooling also play an important role. According to Bhattachary (1979) the impairment of growth and development of children resulted from widely prevalent malnutrition and infection which accounts for the coinage of the term nutritionally battered child referring to the children who are the victims of prolonged and severe protein energy malnutrition. Many studies conducted on the abusing families note that such families are socially isolated. Most of the abused families had no-ongoing relations with individuals outside the family. When abusing parents did make friends outside the family, the relationship was very brief and usually ended in violent quarrels. Few families belong to some sort of social organisation. Large sections of abusing families strongly prevent their children from becoming attached to anyone outside the family. Although the child abuses so rampant in the families in the low-income groups it occur at all socio-economic levels as well. Most of the abused children belong to broken families with abnormal backgrounds.

3. *Possible Child Contributing Factors:* Some children have certain characteristics or behaviours that make it more likely that they will be at risk for abuse or neglect. However, it is important to remember that no matter what characteristics a child has or how they act a child is NEVER responsible for being abused or neglected.
    - illness, especially chronic illness;
    - disability;
    - crying for extended periods;
    - feeding problems;
    - tantrums and whining;
    - biting;
    - toilet learning;
    - disobedience and lying;
    - physical appearance (for example, resembles someone who is viewed negatively by the caregiver);
    - poor grades.

However, the main factors that contribute to the magnitude of the problem of child abuse are poverty, illiteracy, caste system and landlessness, lack of economic opportunities, rural-urban migration, population growth, political instability and weak implementation of legal provisions.

- *Types of Child Abuse:* Child abuse is manifest in various types of behaviour like: physical abuse, emotional abuse, sexual abuse, abandonment, child beggary, child labour, child marriage, branding, pawning, etc.

    (a) physical abuse: physical abuse is the inflicting of physical injury upon a child. This may include: burning, hitting, punching, shaking, kicking, beating or otherwise harming a child. The parent or caretaker may not have intended to hurt the child. It may, however, be the result of over-discipline or physical punishment that is inappropriate to the child's age.

    (b) sexual abuse: sexual abuse is inappropriate sexual behaviour with a child. It includes fondling a child's genitals, making the child fondle the adult's genitals, intercourse, incest, rape, sodomy, exhibitionism and sexual exploitation. To be considered child abuse, these

acts have to be committed by a person responsible for the care of a child (for example a baby-sitter, a parent, or a daycare provider), or related to the child. If a stranger commits these acts, it would be considered sexual assault and handled solely by the police and criminal courts.

(c) *emotional/psychological abuse*: emotional abuse is also known as verbal abuse, mental abuse, and psychological maltreatment. It includes acts or the failures to act by parents or caretakers that have caused or could cause, serious behavioural, cognitive, emotional, or mental trauma. This can include parents/caretakers using extreme and/or bizarre forms of punishment, such as: confinement in a closet or dark room or being tied to a chair for long periods of time or threatening or terrorizing a child. Less severe acts, but no less damaging, are belittling or rejecting treatment, using derogatory terms to describe the child, habitual tendency to blame the child or make him/her a scapegoat.

(d) *child neglect*: it is the failure to provide for the child's basic needs. Neglect can be physical, educational, or emotional. Physical neglect can include not providing adequate food or clothing, appropriate medical care, supervision, or proper weather protection (heat or cold). It may include abandonment. Educational neglect includes failure to provide appropriate schooling or special educational needs, allowing excessive truancies. Psychological neglect includes the lack of any emotional support and love, never attending to the child, substance abuse including allowing the child to participate in drug and alcohol use.

(e) *child prostitution*: prostitution in India has been there since time immemorial and has manifested itself in various forms from time to time. There are no scientific statistics available about the number of prostitutes – least of all about child prostitutes. But according to newspaper reports there are four lakh child prostitutes in India. Reports and studies on prostitutes and prostitution point out that there are some castes and communities in various pockets of the country in which family based prostitution is traditionally practised. This is largely spread in the states like: Karnataka, Maharashtra and Andhra Pradesh.

(f) *kidnapping, abduction and beggary*: apart from poverty, unemployment and other economic pressures and crisis, the perception of girls as an economic liability often result in their abandonment by parents. Several girl children thus are forced to begging and are left to fend for themselves on the streets. This also presents a situation where the street children can be exploited sexually or otherwise by the vested interests. Sale of children by parents/guardians or relatives, to be used for prostitution or begging or bonded labour is also caused by almost the same factors along with the other factor of the father/guardian or caretaker being an alcoholic or drug abuser and thus being always in need of money. Despite efforts, the sale of children, especially girl children, continues in certain states in India.

(g) *drug abuse*: drug abuse and drug trafficking has become a global phenomenon. School children, street children and commonly rag pickers are being affected by the drug problems. It is mostly observed in cities and towns consumed with chocolates and soft drinks etc. Children from alcoholic and drug user families are more observed to be affected by and spread it to their peers and friends quickly. Once addicted, children keep it secret from their parents and involve in more antisocial activities.

(h) *international trafficking*: poverty, the tradition of giving dowry, expenses involved in marriage and societal pressure compel parents to marry their daughters to older men and at times to foreign nationals. These men do not expect a dowry and often give financial compensation to parents for the marriage. Brides are often deserted after a short stay with their husbands. Other incidents of illegal trafficking primarily result in the sale of children. A promise for employment, poverty and ignorance are motivators for parents entrusting their children to brokers. Very often these children are sold to brothels or exported to other countries for undesirable ends. These children get separated from their parents under a false pretext, hence depriving them of their family. Unauthorised adoptions also lead to illegal trafficking.

Fig. 1.4: Types and Nature of Child Abuse

International Perspective of Child Abuse

- The World Health Organisation estimates that 40 million children below the age of 15 suffer from abuse and neglect, and require health and social care.
- A survey in Egypt showed 37 per cent of children reporting being beaten by their parents, and 26 per cent reporting injuries.
- 36 per cent of Indian mothers told interviewers in a survey that they had hit their children with an object within the last six months.
- A 1995 survey in the US showed that 5 per cent of parents admitted disciplining their children through hitting the child with an object, kicking the child, beating the child, and threatening the child with a knife or gun.
- Recent South African Police statistics show 21,000 cases of child rape or assault reported against children as young as nine months old.

National Perspective of Child Abuse

- The situation of children in India is deplorable. Almost 100 million children in India are out of school, despite the proactive stand by the government and the successful implementation of the Education for All programme. Nearly 35 million children are homeless, according to an estimate, although there are homes for just about 36,000 children.
- Studies across India show child abuse to be prevalent in a rampant form. More than four lakh children in India are

reported to be victims of commercial sexual exploitation. In Delhi alone, nearly four to five lakh children live on the streets, 53 per cent of young children suffer from malnutrition and 33 per cent of the 6-14 age group are deprived of schooling.

- An average of 44,476 children are reported missing in India every year (NHRC-UNIFEM, 2003), out of which 11,008 children continue to remain untraced. Most of these children end up in brothels or being abused by tourists.
- The extent of abuse inflicted on children gets reflected from the crime records data. The total crime against children showed a rising trend from 1999 to 2001, as 4,957 cases were registered in 1999 as against 6,087 cases in 2001. However, in the year 2002, such cases went down to 5,972. The total figure for crime against children for the year 2003 (2,084) is not comparable with the figures of the previous year as the figures of child rape are not included for the year 2003. Data on child rape are not collected on a monthly basis.
- Cases of infanticide (134) have increased by 16.5 per cent in 2003 compared to 115 in 2002. Maharashtra reported the highest cases of infanticide (30), which accounted for 22.4 per cent of the total infanticide cases in 2003.
- Cases of female foeticide have decreased by 38.1 per cent during 2003 (52) compared to 84 in 2002. Rajasthan reported the highest number of cases of foeticide (11), which alone accounted for 21.2 per cent of the total cases of foeticide in 2003.
- Incidence of kidnapping and abduction of children was around 700 in 1999 and 2000, which suddenly rose to 2,845 and 2,322 in 2001 and 2002 respectively and again went down to 765 in 2003. The highest number of cases of kidnapping and abduction of children was reported from Maharashtra and Gujarat.
- Cases of procuration of minor girls increased by 37.9 per cent in 2003 (171) compared to 124 in 2002. The highest number of cases was reported from Bihar (47).
- Although incidence of child rape, one of the worst form of sexual abuse, has declined between the periods 1999 and 2002, from 3153 cases to 2532, the unofficial number may have been higher since many cases may have not been reported. So is the case with kidnapping and abduction.

Parental Role to Prevent Child Abuse

Parenting is the most influential responsibility an adult undertakes in life. No one more than the parents has vested interest in protecting children from any societal abuse. Awareness, education and responsible parenting are the best ways for child defence. Child may be more likely to communicate with the parents, if they trust you. Thus, what parents can do to prevent child abuse are as follows:

- Educate the child about the sexual abuse and to identify the difference between acceptable and unacceptable touching. Trust their instincts about people.
- Talking to the child openly, clearly and honestly about the parts of the body including genitals and answering to their questions and allowing them to express openly without feeling anything.
- Develop an environment at home in which sexual topics can be discussed confortably.
- Making the child aware about the signs of abuse and manhandle, so that nobody dare to take advantage of them.
- Explaining the child that no one has the right to hurt, harm or touch him/her in any way that makes the child uncomfortable.
- Build confidence in the child to say NO, if the child feels uncomfortable by any behaviour or conduct of others.
- Trust the child and support him. Many times the child hides such things due to fear and shame. So, open communication between the child and parents is important.
- Be aware of adults who offer children special gifts or toys, or adults who wants to take your child on a special outing.

Child abuse is present in the Indian society in alarming proportions. But we do not know precisely how extensive the problem is due to lack of reporting statistics. They provide some idea about the number of working children, but no data is available on the magnitude of the problems of physically abused, sexually abused and neglected children. However, a large number of children apprehended under the children s Act are the cases of exploitation, victimisation and child beggars. It is recommended that India adopt the prevention of child abuse and neglect as a national purpose and develop a serious commitment to that end. Empirical evidence regarding the magnitude of the problem of child abuse in India, with information about parental characteristics, child factors and conditions is essential to convince policy-makers and to provide them with the ammunition necessary to recommend the allocation of limited government resources for prevention and intervention in the area of child abuse. Due to lack of a system of awareness and information, the problem becomes more challenging. Our children are the assets and future of our country and they need to be protected and their future needs to be secured. Thus, there is need to work together the parents, academicians, researchers, social workers, policy-makers, administrators and others involved in child care for the steps to end this perennial problem and provide our children safe and secure future.

(c) Street Children

UNICEF defines a street child as, "...any girl or boy... for whom the street (in the widest sense of the word, including unoccupied dwellings, wasteland, etc.,) has become his or her habitual abode and/or source of livelihood; and who is inadequately protected, supervised, or directed by responsible adults". It is important to distinguish the group of children that live on their own on the streets because their lives vary greatly from those of children who simply work on the streets; they thus have different needs and require targeted attention. While 18 million children work on the streets of India, it is estimated that only 5 to 20 per cent of them are truly homeless and disconnected from their families. Because the street children in India have unique vulnerabilities – the amount of time they spend on the street, their livelihood depending on the street, and their lack of protection and care from adults, they are a subgroup of the Indian population that deserve specific attention in order to ensure that their needs are known. As the most vulnerable group of children in India according to UNICEF, they need to be understood as much as possible.

- *Causes of being Street Children*: The street children in India choose to leave their families and homes for strategic reasons. Three hypotheses have been put forth in an attempt to explain their choices:
  - ➢ poverty;
  - ➢ aberrant families;
  - ➢ urbanization;
  - ➢ lack of child friendly schooling;
  - ➢ over stressed on academic pressure;
  - ➢ parental burden and pressure;

Most children leave their families to live on the street because of family problems. Family problems include such things as death of a parent, alcoholism of father, strained relationships with stepparents, parent separation, abuse, and family violence. Additionally, street children usually come from female-headed households. Most children who leave home to live on the streets come from slums or low cost housing, both which is areas of high illiteracy, drug use, and unemployment. Children usually transfer their lives to the streets through a gradual process; they may at first only stay on the street a night or two. Gradually they will spend more time away from home until they do not return. Once on the streets, children sometimes find that their living conditions and physical and mental health is better than at home; however, this fact speaks to the poor conditions of their homes rather than good conditions in the street. Street conditions are far from child-friendly. Once they leave home, many street children move around often because of the fear that their relatives will find them and force them to return home.

Life Style of Street Children

The life style of street children are different from children living with their parents at home. They can be described as follows:

- *Economic Activity of Street Children* – Street children must provide for themselves, work is a very important aspect of their lives. Unfortunately, working conditions for street children are often very poor because they are confined to working in the informal sector, which is unregulated by the government. Because of street children s lack of protection from a family and the law, employers often exploit them, making them virtual prisoners, sometimes withholding pay, and abusing them. Employers that would not mistreat the children often will not hire them because they are seen as too great of a risk. Because of the low pay from employers, street children in India often choose to be self-employed or work multiple jobs. In fact, the majority of them are self-employed. One of the most common economic activities done by the children is scavenging for recyclable materials, such as: plastic, paper, and metal. Other jobs include cleaning cars; petty vending, selling small items such as: balloons or sweets; selling newspapers or flowers; begging; shining shoes; working in small hotels; working on construction sites; and working in roadside stalls or repair shops. Street children, especially the older children, are also sometimes engaged in activities such as: stealing, pick-pocketing, drug-peddling, and prostitution, though this is a small proportion. Most of the street children work 8-10 hours total each day in their various economic activities.

- *Spending on the Part of Street Children* – The earnings of street children fluctuate g eatly, but they usually only make enough for subsistence. Most street children in India earn between 200 and 830 rupees a month, with older children making more than younger children. Self-employed children also typically make more than children who are employed under an employer. The largest expense in a street child s budget is food, which often costs 5 to 10 rupees a day. In order to cut down on food expenses, many children drink tea to get rid of hunger. The money street children earn that is not spent on food is usually quickly spent on other things because older children and police frequently steal their money. This lack of ability to save causes severe financial insecurity. While children occasionally send some of their earnings home to their families, they spend most of their extra money on entertainment. Many street children spend 300 rupees a month on movies, though older children also use their money to buy cigarettes, chewing tobacco, alcohol, and drugs. Street children often spend very little on clothing because their employers often provide clothes for work or their families occasionally give them clothes if they know where they are living. Also, the boys among them do not bother wandering fully or partially naked in public because it adds to the people s sympathy for them.
- *Education* – The education of street children in India is very poor and often non-existent. A study of street children in Bombay in 1989 found that 54.5 per cent had never been enrolled in school and 66 per cent of the children were illiterate. A 2004 study of street children in Bombay revealed that circumstances were largely the same: 60 per cent of the children had never attended school and approximately two-thirds were illiterate. Thirty per cent had been to elementary

school, while only 10 per cent had been to middle or high school. In fact, many children in the 2004 study said that one of the reasons they ran away from home is because they did not want to be forced to work and unable to attend school. Obviously, however, the demands of living alone make it very unlikely that they will be able to obtain education through leaving.

- *Relationships and Coping by Street Children* – The street children in India are especially vulnerable among low-income children because they do not have the support structures that other children normally have, namely: families, the psychological and monetary support they offer. Thus, street children adopt strategies to cope with the harsh realities of their lives. For many, these strategies include developing a tough exterior and strong independence to hide their vulnerability. They live in survival-mode, constantly having to be aware of their surroundings and fight for their safety. These circumstances lead children to engage in behaviours that children in families typically do not, such as: creating a new identity, using aggression frequently, and valuing relationships based on what can be gained from them. While the majority of street children in India have been found to use positive coping mechanisms to deal with the stress of their lives, some choose maladaptive strategies, such as: drinking alcohol, using drugs, and visiting prostitutes. When questioned about their substance use, many street children in Bombay reported that the cause was frustration concerning living on the street or conflicts in their family which caused them to leave home.

Fortunately, street children are not entirely on their own. Many form groups with other street children to protect themselves. These groups normally have a leader and specific territory; unfortunately, though these groups bring safety to most, younger children are sometimes used by the leader to steal or do other illegal activities. Street children are mostly rely on their friends for help when they are sick, money when they run out, and information about work when they need a job. Street children spend much of their free time with their friends, often going with them to the movies. Among the most important deprivations faced by street children is the lack of a protective and guiding adult, but some street children manage to find individuals to fulfil this role. Though most live on their own or with friends, some street children form connections with families that live on the streets or in slums and see these families as their substitute families. Many of these children find a 'mother-figure' that cares for them when they are ill and is interested in their well-being.

- *Health and Nutritional Status of Street Children* – Street children in India face additional vulnerability because of their lack of access to nutritious food, sanitation, and medical care. Street children lack access to nutritious food because many are dependent on leftovers from small restaurants or hotels, food stalls, or garbage bins. Lack of sanitation in bathing, toilets, and water also contributes to poor health. Open air bathing of street children is in fact a very common sight in all parts of India. These children have to put their naked bodies on display for a very long time before, during and after bathing. As a result they develop hardly any sense of modesty. They as well as the onlookers have a casual approach to this phenomenon. Street children also lack restroom facilities, demonstrated by the fact that these children used the roadside or railway line for their toilet. For water, the children use public pipes and water taps. Most of the street children in India also lack access to medical care, which is especially detrimental during times of illness or injury. Moreover, most street children do not have winter clothing, leaving them more vulnerable to illness during the winter.
- *Abuses faced by Street Children* – Street children in India are frequently exposed to abuse and extortion. Because they have no social status and no adults to protect them, street children identify being physically threatened and intimidated by adults as the one factor that contributes most to the misery of living on the streets. The primary cause for this treatment is the views that the police and general public hold toward them: most scorn them and react to them with hostility. Many street children have reported that police will beat them in order to coerce them into giving them a 'cut' for working in certain areas. Police often arrest street children under the Vagrancy Act, and, having no formal way to appeal their arrest, the children must bribe or work at the police station until their 'debt' has been paid.

Many factors contribute to the police abuse of street children, including the police perceptions of the children, widespread corruption, and a culture of police violence, the inadequacy and non-implementation of legal safeguards, and the level of impunity that the police enjoy. Though the Juvenile Justice Act, which applies to all the states and Union Territories in India except Jammu and Kashmir, prohibits detaining neglected or delinquent juveniles in police lock-ups or jails, it is rarely enforced.

The Problems of Street Children

1. *Abuse*: Many of the street children who have run away from home have done so because they were beaten or sexually abused. Tragically, their homelessness can lead to further abuse through exploitative child labour and prostitution. Not only does abuse rob runaway children of their material security, but it also leaves them emotionally scarred. Many of the abused children are even traumatised and some refuse to speak for months. To aggravate matters, children often feel guilty and blame themselves for their mistreatment. Such damage can take years to recover from in even the most loving of environments; on the streets it may never heal.
2. *Child Labour*: Most Indian street children work as child labour in various unorganised sectors. The children usually rise before dawn and carry their heavy load in a large bag over their shoulder. Rag-pickers can be seen alongside pigs and dogs searching through trash heaps on their hands and knees. Other common jobs are the collecting of firewood, tending to animals, street vending, dyeing, begging, prostitution and domestic labour. Children that work are not only subject to the strains and hazards of their labour, but are also denied the education or training that could enable them to escape the poverty trap.
3. *Gender Discrimination*: In Indian Society females are often discriminated against. Their health, education, prosperity and freedom are all impacted. The problem is worse in conservative Rajasthan than almost anywhere else in India. For example, because girls carry the liability of dowry and leave the family home after marriage, parents may prefer to have male offspring. Many babies are aborted, abandoned or deliberately neglected and underfed simply because they

are girls. This can be seen in the fact that female mortality rates amongst 0-4 year olds in India are 107 per cent of male mortality rates, whereas the comparable number in Western Europe is 74 per cent. The rate is 119 per cent in Rajasthan. Further evidence of the imbalance is that the female/male ratio within the general population of India is unnaturally low at 927/1000, and even lower in Rajasthan at 909/1000. Gender discrimination is particularly evident in education where boys are more likely to attend school and to do so for more years. The traditional place of the woman is in the home and so many parents and children consider education for girls to be a waste of time, especially when the child can instead be working or performing domestic chores. Only 38 per cent of Indian women are literate and, at 64 per cent, the gender parity between literacy rates amongst Indian women and men is one of the most unequal in the world. Child Marriage is another way in which girls are disadvantaged. In addition to limiting educational possibilities and stunting personal development, early marriage carries health risks. A girl under 15 is five times more likely to die during pregnancy than a woman in her twenties; her child is also more likely to die.

4. *Health*: Poor health is a chronic problem for street children. Half of all children in India are malnourished, but for street children the proportion is much higher. These children are not only underweight, but their growth has often been stunted; for example, it is very common to mistake a 12 year old for an 8 year old. Street children live and work amidst trash, animals and open sewers. Not only are they exposed and susceptible to disease, they are also unlikely to be vaccinated or receive medical treatment. Only two in three Indian children have been vaccinated against TB, Diphtheria, Tetanus, Polio and Measles; only one in ten against Hepatitis B. Most street children have not been vaccinated at all. They usually cannot afford, and do not trust, doctors or medicines. If they receive any treatment at all it will often be harmful, as with kids whose parents place scalding metal on their bellies as a remedy for persistent stomach pain.

There is much ignorance about reproductive health and many girls suffer needlessly. A girl made infertile by an easily-preventable condition may become not able to get marriage and so doomed to a life of even greater insecurity and material hardship. The HIV/AIDS rate amongst Indian adults is 0.7 per cent and so has not yet reached the epidemic rates experienced in Southern Africa. However, this still represents 5 million people, or about 1 in 7 in of those in the world who have the disease. The rate amongst children is lower, but because street children are far more sexually active than their Indian peers and because many are even prostitutes they are thus hugely at risk of contracting the disease. AIDS awareness, testing and treatment exist, but less so for street children than other demographic groups.

5. *Homelessness*: Street children in India may be homeless because their family is homeless through poverty or migration, or because they have been abandoned, orphaned or have run away. It is not unusual to see whole families living on the sidewalks of Jaipur, or rows of individual children sleeping around the railway station. Homeless children have the odds stacked against them. They are exposed to the elements, have an uncertain supply of food, are likely miss out on education and medical treatment, and are at high risk of suffering addiction, abuse and illness. A single child alone on the streets is especially vulnerable.
6. *Poverty*: Poverty is the prime cause of the street children crisis. Children from well-off families do not need to work, or beg. They live in houses, eat well, go to school, and are likely to be healthy and emotionally secure. Poverty dumps a crowd of problems onto a child. Not only do these problems cause suffering, but they also conspire to keep the child poor throughout his/her life. In order to survive, a poor child in India will probably be forced to sacrifice education and training; without skills the child will, as an adult, remain at the bottom of the economic heap.

- *Government Involvement:* Street children in India are "a manifestation of societal malfunctioning and an economic and social order that does not take timely preventative action".

Thus, many scholars believe that fixing the problems of street children depend on addressing the causal factors of their situations.

Additionally, as these causal factors are addressed, help for the immediate situation of street children must also be given. India has set in place various forms of public policy concerning street children over the past two decades, but they have largely been ineffective because they are uniformed by sociological, anthropological, and geographical research on street children, meaning they do not always correctly assess and address needs.

Prior to 1993, the 'Official Vocabulary' of post-independence India did not contain the term 'street child,' and street children were only helped because they were grouped with other children that worked on the streets. For instance, the Co-ordination Committee for Vulnerable Children worked to give identity cards to children working on the streets in order to help protect them from police violence. In the early 1990s, facing pressure from non-governmental organisations (NGOs), the Indian government created the 'Scheme for Assistance to Street Children,' which launched in February 1993. Though many NGOs had meetings with the government to give feedback about the scheme and suggestions to improve it, none of these recommendations were included in the final draft, making it very difficult for NGOs to participate in it. Since their entrance into the policy arena and the Scheme was set in place, street children have been included in some other policies and programmes as well. The Indian Council of Child Welfare has included street children in their programmes, and in the 8th Five-year Plan a scheme for children in 6 metropolitan cities was set in place. The Ministry of Labour, Government of India has also included street children in their livelihood training programmes, though this has been met with minimal success because many street children do not have the education necessary to participate in the programmes.

Educational Status of Children

A basic quality education is a human right, yet more than 130 million primary-school-age children in developing countries are out of school. Nearly 60 per cent of them are girls, many saddled with domestic obligations and household chores; many others limited by traditions in which families consider school costs too high to pay when it comes to their daughters; and still others living such long distances from school and travel is a risk to their health and well-being. Too often, girls and boys abandon their education when they are forced to work despite their young age or the hazards of their labour, when armed conflict and other emergencies disrupt their lives, when poverty surrounds them or when adults exploit them sexually or buy and sell them like commodities.

Education does not begin when the child sets foot in primary school, nor does it end when the school bell rings and class lets out. Learning begins at birth; it occurs in the family, in neighbourhoods, in communities, during play. Life's teachers are parents, siblings, peers, work places, and the mass media.

Article 45 of the Directive Principles of State Policy promises free and compulsory education to all children up to the age of 14 years and instructed the State to do so within 10 years of its creation. Though never actualised, Article 45 is nevertheless seen as a bench mark of what this country hoped to achieve for its children in the name of education. The role of education is for growth and development of individual personalities. It is not only a basic need but also a means of meeting other needs through development of basic skills and abilities. However, in India the educational status of the children is not very satisfactory. In the last few censuses of India, children below 5 years of age were treated as illiterates. Ability to read and write with understanding is not ordinarily achieved until one had some schooling or had at least some time to develop these skills. It was felt by the Ministry of Human Resources Development and Planning Commission that the population aged 7 years and above is to be classified as literate or illiterate. Only 62 per cent primary school children reach class five and the incidence of dropout and stagnation amongst girls is nearly twice that of boys. Nearly one-third of girls in class one never reaches class two. Even in non-formal education centres, girls form only one-third of total enrolment.

Despite the best efforts by the Government, dropout rates in the primary schools are significant; retention of children in schools is low; and wastage in primary and elementary school level is considerable. It is a matter of concern, however, that a sizeable number of schools denote to have minimum facilities required to impart good quality education to all. More than 14 per cent primary schools and 4 per cent middle schools are run in open spaces or in tents or thatched huts. Another 14 per cent of the primary schools and 8 per cent of the middle schools are run in Kutcha buildings. Information about some other facilities available for 1986, which are directly related to the state of functioning of schools that could also affect the enrolments and retention rates, provide a dismal picture. Available information indicates that 54 per cent of primary schools and 34 per cent middle schools did not have drinking water facility. Likewise, nearly 80 per cent of the primary schools and 60 per cent of the middle schools were without urinals and lavatories. Micro studies on the status of children in diverse situations urban and rural, reveal that – a shocking 60 per cent of children under six may be left in each other s care, 48 per cent of sibling care givers may be 4-8 years old. Of children not in school, one fifth specifically do not attend because of childcare responsibilities. Of these, 70-80 per cent are girls. Both sets of children thus lose out on educational opportunities. The younger child suffers from the lack of stimulation that only an aware, experienced and caring adult can provide and the older child is unable to access schools. Thus the underprivileged child suffers an almost insurmountable educational handicap from the time she is born, all for the lack of the single component of early care and education (ECE).

Profile of the Child Population in India

- The child population (0-6 years) is 158 million.
- One-third of babies are born with low birth weight.
- Only 42 per cent children (12-23 months) are fully vaccinated.
- 14 per cent are not vaccinated at all.
- India has the largest number of malnourished children in the world.
- 47 per cent of all children below 2 years are malnourished.
- 5 per cent of all children 0-6 years suffer from severe or moderate anemia.
- 25 million children are born every year.
- The Infant Mortality Rate (IMR) is 70 per 1,000 live births.
- 60 million children (< 5 years) live in poverty.
- Of them, only 19.4 million children (3-5 years) are getting preschool education under ICDS.

UNIVERSAL RIGHT'S OF YOUNG CHILDREN

The importance of the child in the context of Human Resource Development, National Development and Global Development is recognised and unequivocally accepted by all. The future of any nation is largely determined on how its children grow and develop. This is particularly so in the case of India, which is the home for over 375 million children, the largest number for any country in the world. There are several provisions in the Constitution of India, either as Fundamental Rights or as Directive Principles of State Policy that have been used to promote ECCE services in the country. As a Fundamental Right, Article 15(3) of the Constitution of India empowers the State to practice positive discrimination favouring economically and educationally weaker groups, which allows for special provisions for girls and children of disadvantaged social groups, and in difficult situations not to discriminate against any citizen. Article 15(3) asserts, "*Nothing in this article shall prevent the State from making special provisions for women and children.*" Specific Articles under the Directive Principles of State Policy of the Constitution of India that provide a supportive framework for ECCE in India are as follows:

Article 39 (f) – Opportunities and facilities for children to develop in a healthy manner and in conditions of freedom and dignity and that childhood and youth are protected from exploitation.

Article 42 – With direct relevance to working women: "*enjoins the State to secure just and humane conditions of work and maternity relief.*" (*Children* are also benefited by this statutory provision.)

Article 45 – Until the Constitution (Eighty-sixth Amendment) Act, 2001 was passed, Article 45 (Directive Principles of State Policy) of the Constitution of India directed the State to provide free and compulsory education to all children up to the age of fourteen. The earlier inclusion of 0-6 year old children within this constitutional directive implied the intent to provide conditions for holistic child development, with preschool education as an important component.

Article 47 – The State shall endeavor to raise the level of nutrition and the standard of living of its people to improve health.

Imparting meaningful rights to children so as to create an environment conducive to their growth and well being can no longer be regarded as a matter of government largely, but a fundamental social requirement. Unfortunately, the quest to safeguard children s rights to survival, development and protection remain largely unfinished for a large majority of children in our country. The preamble of the Convention on the Rights of the Child recalls the basic principles of the United Nations and specific provisions of certain relevant human rights treaties and proclamations. It reaffirms the fact that children, because of their vulnerability, need special care and protection; and places special emphasis on the primary caring and protective responsibility of the family. It also emphasises on the need for legal and other protection of the child, before and after birth, the importance of respect for the cultural values of the child s community, and the vital role of international co-operation in achieving the realisation of children s rights. The great concern for the welfare of children at the international level is reflected in various international conventions. The Universal Declarations of Human Rights recognised the fact that children are entitled to special care and protection. It is stated in Article 24 of the Declaration that –

> *"Every child regardless of his/her race, colour, sex, language, religion, national, ethnic or social origin, property or birth, disability, has the right to such measures of protection as are required by his status as a minor, on the part of his family, society and the State".*

This was followed by the '*Declaration of the Rights of the Child*' adopted by the UN General assembly in 1959. The Declaration in its Preamble points out that the "*child by reason of his physical and mental immaturity, needs special safeguards and care, including appropriate legal protection, before as well as after birth*". It proceeds to outline several principles in this behalf. The International Covenant on Economic, Social and Cultural Rights, 1966 also mandates that "*special measures of protection and assistance should be taken on behalf of all children and young person without any discrimination for reasons of parentage or other conditions. Children and young person should be protected from economic and social exploitation ....*" However, the most significant milestone in the quest for children s rights has been the UN Convention on the Rights of the Child, adopted by the UN General assembly in 1989. It is perhaps the only almost universally ratified international convention. This Convention was followed by the "World Summit on Children" in 1990 which was the first major global action for the implementation of the Convention. The World Summit adopted the 'Declaration on the Survival, Protection, Development and Participation of Children' along with a 'Plan of Action' for implementing the Declaration. The UN Convention of the Rights of the Child is a statement of an ideal, which only a few of the nations have so far achieved. The

Convention enumerates the various political, social, economic and cultural rights of every child in particular the right of survival, development, protection and participation. The details of CRC are as follows:

Guiding Principles of CRC

Article 1: Everyone under 18 years of age has all the rights in this convention.

Article 2: The convention applies to everyone whatever the race, religion, abilities, whatever child think or say, and whatever type of family the child comes from.

Article 3: All organisations concerned with children should work towards what is best for each child.

Article 4: Governments should make these rights available to all children.

Article 6: You have the right to life. Governments should ensure that the child survive and thrive.

Article 12: The child has the right to say what he/she think should happen, when adults are making decisions that affect child, and to have his/her opinions taken into account.

Types of Child Rights

The broad types of Child Rights are as follows:

1. *Survival and Development Rights:* The basic rights to life and achieving one s full potential.

Article 7: Child has the right to a legally registered name and nationality. Child also have the right to know and, as far as possible, to be cared for, by parents.

Article 9: Child should not be separated from parents unless it is for child s own good, for example, if a parent is mistreating

or neglecting a child. If the parents have separated, child have the right to stay in contact with both parents, unless this might hurt the child.

Article 20: If child cannot be looked after by own family child must be looked after properly by people who respect child s religion, culture and language.

Article 22: If child have come into the country as a refugee, child should have the same rights as children born in this country.

Article 23: If child have any kind of disability, child should have special care and support, so that the child can lead a full and independent life.

Article 24: Child have the right to good quality health care, to clean water, nutritious food and a clean environment, so that he will stay healthy.

Article 25: If children are looked after by the local authority, rather than by their parents, they should have the situation reviewed regularly.

Article 26: The child or guardians have the right to help from the Government if children are poor or in need.

Article 27: Child has a right to a standard of living that is good enough to meet physical and mental needs. The Government should help child s family if it cannot afford to provide this.

Article 28: Children have a right to an education. Primary education should be free.

Article 29: Education should develop the child s personality and talents to the fullest as possible. It should encourage the child to respect parents, and own and other cultures.

Article 30: The Child has a right to learn and use the language and customs of his family, whether these are shared by the majority of people in the country or not.

Article 31: The child has a right to relax and play and to join in a wide range of activities. Article 42: The Government should make the convention known to all parents and children.

2. *Protection Rights:* Keeping safe from harm.

Article 19: Governments should ensure that children are properly cared for; and protected from violence, abuse and neglect by parents, or anyone else who looks after.

Article 32: The Government should protect the child from work that is dangerous, or that might harm the child health or education.

Fig. 1. 5: Children's Rights in School

Article 36: The child should be protected from any activities that could harm his development.

Article 35: The Government should make sure that children are not abducted or sold.

Article 11: The Government should take steps to stop from being taken out of child s own country illegally.

Article 34: The Government should protect child from sexual abuse.

Article 37: Child should not receive any cruel, inhuman or degrading treatment or punishment.

Article 40: If children are accused of breaking the law you should receive legal help. Child should not be put in prison with adults and should be able to keep in contact with his family. Prison sentences for children should only be used for the most serious offences.

3. *Participation Rights:* Having an active voice.

Article 13: Child has the right to get and to share information, to meet together and to join groups and organisations as long as it is not damaging to the child or to others.

Article 14: The child has the right to think and believe what he wants, and to practice his religion, as long as he is not stopping other people from enjoying their rights. Parents should guide the child on these matters.

Article 15: Child has the right to meet together and to join groups and organisations, as long as this does not stop other people from enjoying their rights.

Article 16: Child has a right to privacy. The law should protect him from attacks against his way of life, his good name, his families and his homes.

Article 17: Children have the right to reliable information from the mass media. Television, radio and newspapers should provide information that they can understand, and should not promote materials that could harm them.

Source: UNICEF.

Significant Features of the UN Convention on the Rights of the Child (CRC)

- Applies equally to both girls and boys up to the age of 18, even if they are married or already have children of their own.
- The convention is guided by the principles of Best Interest of the Child and Non-discrimination and Respect for views of the child.
- It emphasises the importance of the family and the need to create an environment that is conducive to the healthy growth and development of children.

LEGISLATIONS FOR PROTECTION OF CHILD RIGHTS IN INDIA

Much before the various International Conventions, the Indian Constitution provided a framework within which provisions were available for protection, development and welfare of children. The framers of the Indian Constitution were fully conscious of their responsibility towards children. Consequently, this responsibility is reflected in some of the Constitutional provisions passed for protecting the rights and well being of children, such as:

- Article 15(3) enables the state to make special provisions for women and children.
- Article 23 prohibits the trafficking in human beings and forced labour in all its forms.
- Article 24 prohibits employment of children below the age of 14 years in hazardous jobs.
- Article 37(e) makes it a duty of the State to prevent the children from entering into jobs unsuited to their age.

- Article 39(e) mandates that the health and strength of workers, men and women, and the tender age of children are not abused and that citizens are not forced by economic necessity to enter avocations unsuited to their age and health.
- Article 39(f) recommends that children are given opportunities and facilities to develop in a healthy manner and in conditions of freedom and dignity and that childhood and youth are protected against exploitation and against moral and material abandonment.
- Article 45 directs the States to provide free and compulsory education to all children up to 14 years of age within the time limit of 10 years.

The family and immediate community environment are fundamental to ensuring the rights of the child.

In spite of these Constitutional provisions the state, children in India present a gloomy picture. Despite the fact that India has made significant progress in assuring children their rights to survival, there are still many miles to go. The apathy and inability of the State machinery in tackling the various problems confronting children is quite apparent. Government bear enormous responsibilities in ensuring the promotion and protection of child rights in all their aspects. Further, children s rights cannot be secured through piecemeal measures. Child welfare and development should become an integral part of comprehensive national planning instead of being adjunct to isolated welfare services. The Fundamental Rights and Directive Principles of the Indian Constitution provide the framework for child rights. Several laws and national policies have been framed to implement the commitment to child rights.

National Policies

The major policies and legislations formulated in the country to ensure child rights and improvement in their status include:

1. National Policy for Children, 1974.
2. National Policy on Education, 1986.
3. National Policy on Child Labour, 1987.
4. National Nutrition Policy, 1993.
5. Report of the Committee on Prostitution, Child Prostitutes and Children of Prostitutes and Plan of Action to Combat Trafficking and Commercial Sexual Exploitation of Women and Children, 1998.

6. National Health Policy, 2002.
7. National Charter for Children, 2004.
8. National Plan of Action for Children, 2005.

Of these, two major policies are discussed below:

(i) *National Charter for Children, 2004:* Underlying the National Charter for Children 2004, is the intent to secure for every child the right to a healthy and happy childhood, to address the root causes that negate the healthy growth and development of children, and to awaken the conscience of the community in the wider social context to protect children from all forms of abuse, while strengthening the family, society and the nation. This Charter has the following sections on child protection:
   - survival, life and liberty;
   - protection from economic exploitation and all forms of abuse;
   - protection of the girl child;
   - care, protection, welfare of children of marginalized and disadvantaged communities;
   - ensuring child-friendly procedures;

(ii) *National Plan of Action for Children (NPAC), 2005*: The National Plan of Action for Children was formulated by the then Department of Women and Child Development (now MWCD) in 2005. The Plan is being monitored by the Prime Minister's Office. The Action Plan aims at ensuring all rights to children up to the age of 18 years. It affirms the government's commitment towards ensuring all measures for the survival, growth, development and protection of all children. It also aims at creating an enabling environment to ensure protection of child rights. States are being encouraged to formulate State Plans of Action for Children in line with NPAC. The National Plan has identified several key priority areas that include children's right to survival, development, protection and participation besides monitoring and review of policies and programmes. The NPAC also stresses the need for budgetary allocations to achieve child protection goals.

National Legislations

National legislations for protection of Child Rights in the country are as follows:

- Guardian and Wards Act, 1890.
- Factories Act ,1954.
- Hindu Adoption and Maintenance Act, 1956.
- Probation of Offenders Act, 1958.
- Bombay Prevention of Begging Act, 1959.
- Orphanages and Other Charitable Homes (Supervision and Control) Act, 1960.
- Bonded Labour System (Abolition) Act, 1976.
- Immoral Traffic Prevention Act, 1986.
- Child Labour (Prohibition and Regulation) Act, 1986.
- Prevention of Illicit Traffic in Narcotic Drugs and Psychotropic Substances Act, 1987.
- Pre-natal Diagnostic Techniques (Regulation and Prevention of Misuse) Act, 1994.
- Persons with Disabilities (Equal Protection of Rights and Full Participation) Act, 2000.
- Juvenile Justice (Care and Protection of Children) Act, 2000.
- Commission for Protection of the Rights of the Child Act, 2005.
- To regard the child as an asset and a person with human rights.
- To address issues of discrimination emanating from biases of gender, class, caste, race, religion and legal status in order to ensure equality.
- To accord utmost priority to the most disadvantaged, poorest of the poor and the least served child in all policy and programme interventions.
- To recognize the diverse stages and settings of childhood, and address the needs of each, providing all children the entitlements that fulfil their rights and meet their needs in each situation.

The Guiding Principles of the NPAC 2005 is Prohibition of Child Marriage Act 2006. Some of the important legislations are discussed below. Under each Act relevant sections have been enumerated:

(i) ***The Indian Penal Code***

(a) Foeticide (Sections 315 and 316).

(b) Infanticide (Section 315)

(c) Abetment of Suicide: Abetment to commit suicide of minor (Section 305).

(*d*) Exposure and Abandonment: Crime against children by parents or others to expose or to leave them with the intention of abandonment (Section 317).

(*e*) Kidnapping and Abduction:

- kidnapping for extortion (Section 360);
- Kidnapping from lawful guardianship (Section 361);
- kidnapping for ransom (Section 363 read with Section 384);
- kidnapping for camel racing etc. (Section 363);
- kidnapping for begging (Section 363-A);
- kidnapping to compel for marriage (Section 366);
- kidnapping for slavery etc. (Section 367);
- kidnapping for stealing from its person: under 10 years of age only (Section 369);

(*f*) Procurement of minor girls by inducement or by force to seduce or have illicit intercourse (Section 366-A)

(*g*) Selling of girls for prostitution (Section 372).

(*h*) Buying of girls for prostitution (Section 373)

(*i*) Rape (Section 376)

(*j*) Unnatural Sex (Section 377).

(*ii*) *The Pre-natal Diagnostic Techniques (Regulation and Prevention of Misuse) Act, 1994:* This is an Act for the regulation of the use of pre-natal diagnostic techniques for the purpose of detecting genetic or metabolic disorders, chromosomal abnormalities or certain congenital malformations or sex linked disorders, and for the prevention of misuse of such techniques for the purpose of prenatal sex determination leading to female foeticide and for matters connected therewith or incidental thereto.

(*iii*) *The Juvenile Justice (Care and Protection of Children) Act, 2000*: The Juvenile Justice (Care and Protection of Children) Act, 2000 is a comprehensive legislation that provides for proper care, protection and treatment of children in conflict with law and children in need of care and protection by catering to their development needs, and by adopting a child friendly approach in the adjudication and disposition of matters in the best interest of children and for their ultimate rehabilitation through various institutions established under the Act. It conforms to the UN Convention on the

Rights of the Child, the UN Standard Minimum Rules for the Administration of Juvenile Justice (The Beijing Rules) 1985, the UN Rules for the Protection of Juveniles Deprived of their Liberty and all other relevant national and international instruments. It prescribes a uniform age of 18 years, below which both boys and girls are to be treated as children. A clear distinction has been made in this Act between the juvenile offender and the neglected child. It also aims to offer a juvenile or a child increased access to justice by establishing Juvenile Justice Boards and Child Welfare Committees. The Act has laid special emphasis on rehabilitation and social integration of the children and has provided for institutional and non-institutional measures for care and protection of children. The non-institutional alternatives include adoption, foster care, sponsorship, and after care. The following sections of the Act deal with child abuse:

Section 23: Punishment for Cruelty to Juvenile or Child: The Act provides for punishment (imprisonment up to six months) if a person having the actual charge of, or control over, a juvenile or the child, assaults, abandons, exposes or wilfully neglects him/her, causes or procures him/her to be assaulted, abandoned, exposed or neglected in any manner likely to cause such juvenile/child unnecessary mental or physical suffering.

Section 24: Employment of Juvenile or Child for Begging: The Act provides for punishment (Imprisonment for a term which may extend to 3 years and fine) if a person employs or uses any Juvenile/child for the purpose or causes any juvenile to beg.

Section 26: Exploitation of Juvenile or Child Employee: The Act provides for punishment (Imprisonment for a term which may extend to 3 years and fine) if a person ostensibly procures a Juvenile/child for the purpose of any hazardous employment, keeps him in bondage and withholds his earnings or uses such earning for his own purposes

(iv) *The Immoral Traffic (Prevention) Act, 1956*: In 1986, the Government of India amended the erstwhile Suppression of Immoral Traffic in Women and Girls Act 1956 (SITA), and renamed it as the Immoral Traffic (Prevention) Act (ITPA) to widen the scope of the law to cover both the sexes exploited sexually for commercial purposes and to provide enhanced.

Section 3: Stringent action and punishment for keeping a brothel or allowing premises to be used as a brothel;

Section 4: Living on the earnings of prostitution;

Section 5: Procuring, inducing or taking a person for the sake of prostitution;

Section 6: If any person is found with a child in a brothel it shall be presumed, unless the contrary is proved, that he has committed an offence of detaining a person in premises where prostitution is carried on;

Section 6(1B): The punishment consists of imprisonment of either description for a term which shall not be less than 7 years, but which may be for life or for a term, which may extend to 10 years and shall also be liable to fine, with a provision for less than 7 years under special circumstances;

Section 6(2A): A child or minor found in a brothel, on medical examination, detected to have been sexually abused, it shall be presumed, unless the contrary is proved, that the child or minor has been detained for purposes of prostitution or, as the case may be, has been sexually exploited for commercial purposes;

Section 21: Establishment of Protective Homes by the State Government. 28 Instruments and Standards for Protection of Child Rights.

(v) *Child Labour (Prohibition and Regulation) Act, 1986*: The Act was formulated to eliminate child labour and provides for punishments and penalties for employing children below the age of 14 years in from various hazardous occupations and processes. The Act provides power to State Governments to make Rules with reference to health and safety of children, wherever their employment is permitted. It provides for regulation of work conditions including fixing hours of work, weekly holidays, notice to inspectors, provision for resolving disputes as to age, maintenance of registers etc. Through a recent notification, child domestic workers up to 14 years of age working in hotels and dhabas have been brought within the purview of the Act. It is one step towards the total elimination of child labour.

(vi) *The Prohibition of Child Marriage Act, 2006:* The Child Marriage Restraint Act, 1929 has been repealed and the major provisions of the new Act include:

- every child marriage shall be voidable at the option of the contracting party who was a child at the time of the marriage;
- the court while granting a decree of nullity shall make an order directing the parties, parents and guardians to return the money, valuables, ornaments and other gifts received;
- the court may also make an interim or final order directing the male contracting party to the child marriage or parents or guardian to pay maintenance to the female contracting party to the marriage and for her residence until her remarriage;
- the court shall make an appropriate order for the custody and the maintenance of the children of child marriages;
- notwithstanding that a child marriage has been annulled, every child of such marriage shall be deemed to be a legitimate child for all purposes;
- child marriages to be void in certain circumstances like minor being sold for the purpose of marriage, minor after being married is sold or trafficked or used for immoral purposes, etc;
- enhancement in punishments for male adults marrying a child and persons performing, abetting, promoting, attending etc., a child marriage with imprisonment up to two years and fine up to one lakh rupees;
- states to appoint Child Marriage Prohibition Officers whose duties include prevention of solemnization of child marriages, collection of evidence for effective prosecution, creating awareness and sensitization of the community etc.

(vii) *The Commissions for the Protection of Child Rights Act, 2005:* The Act provides for the Constitution of a National and State Commissions for protection of Child Rights in every State and Union Territory. The functions and powers of the National and State Commissions will be to:

- examine and review the legal safeguards provided by or under any law for the protection of child rights and recommend measures for their effective implementation;
- prepare and present annual and periodic reports upon the working of these safeguards;

- inquire into violations of child rights and recommend initiation of proceedings where necessary;
- undertake periodic review of policies, programmes and other activities related to child rights in reference to the treaties and other international instruments;
- spread awareness about child rights among various sections of society;
- children's Courts for speedy trial of offences against children or of violation of Child Rights;
- state Governments and UT Administrations to appoint a Special Public Prosecutor for every Child s Court.

Apart from these laws mainly concerning children, there are a host of related social legislations and criminal laws which have some beneficial provisions for the care, protection and rehabilitation of children. The laws relating to commerce, industry and trade have some provisions for children, but they hardly provide any protection or cater to their developmental needs. Some states have formulated state specific legislation to deal with child abuse *e.g.*, Goa and Tamil Nadu Despite the above mentioned legislations, there are still major gaps in the legal provisions relating to child abuse in myriad situations, particularly in cases of trafficking, sexual and forced labour, child pornography, sex tourism and sexual assault on male children. The Ministry of Women 51 and Child Development is therefore formulating a comprehensive legislation on Offences against Children.

Schemes and Programmes on Child Protection

Some of the existing child protection schemes and programmes include:

1. *A Programme for Juvenile Justice* for children in need of care and protection and children in conflict with law. The Government of India provides financial assistance to the State Governments/UT Administrations for establishment and maintenance of various homes, salary of staff, food, clothing, etc., for children in need of care and protection and juveniles in conflict with law. Financial assistance is based on proposals submitted by States on a 50-50 cost sharing basis.
2. *An Integrated Programme for Street Children* without homes and family ties. Under the scheme NGOs are supported to run 24

hours drop-in shelters and provide food, clothing, shelter, non-formal education, recreation, counselling, guidance and referral services for children. The other components of the scheme include enrolment in schools, vocational training, occupational placement, mobilizing preventive health services and reducing the incidence of drug and substance abuse, HIV/AIDS etc.

3. *Childline Service* for children in distress, especially children in need of care and protection so as to provide them medical services, shelter, rescue from abuse, counseling, repatriation and rehabilitation. Under this initiative, a telephone helpline, number 1098, runs in 74 urban and semi-urban centres in the country.
4. *Shishu Greha Scheme* for care and protection of orphans/abandoned/destitute infants or children up to 6 years and promote in-country adoption for rehabilitating them.
5. *Scheme for Working Children in Need of Care and Protection* for children working as domestic workers, at roadside dhabas, mechanic shops, etc. The scheme provides for bridge education and vocational training, medicine, food, recreation and sports equipments.
6. *Rajiv Gandhi National Creche Scheme for the Children of Working Mothers* in the age group of 0- 6 years. The scheme provides for comprehensive day-care services including facilities like food, shelter, medical, recreation, etc., to children below 6 years of age.
7. *Pilot Project to Combat the Trafficking of women and Children for Commercial Sexual Exploitation in Source and Destination Areas* for providing care and protection to trafficked and sexually abused women and children. Components of the scheme include networking with law enforcement agencies, rescue operation, temporary shelter for the victims, repatriation to hometown and legal services.
8. *National Child Labour Project (NCLP)* for the rehabilitation of child labour. Under the scheme, Project Societies at the district level are fully funded for opening up of Special Schools/Rehabilitation Centres for the rehabilitation of child labourers. These Special Schools/Rehabilitation Centres provide non-

formal education, vocational training, supplementary nutrition and stipend to children withdrawn from employment.

9. *INDO-US Child Labour Project (INDUS):* The Ministry of Labour, Government of India and the US Department of Labour have initiated a project aimed at eliminating child labour in 10 hazardous sectors across 21 districts in five States namely: *(i)* Maharashtra, *(ii)* Madhya Pradesh, *(iii)* Tamil Nadu, *(iv)* Uttar Pradesh and *(v)* NCT of Delhi.

SUMMARY OF THE CHAPTER

Who are the Pre-Schoolers?

- Children between the age group of 2 to 6 years are called 'Pre-school' children.
- Because of its nature, this period in life is also known as – pre-gang age, trouble-some age, imitative age, period of plasticity, exploratory age, formative age and foundation age etc.

Significance of Pre-School Years

- It is during this period that interests, habits, attitudes and values of the individuals are learnt.
- The rate of development in all areas is the most rapid during these years.
- This period paves the way for effective learning and the child is prepared in all respects to profit from formal schooling.

Needs of the Young Children

- There are certain basic and essential needs of the children, which need to be satisfied and taken care of for normal growth and development.
- Various types of children s needs are – physical needs and psychological needs.
- If these needs are not satisfied by the children, they develop different forms of maladjustments and behaviour disorders.

Status of Children in India

- *Status of Children in India*: The general status of the Indian children is far from satisfactory in comparison to many other countries of the world.
- Malnutrition among children in India is the biggest contributing factor to the high infant mortality and morbidity.
- India has several million children living under especially

difficult circumstances such as: street children, prevalence of child labour, child abuse etc.

- Despite the best efforts by the government, dropout rates in the primary schools are significant, retention of children in school is low; and wastage in primary and elementary school level is considerable.

Universal Rights of Children

- Every child born into the world has basic rights to be enjoyed – to be born wanted, to get nutritious food, to be protected, to have family, to get free education and health care facilities, to express his feelings, to get free medical and legal aid, to get a name from birth etc.

Legislation for Protection of Child Rights in India

- Indian Constitution is fully conscious towards children, which are reflected in some of the Constitutional provisions passed for protecting the rights and well being of children.
- The Fundamental Rights and Directive Principles of the Indian Constitution provide the framework for child rights.
- Several laws and policies have been framed to implement the commitment to child rights in India.

2

Development of Pre-school Children

"Small, vulnerable and wordless though the baby may be, it is at the same time power packed with astonishing potential".

The period of pre-school begins after babyhood and continues up to the age of six. This is a very critical period for the child for his growth and development when especially the child starts showing his independent behaviour and working without others help. However, there are two basic assumptions, which enable to understand the children during the period in a better way. *Firstly,* children are very much more alike, than they are different. Important difficulties in culture, life style, and communal needs and wishes must not be obscured; however, there is a natural biological and evolutionary similarity in children s body and minds – a similarity in their drives, feelings, wishes, and ideas that cuts across social, ethnic, racial and sexual distinctions. *Secondly,* each child is a unique and precious individual. He/she have a specific endowment, as well as his own history and experiences, all of which allow children to differ in their sensitivities and their ways of understanding, reacting and coping. Three areas are critical foundations for healthy child development: stable, responsive and nurturing care giving with opportunities to learn; safe, supportive, physical environments; and appropriate nutrition.

PRE-CONDITIONS OF DEVELOPMENT

There are many necessary pre-conditions for a healthy development of the child to be possible. Hence, some of these have to be met even before the child is born and some after the birth of the child. Even some pre-conditions deal with factors that affect the child s physical growth, others relate to his mental and emotional well being. For a child to have the chance of developing to his fullest potential, these preconditions must be met. These are as follows:

Healthy Genetic Endowment

Everyone recognise the importance of a child s natural endowment. It can set limits on what the child can achieve even with the best opportunities. Though all parents would like to endow their children with the most positive abilities and characteristics, some families have a history of conditions, which could pass serious mental or physical problems into their children. For such families, the medical science of genetics can provide counselling and testing during pregnancy. Though genetic counselling, couples can be advised about their chances for having a healthy baby. After a child is conceived, tests on samples of the amniotic fluid that surrounds the foetus can detect any of over 100 problem conditions present in the unborn child. The use of both these relatively recent medical services can help lower the frequency of genetic disease.

Parental Care

Even before a woman conceives, she should be medically fit, adequately nourished, physically mature, and psychologically prepared to have a child. For healthy development of her unborn child, the mother must eat well-balanced food and should receive proper medical attention to prevent anaemia, infection, high blood pressure, and excessive weight gain, which is very common among the pregnant women of our country. She should also avoid the exposure to unnecessary medication and X-rays, which could seriously affect the foetus.

One of the major goals of parental care is to maintain pregnancy to full term and give birth to a healthy baby. It is evident that the major cause of infant and maternal mortality in our country is prematurity which can be easily prevented through early medical care. Unfortunately, prematurity most often occurs among poor families who cannot afford the special medical care attention, and nutrition which the infant and mother needs most during first few months of baby s birth.

Physical Care, Love and Attention

Another essential precondition to development is the physical well-being of each child. Physical care includes adequate nutrition, immunisations, and regular medical check-ups. In the process of receiving such continuous, attentive care during the first months of life, a child also receives affection, intellectual stimulation, and the opportunity to form secure social attachments – all essential for further development. Children need attention, yet the kind of attention they receive is most important. When adult reactions are active and responsive to the child s own behaviour, the child learns about the value of his own actions and about the responses he can expect from other people. Such experiences, repeated with people who love him, help the child to gain a sense of identity and develop as a social being.

The child must also have the opportunity to learn about limits and structure: to know what responses he can reasonably expect from adults, what standards he is expected to uphold, and what consequences he can predict for both his acceptable and unacceptable behaviour. At the same time, he needs flexibility and diversity to estimate his curiosity. As the child matures, limits and rules have to change, and new and more complex expectations have to be introduced. An individual balance between the child s need for stimulation, stability and predictability will encourage healthy intellectual and social development.

Parental/Adult Care takers as Role Models

As children move from infancy into the pre-school years, they begin to identify with and to imitate the actions and attitudes of adults important to them. These adults care takers around children, whether they are aware of it or not, serve as role models for the children. For a child to develop socially acceptable behaviour, he needs the presence of respected adults caretakers who themselves act in acceptable ways and who will reward the child for behaviour that they feel is good and worthwhile.

All these factors are only preconditions for development. Their fulfilment cannot guarantee intelligence nor any other quality or ability. When these preconditions are not met, the effects on the child s development are often painfully clear by the age of three. Unfortunately, by this age, they may not be completely reversible.

MAJOR ASPECTS OF GROWTH AND DEVELOPMENT

Children do not just grow in size. They develop, evolve, and mature, mastering ever more complex understandings of the people, objects, and challenges in their environments.

The term '*growth*' and '*development*' are very often used interchangeably. However, these two terms are different from each other. *Growth* refers to measurable quantities such as: height and weight, whereas development refers to the process of functional maturation, that is, maturation of the roles played by the body s systems, in its purest sense. Growth does not restrict its reference only to outward physical growth but that of internal organs like: brain. *Development* by contrast, refers to 'qualitative changes'. It is not merely a matter of adding inches to stature or ability to ability, instead, it is a complex process of integrating many structures and functions. According to Hurlock, Development may be defined as '*a progressive series of orderly coherent changes*'. 'Progressive' signifies that the changes are directional that they lead forward rather than backward. 'Orderly' and 'Coherent' suggest that there is a definite relationship between a given stage and the stages, which proceed or follow it. It is the emerging and broadening of the child s ability to function on a higher level, whether in the psychomotor, cognitive or affective domains of human behaviour. The more and more information the child receives from his own body, his perception, his physical motor activities, he understands the world better. Whatever the child does from his birth to pre-school-stage, does lay foundation not only for later physical motor skills, but also for cognitive progresses and socio-emotional and aesthetic development as well. Therefore, inter-relatedness among all the aspects of growth and development should always be recognised. Moreover, we need to know the children with deeper insight and have a clear understanding of how they develop and learn in the early years so that we will have a point of departure for planning, administering and supervising a solid base on which to make our appropriate decisions (Refer figure 2.1).

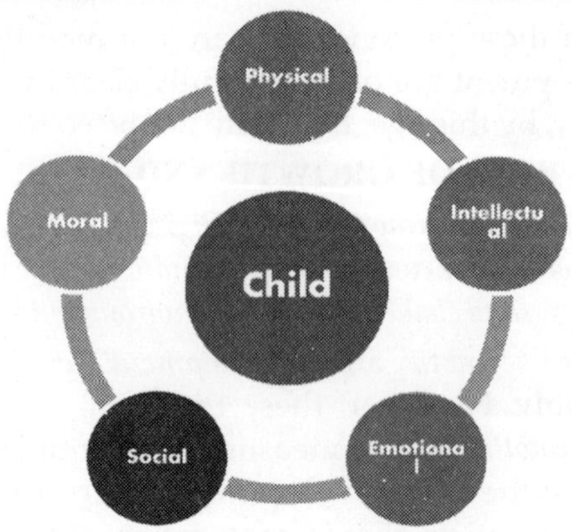

Fig. 2.1: Interactive Nature of Child Development

Physical Growth

The rate of physical growth is slow during the pre-school years compared to infancy and toddler-hood. However, preschool children show a steady gain in height and weight. They gain two to three inches in height every year. On an average, most six years olds are 44 inches tall. At the same time, the weight increases by about two kilograms every year. The following Table 2.1 gives the average height and weight of normal healthy pre-schoolers.

Table 2.1: Average Weight and Height of Indian Pre-school Children

Age in Years	Weight in Kgs.		Height in Cms.	
	Boys	Girls	Boys	Girls
2+	13.0	12.6	90.7	89.8
3+	14.8	14.4	99.1	98.2
4+	16.5	16.0	105.7	105.1
5+	18.2	17.7	111.5	111.0
6+	20.4	20.0	118.5	117.5

Source: A Report of the Expert Group of the Indian Council of Medical Research (ICMR), 2010.

A steady gain in height and weight usually indicates good physical growth. During preschool years, along with the changes in height and weight, there are other changes in the muscle tissue, adipose tissue, internal organs and various systems of the body.

The process of hardening and growth of bones continues during preschool years. However, pre-schooler s bones are still plastic, *i.e.,* they do not break easily and when damaged, mend more rapidly than bones that are mature. The bones of the arms and legs and trunk grow rapidly. By the age of six years, the legs of the pre-schoolers account for half his/her body length. This ratio is the same as the ratio of the adult body.

The brain continues to develop and reaches 75 per cent of its adult weight by five years of age and 90 per cent of its adult weight by the time the child is six years old. As a result of this development, the control over movements becomes better. Pre-school children tend to be farsighted as the eyes are still developing. It is only when the child is about eight years old, that the eyes are fully developed. The implication of this fact is that the reading material for pre-schoolers should be in large and bold print.

Around the age of four years, the muscles of the child grow rapidly. This growth in muscles accounts for more than half of the increase in weight. As the muscle fibre thickens and becomes stronger, the body movements become more efficient. Consequently, the child is able to participate in many more physical activities and games. The muscular growth, along with the steady increase in height, brings about a change in body proportions. Hence, the pre-schooler looks more slender. This is because, during the preschool years, the muscles around the abdomen become firm, the baby-like round stomach flattens and the child s arms and legs become longer. At the same time, the layer of the fatty tissue becomes thinner.

The change in body proportions along with improvement in muscle tone and strength, skeletal development and maturation of the nervous system contribute to an improvement in the child s balance and posture. This helps the pre-school child to become steadier on her feet. Her movements become graceful and well co-ordinated. Moreover, many other physiological changes also occur during pre-school years. As the expansion and contraction of lungs become better controlled, the child s breathing becomes lower and deeper. The heart also beats more slowly and steadies. As a result of better breathing and better blood circulation, most children are ready for the increased physical demands that will be placed on them in middle childhood.

Motor Skills

The pre-school years are marked by great advances in strength, speed and co-ordination. The child s body in preschool years is flexible and this enables her to learn many more skills. The pre-schooler enjoys learning new skills and spends a lot of time practising and refining them. Despite falling and stumbling, she jumps from stools and runs across open stretches. She takes part in many more physical activities and also interacts more frequently with other children. Her physical and motor skills also give her greater independence and she uses these skills to explore the environment and to do things on her own. The pre-school child is testing her skills and likes to have a sense of mastery in eating quickly, in running and in climbing to the top of the stairs.

- *Gross Motor Skills:* Most children between three and four years can run. At this stage, as they strive for better control, they delight in running with sudden starts and stops and turn corners rapidly as they do so. By five years, they are able to control their speed and direction. They can now start and stop smoothly. The length of their strides increases. Pre-schoolers seem to prefer to run instead of walking from one place to another. This is evident as they race each other and go up and down the stairs, weaving through crowded places and dodging obstacles. Children also learn to jump in a co-ordinated and graceful manner only after they have gained the strength and balance to leave the ground with both feet at the same time. This jumping pattern becomes smother during the pre-school years as they learn to crunch and use their arms to thrust themselves up while jumping. As the motor skills develop, they enable greater control, co-ordination and balance. Walking, running, and jumping are basic skills that develop naturally during the early childhood years. However, some skills need to be learnt and practised after the child has acquired the basic skill. For example, riding a cycle, turning cartwheels, climbing a tree, swimming etc.

Nearly all children develop their motor abilities in the same sequence, but the exact age at which they acquire these skills varies considerably. Most of the basic motor skills – running, jumping, climbing are achieved by the age of five or six years. In the pre-school years, children refine these skills and develop a wide range of new abilities.

- *Fine Motor Skills:* The development of fine motor control can be seen in the way a child writes with a chalk or a pencil. Control over scribbling emerges at the same time as the child masters other manipulative skills. Four year olds hold a crayon firmly and are better able to use the small muscles or their fingers. By five years of age, the child s drawings are quite distinguishable, as people, animals or trees. Typically, the pre-schooler s first representation of a human figure is drawn with a circle for a head and two vertical lines for legs. Six years old include greater detail in their drawings and the figures begin to take or realistic proportions.

The development of fine motor skills is also reflected in the way Pre-schoolers manipulate materials. At three years of age, using a pair of scissors can be frustrating for the child, but by four years, the child can cut paper and use a pair of scissors efficiently. Five-year-olds are able to cut along a straight line with scissors. By the time they are six years old, they can follow a line to cut out squares from thick paper. This would be difficult for them if the paper is thin or limp as it would bend easily. When children discover that they can cut things and paste them together in new combinations or convert raw materials into a design, they have found a new field of creative play. Drawings, colouring, paper-folding, pasting and threading the beads are usually the favourtie activities of the pre-schoolers. Moreover, during pre-school years, children become increasingly proficient in the area of self-help skills, *i.e.*, they learn to look after their own needs. The advances in gross and fine motor control not only give Pre-schoolers greater independence, but also allow them to help in activities within and outside the home.

Cognitive Abilities and Development of Concepts

Cognitive abilities refer to the process involving knowledge about the world, capacity to infer, to think and to understand a phenomenon rightly. This emphasises on the ability to generalise and formulate idea to solve-problems. Hence, cognition includes: thinking, remembering, problem-solving planning, imaging judging and deciding. Cognitive change at any period in the life span is affected to certain extent by perceptual development. As the child grows, much of his development of cognition comes first from the organisation of the perceptual processes. When the child receives numerous stimuli through his sense organs he categories those stimuli in order to give significance to the information they bring him. The young child s perception is bound to the physical aspects of perception and depends on his attitudes, values, and cultural meanings with which he interprets perceptual world. The cognitive framework of a young child is less complex than an older child as a result he fails to recognise the distinctive features among similar objects. Jean Piaget has classified cognitive development into four different sequential stages:

1. Sensory Motor Period – First sixteen (16) months.
2. Preoperational Period – Lasting from seventeen months to seven years.
3. Concrete Operational Thought Period – Lasting from seven to eleven years.
4. Formal Operational Period – Early adolescence.

During preoperational period the child acquires the skill of using symbols and languages and he learns to separate physical and mental realities and understands mechanical causation. The child s rapidly developing language, participation in make-believe play and drawings are reflections of her symbolic thinking. Piaget stated that pre-schooleres are not able to look at things from another perspective, that they do not have reversibility of thought and that they tend to centre because of which they are not able to classify, seriate or conserve. However, recent research has shown that pre-schoolers may develop these abilities a little earlier. They show these abilities provided the tasks are simple, distractions are removed and they are given some clues.

The pre-school years are the period when the child is learning many new concepts. She learns about everyday happenings and things she sees around her. During this period pre-school child is forming ideas about things and events, air, water, plants, trees, stars, festivals, colours, numbers and so forth. Concepts of objects like: dog, house, chair, tree, bus, flowers and so forth are acquired relatively early. The abstract concepts of numebr, shape, size and so forth are acquired more slowly. Understanding abstract concepts of number, time, space, size etc., are more difficult but non-the less the pre-schooler makes some head way in these. Moreover, a pre-school year sees the child sharpening her reasoning skills. The child tries to find out the cause of things. The foundations of problem-solving, hypothesis testing and scientific tempers are laid, as the child makes observations and collects information. The pre-schoolers also have the ability of matching and identifying common relations.

Research data in cognitive studies done with children provide much support for Piaget s explanation. In its application to education this cognitive theory dictates responsibility for a comprehensive programme with specific criteria for suitable environmental input, and for the nature and quality of the interaction between child and adult.

Language Skill

A child s language progresses at an amazing rate from babbling to one ward communication to complex sentences. There is a direct relationship between the child s growing vocabulary and her rapidly developing cognitive abilities. In addition to knowing how a word is used, the child must also understand the concept of which the word is a symbol. The understanding of the world is thus related to the understanding of the concept. Research findings show that in the normal course of growth, children are able to find and use the right word, only when they have understood the concept. Children in pre-school years are able to use and understand words that make comparisons between two objects or people, *i.e.*, comparative terms such as: larger, shorter, less etc. Initially, when a child hears the words being used in reference to a particular object in a situation, she may use the words only in the identical way.

Later the generalisation to other situations follows. By three years of age, a child is able to sort objects into two categories, for example – *(i)* big and; *(ii)* small. Gradually children learn to use words that convey this contrast. Children begin to develop an understanding of the concepts of space, movement and causation they begin to use location words like here there and in front of behind. By four years of age the child does not confuse the words that signify location. Children during pre-school years are able to contract longer and more complex sentences. The four-year-olds sentences are usually shorter than those of a five or six year old. As the child understands the concept of time, she begins to use tenses precisely. The use of the future tense in speech comes later than the past and present tense. This is because the immediate past in the child s actual experience is remembered more readily than something which has not actually happened. Being able to use the future tense appropriately, on the other hand, involves thinking, anticipating and planning ahead. It also requires the ability to use language as a means of thinking out problems and ideas. It is only when children are four to four and a half years of age, that they use future tense appropriately. However, children sometimes do get confused about the tenses even till eight to ten years of age.

The child learns language especially from the parents through imitation. The important implication for parents and teachers is that they should themselves serve as good role models, for the child to imitate. If the parent uses impolite or abusive language, the child will learn the same. Hence, the child must be exposed to a great deal of language and that too of a standard quality to be able to learn the same.

Social Relationship

Social development during preschool years is parallels cognitive and self-development in many ways. Most of this occurs during play, in which the child s interests evolve slowly and gradually from a primary concern with exploration and mastery of physical objects to a primary concern with peers and peer relationships. Early in this stage, the children are concerned primarily with whatever activities they are engaged in at the moment. The presence or absence of peers is relatively unimportant to them. Later, they become strongly motivated to seek out and play with peers, and objects are of interest primarily for social play rather than as vehicles for individual exploration or mastery.

Social activities of two-year-olds involving peers usually are restricted to 'parallel play'. It placed near each other and given similar toys to play with, two children during this stage usually will begin to play in similar fashion. However, they will play mostly as if they were alone, showing little or no interest in the other child and rarely if ever making attempts to interact. As children s peer orientation and social skills develop, they move into what has been called 'associative play'. They still play separately and individually, but they show much more awareness of each other s presence and much more social speech, even though their speech is heavily egocentric. Much of child s development, especially his social development and behaviour, during this stage is determined by two factors:

(i) Self-concept.

(ii) Personal Control.

During pre-school years the concept of self-broadens. The pre-schooler begins to define herself in terms of her physical characteristics, beliefs, likes and dislikes. The self-concept develops as others tell the child about herself and as she herself finds out about her abilities. By five years of age, the child is clear about his/her own gender. Sex-role stereotypes are learnt early in the childhood years and this is not surprising since adults behave differently towards boys and girls and so do expect differently. Moreover, development of strong interests in peers and in playing with them appears to occur spontaneously once children master the sensorimoter schemas involved in basic development tasks. Through contacts with playmates and neighbours, contacts with older siblings or relatives, and input from television, books and other sources, children gradually come to understand that children of their age typically play with similar children and that certain toys and games are meant especially for them and are for them to use. Further, it leads to the age and sex typical characteristics of early childhood, and eventually to a strong interest in playing with peers rather than spending time with or around parents.

General Characteristics of Pre-School Child

The different stages in the child s overall development constitute markers providing parents and educators with essential elements for assessing the child s progress and providing him with the necessary care and stimulation. All children throughout the world go through the same stages, but with certain relativity due to their specific personal and socio-cultural characteristics. However, account must be taken of the progress made between several successive assessments, and it is a series of several photographs accounts, which best gives a dynamic view of the process of development. Below are described the general characteristics of pre-school child. Most of the children during this period proceed in the following manner, but there may be few exceptions.

From 2 ½ to 4 Years

- Walks around on his own and visit neighbours.
- Can walk on tiptoe.
- Learns to dress and undress alone.
- Acquires toilet training at night.
- Imitates a cross, draws a figure with a head and trunk, sometimes other parts of the body.
- Recognises two or three colours.
- Speaks intelligibly, but still using childish language.
- Can state his name, sex, and age.
- Ask many questions, and is interested in how children are born.
- Recognises top and bottom, front and back.
- Listens to stories and asks for those he likes to be told again.
- Plays with other children and begin to share things.
- Shows affection for younger brothers and sisters.
- Becomes able to perform simple tasks.

From 4 to 5 Years

- Leaps, jumps, swings.
- Walks down stairs putting one foot on each step.
- Draws a figure with head, and principal limbs and parts of the body.
- Copies a square and a triangle.
- Speaks quite intelligible.
- Knows how to count his fingers.
- Knows his age and the day of the week.
- Listens to a story and can repeat its substance.
- Still asks many questions, takes an interest in new words and their meaning.
- Protests vigorously when prevented from doing what he wants.
- Can recognise four colours.
- Can assess shape and size, distinguish large from small.
- Takes an interest in the activities of adults.

From 5 to 6 Years

- Knows how to climb trees and dance to music.
- Can catch a ball thrown from a distance of one metre.

- Can remain motionless for one minute.
- Speaks correctly, relinquishes childish language.
- Draws a figure with head, trunk, limbs and hands.
- Begins to distinguish right from left, yesterday from tomorrow.
- Asks for meaning of abstract words.
- Takes an interest in the activities of the home and the quarter.
- Takes an interest in the age of young people and old people.
- Distinguishes between sweet, salt, sharp and bitter flavours.
- Invents games and changes the rules while they are proceeding.
- Detests authority imposed on him and carries out orders slowly.
- Performs simple tasks with interest.

PROBLEMS IN DEVELOPMENT

Every stage of development has its related problems. In order to understand a child s problems, it can be viewed in the context of:

- The stage of development the child has reached.
- The developmental tasks which the child is facing.
- The normal ranges and patterns of behaviour found in children at that particular stage of development.

Every child experiences some difficulties with his feelings, which create concern in those who care for him, specially the parents. Even when things do go well, however, every child between the ages of 3 and 6 still faces the normal aches and pains and crises of growing up. The children s problems thus can be identified by symptoms (such as: bed-welting or destructiveness); by underlying cause (such as: insecurity or family upheaval); by the system of functioning which has been affected (such as: disturbances of language functioning or emotional control); by very broad categories (such as: disturbances in the normal rate or progress of development). Most common problems in development are:

Disturbances in Developmental Progress

Children develop at their own rates, and there are broad ranges of what can be considered normal or typical behaviour for any given age. In any group, there are children with more mature speech, personality, and general behaviour than that of most children of their age, and there are others whose development lags behind. A child is said to be developmentally lagging or having developmental retardation. When the child, for any reason, is significantly lacking what can be expected of typical children of the same age. It usually applies to a child who is quite clearly slow in developing intellectual abilities and social and motor skills. Such a child can be recognised by his need for more assistance than other children of the same age, by his bewilderment or unco-operativeness in situations that most children master easily, or because he does not engage in the typical activities expected of children of his age. The parents of a developmentally lagging child often recognise the child s slowness or inability to keep up with other children. There are many causes of for developmental lag or retardation. The main causes are:

(a) *Sensory Problems*: Children having specific perceptual, visual or hearing problems is frequently not discovered until the child reaches pre-school or even school age.

(b) *Mental Retardation:* Children whose mental retardation is organic in nature – caused by, Down s syndrome, usually have very severe developmental disabilities. Those children, whose mental retardation is from nonorganic causes, usually have significant difficulties in behaving according to the norms for their age.

Attention Problems

There are some children, who are always physically active and unable to pay attention to any one thing/activity for more than few seconds. Such children may be hyperkinetic, which means that they are very active and has short attention span. They cannot concentrate long enough to listen to a story till the end. Some time, though their bodies may be still, their thoughts are perpetually active.

To control these difficult kinds of behaviour, parents and caregivers often resort to threats or punishment, but to non-avail. Punishment may make the child even more upset and less able to pay attention. Rather careful attention to these children, both at home and nursery school will enable to recognise the needs of the individual child and appropriate stimulation with reasonable structures can be carefully balanced. Many children with these problems show profound changes in their behaviour with carefully planned care at home and at the pre-school.

Language Problems

Many children between ages 2½ and 4 experience two kinds of language difficulty: *(i)* cluttering and *(ii)* speech immaturity. For even some, these difficulties continue through their first few years in school.

(a) *Cluttering*: Many children show cluttering when they become excited. At certain stages of development, 25 per cent or more of a child s speech may be cluttered. Even a 6 year old will culture his speech with repetitions when he is excited, tired, or not concentrating on what he is trying to say – when, for example, his mother asks what he has done at school and he wants to run out to play. The child whose parents treat cluttering or other early speech difficulties as abnormal is probably more likely to develop a serious and enduring speech problem. If a child who clutters is constantly interrupted and corrected, he is unlikely to develop pleasure or confidence in his speech fluency.

(b) *Speech Immaturity:* It is the other common childhood language difficulty. Speech immaturity is usually thought to be cute, and amused parents may encourage the child to continue to mispronounce 'w' for 'r', 'th' for 's' or 'woes' for 'rose'. Speech immaturities usually represent a phase, a passing stage in the child s acquisition of mature pronunciation.

Parents and teachers must understand that, cluttering and speech immaturities are problems in talking, not in understanding or using language for communication or thought. If ignored, they correct naturally as the child develops. There are however, several serious language problems that will not correct without treatment. Children with severe speech difficulties require expert evaluation since causes can include deafness, mental retardation, severe developmental disturbances (such as: childhood autism) aphasia and other significant disabilities. Children from bilingual homes or from families with limited verbal interaction may be silent or soft-spoken when they first enter pre-schools. The child whose limited speech is the result of fear and in security usually shows that he can understand what is said to him and when placed in a secure setting eventually begins to speak readily and clearly.

Social Problems

Children are socialised by their parents and immediate culture to become certain kinds of adults. Some children however clearly have difficulty relating to adults and peers. In the preschool years, there are three main types of social disability: *(i)* over inhibition *(ii)* over – excitability, and *(iii)* disorganisation.

Overly inhibited children may range from those who are simply shy to those who are fearful of strangers and new situations, uncommunicative, and not playful. In a supportive preschool setting the children may be allowed to respond at their own pace, the shy child can gradually begin to relate first with his caregiver and then with children of his age. A three year old entering preschool for the first time may have major difficulties leaving his parents and may show signs of real panic if this separation is handled roughly. Hence, by informing the caregiver of possible problems, parents can make the situation easier for both the child and the caregiver. The fearful child should enter preschool slowly. There might be several visits with a parent to the preschool and then a visit or two in which the parent leaves for a short time. When a child realises that his parents trust him there and that they will return, his initial fears of separation are usually reduced.

The social difficulties of the overly excitable child are quite different from those of the inhibited child. Excitable children often exhibit characteristics similar to those of hyperkinetic behavioural disturbance. For these children, quiet play may be difficult, and any change or stimulation may lead to a stream of wild, joyless activity. Their excitability may be associated with excessive and inappropriate responses, such as: laughing too much at a joke or becoming too angry over a disagreement. It is important to distinguish the excitable child from one who is normally lively, vigorous, and enthusiastic. Being with an overtly excitable child is like walking a tight rope, even when the child is quiet, he may at any time explode and release his pent-up energy. The proper choice of a preschool setting is as important for the excitable child as it is for the inhibited one; in each case, the child s general welfare must be the prime concern. A caregiver in the preschool can try to prevent the child who exhibits episodic anger from becoming too frustrated or upset by helping him choose activities that he can perform successfully. For the child whose aggression is triggered by losing in a competitive game or situation the caregiver can help find activities that do not involve winners and losers.

The child whose behaviour is disorganised may exhibit features of both the inhibited and the overlay excitable child. Behaviourally disorganised children lack systematic play and pleasant, satisfying social relations. Such a child may move quickly from one activity to another, show little capacity for long, thematic kinds of play – such as: playing store or house – and may never form attachments to other children or adults. His behaviour may be grossly immature in some ways and odd in others: for example, he may speak poorly or wet his pants, have unusual mannerisms or gestures, or may continually repeat the same word or phrase. For these children, professionals capable of providing therapy as well as education and care must supervise pre-school. Parents and teachers in a pre-school must learn to recognise the difference between a young child s normal silliness and immaturities and those that characterise developmental delay.

Physical Problems

Every child will most likely suffer some physical problems such as: cold, cough, fever, measles etc. Most children between ages 3 and 6 will have some problems in eating, sleeping, and toileting. Even though such problems are normal, the parents/preschool teachers should be alert to their nature and to any additional troubles which could indicate a more serious problem. For example, it is fairly typical for a child to bed-wet occasionally; however, one who suddenly reverts to regular bed-wetting and who exhibits other unusual behaviours may be undergoing a period of stress or reaching to some other emotional or developmental problem.

There are certain physical problems, which are directly associated with the emotions, such as: asthma, chronic diarrhoea, and nose stuffiness and vomiting, eczema etc. These are not actually caused by the child s state of mind, rather from the child s inability to cope with his feelings and anxiety. Such illnesses are often part of a stress cycle: the greater the child is upset, the worse the affliction gets; the less the upset, the milder the affliction. The proper functioning of a child s body is related to how he feels about himself and to how he is valued and treated by others.

Understanding Developmental Problems

Each child s behaviour reflects what he is as a whole person – a person with a mind, a body, a family, a culture, a history, and a current life situation. Awareness of problems in a child s development must cut across labels, so that his specific needs can be identified and met. Understanding how a child s social, emotional, intellectual, and physical growth are so closely related allows us to see the importance of preschool programmes which deal with the whole child. Quality preschool depends on preschool teachers own commitment, competence, and concern. In order to provide continuing positive support to the child s development, that a child normally experiences at home, preschool has to meet four essential conditions, such as:

- It promotes the child s physical health by identifying problems, helping the family to obtain medical help, and working to prevent the occurrence of new disease.
- It provides the child meaningful social experiences with competent and concerned pre-school teachers and with children of the same age.
- It creates opportunities for learning by making materials and situations available in an organised, thoughtful manner.
- It supports the child s family life by involving parents in the care of their children, keeping them informed about their children, making parenthood a pleasant and rewarding opportunity rather than an extra burden. It helps the parents feel secure that their children are receiving quality care.

All parents want their children to become certain kinds of adults. Hence, it must support their values and goals, while helping parents to find the best ways to reach the goals they have for their children and for themselves as parents.

SUMMARY OF THE CHAPTER

Pre-Conditions of Development

- Pre-school age is very critical period for the child s growth and development.
- Various preconditions of children s developments are – healthy genetic endowment, parental care, physical care, love and attention and models.

Major Aspects of Growth and Development during Pre-School Years

- Major aspects of growth and development in children include: physical growth, motor skills, cognitive abilities, concept formation, language skills and social relationships.
- The rate of physical growth is slow during the pre-school years compared to infancy and toddler-hood. However, preschool children show a steady gain in height and weight.
- The pre-school years are marked by great advances in strength, speed and co-ordination.
- The cognitive framework of a young child is less complex than an older child as a result he fails to recognise the distinctive features among similar objects.
- A child s language progresses at an amazing rate from babbling to one ward communication to complex sentences.
- Social development during preschool years is parallels cognitive and self-development in many ways.
- The different stages in the child s overall development constitute markers providing parents and educators with essential elements for assessing the child s progress and providing him with the necessary care and stimulation.

Problems in Development

- Various problems in development during preschool years are disturbances in developmental process, attention problems, language problems, social problems and physical problems.
- Understanding developmental problems of pre-school children enables the parents and preschool teachers to develop positive and quality environment for their optimal growth and development.

3

Care for Pre-School Children

"Everyone who loves, cares, and plays with children can help them to Learn and Develop. Care in Early Childhood is about celebrating the Present with an eye on the Future".

The ultimate objective of *"Development* of any country must be the improvement of the *quality of life of its people.* It is generally agreed that the years of early childhood are the most influential in a child's life. By the time most children start Pre-school, aged around three, the most important building blocks for learning have already been put in place. The importance of early stimulation, early nutrition and optimum interactional environment are widely recognised. The challenge of early childhood is to work out how development can best take place, and equally important to judge what should be the role of parents, the community, the state and the professionals in determining and bringing about the development. Since, the foundations for physical, psychological and social development are laid in early childhood services provided in an integrated manner at this stage can help ensure such improvement. The current situation reflects the growing realisation among policy-makers of the need for a supportive environment for a happy and healthy childhood.

MEANING AND DEFINITIONS OF CHILD CARE

The term 'care' in the context of Early Childhood Years is universally recognised as the fulfilment of all the basic needs of children for overall growth and development – Physical, social, intellectual, moral, speech, behaviour and habit formations. Moreover, the concept of children's care includes both 'caring' and 'nurturing' in an enabling and stimulating environment to develop to its full potential which are considerably and often irreversibly reduced. The care during early childhood years ensures holistic development of children to the maximum, bringing continuity of development in later life.

Early childhood care is one of the best ways to assure the child a smooth transition into primary school. It is also a critical factor in the child's subsequent transition to adulthood, influencing both social skills and behavioural choices.

Hence, child care is defined as the integrated set of actions that ensure for children the synergy of protection and support for their health, nutrition, physical, psychological and cognitive aspects of development. It is the caring for and supervision of a child or children, usually from birth to age thirteen. Child care is the action or skill of looking after children by parents, a day-care centre, babysitter, or other providers. Child care is a broad topic covering a wide spectrum of contexts, activities, social and cultural conventions, and institutions. Children, age five and younger, are being jointly cared for by parents and early childhood educators, relatives or other child-care providers. Early child care is a very important and often overlooked component of child development. Child care providers are our children's first teachers, and therefore play an integral role in our systems of early childhood education. Quality care from a young age can have a huge impact on the future successes of children. Quality child care may be defined as child care services that provide a responsive, developmentally appropriate environment for young children. This quality care, added to a quality home environment, leads to the best possible physical, intellectual, and social-emotional development in the child. Parents who know that their child is receiving quality child care can be assured that their child is safe, nurtured, and challenged to learn. Moreover, care does not take place in a void. The survival, well-being and development are dependent on and built around close relationships with parents, siblings, peers, other family members, neighbours and sometime other attachment figures in the community. Thus, the current situation reflects the growing realisation among policy-makers of the need for a supportive environment for a happy and healthy childhood.

BENEFITS OF CHILD CARE

Care of children up to six to eight years is of utmost importance as it lasts a life time. Early childhood years not only lays the foundation of later years, but globally acknowledged as the most 'critical' period for the development of several cognitive, social and psychomotor competencies, which contribute to later success in life. Hence, this critical period if not taken care of or supported by a stimulating and enriching physical and psychosocial environment, the chances of child's brain development to its fullest potential is hindered. Early childhood stage is even more crucial as the foundation for inculcating of social and personal values, habits, behaviour and attitudes gets developed and that too lasts a life time. So, it is the right of every child to gets a good 'head-start from the family, school and the community that will have a strong impact on the precious human capital available to a country like India. These assets of today will be in the years to come the 'youth power' of tomorrow.

- Early care ensures children's survival, well-being and development in healthy and normal way – meeting the basic needs of protection, food and health care, affection, safety, security and learning in a stimulating environment. It is concerned with holistic development of children.
- Fosters in children the natural need for discovery and curiosity, and their desire to learn, which forms the basis of lifelong learning. Such interest is an asset that stays with them for the rest of their lives and helps them to do better in later life.
- Early child care go much beyond school readiness, by preparing children for life and encourage them to be open for learning and for life's opportunities. It also increases in children, self-confidence and other learning potential, improved social skills, more creative ways of thinking and problem-solving.
- Supports parents in their skills as parenting, training on literacy, child development, health and nutrition, stimulate and create a good developmental environment for children.

- Parents/caregivers builds confidence, encourages parenting skills and becomes involved in their children's learning and development process, there by become an integrated part of child care services.
- Child Care can reduce inequality in society by giving girls and children from disadvantaged backgrounds learning experiences/opportunities in schools and a chance in life for building a better future.

So, if children are not given experiences and opportunities to think and act independently they may grow up unable to make decisions for themselves, not knowing how to think for themselves or help themselves, they will always be waiting for others to help them. On the other hand, if children grow up from an early age in a stimulating environment, they will experience the feeling of confidence and self-respect that comes from being able to act as an independent human being. Thus, making them more competent and prepared them to face the challenges of future life.

IMPORTANCE OF CHILDREN'S ENVIRONMENTS

Young children's environments have a major impact on their 'being' and the 'ability to grow' as independent individuals.. Their developmental environments are largely established by their parents, siblings, relations, teachers, school and other members of their community. The family is the child's initial and most important source of stimulation. It is in the family that children first learn socialisation skills, and where their initial emotional, physical and intellectual needs are met and get shaped. In psychological theorisation, environment has always been regarded as crucial factor. Every child is a part of many social settings, such as: family, school, neighbourhood and the larger community. Interaction between these settings takes place as and when he grows and develops. During early childhood years, a safe and stable environment, good health, adequate nutrition, responsive care giving, opportunities for emotional connections and attachment, and stimulation (opportunities to learn) are important to ensure healthy development in the child. In these years, it is important also to address maternal mental health, as this influences the quality of caregiver – child interaction. Maternal depression puts children at special risk of deprivation and inadequate stimulation. In return, interventions to support care for child development positively impact on the caregiver's mental health and well-being. Hence, healthy and stimulating environment (physical, psycho-and social) can help children to improve their competencies (Refer Figure 3.1). The environment of the child is further important, because it provides parents with a culturally based history of attachment experiences and child-rearing attitudes, behaviour and norms, that influence their parental style of responding to the children's attachment needs, and preparing them for adaptation to the specific 'niche' in which they were born.

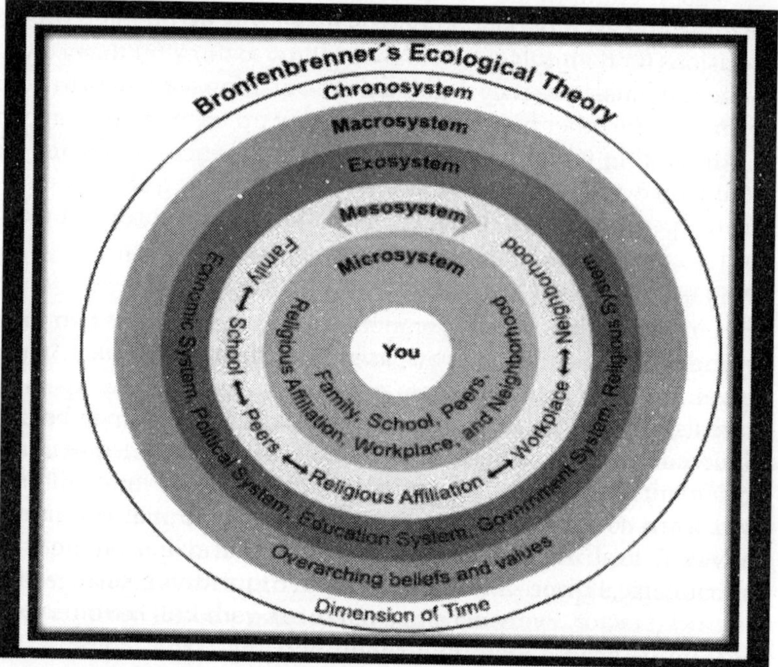

Fig. 3.1: Bronfenbrenner's Ecological Theory of Development (1995)

In order to provide still better understanding about how the child grows in its own environment Uri Bronfenbrenner's 'Ecological theory' on child development (Figure 3.1) will be of great significance. This theory has proposed a strong ecological and contextual view of development, which consists of five environmental systems ranging from the five-grained inputs of direct interactions with social agents to the broad based inputs of culture. Children are depicted as growing up in the context of the Micro-systems of family and pre-school. With each Microsystems, the impact of the environment is powerfully mediated by the beliefs and expectations of care givers, as expressed through the extent and character of the specific interactions with children. The relationship between the Micro-systems, in terms of shared or conflicting mutual beliefs of care givers as well as active points of contacts constitutes the Meso-system. Of course, Children's experience of their environment not mere as tidy' as the model suggests: there may be multiple, overlapping changing Micro-systems.

Further, the quality of children's home environment, in terms of quality of stimulation and learning opportunities, is closely associated with their well-being. Having access to material learning resources and nurturing learning experiences consistently during the first few years of life affords children with the foundations for healthy development and lifelong learning. Research reveals the following findings on environmental influences on infant and on young children:

- For healthy brain development child needs a good diet, sufficient rest and sleep.
- A child's visual system is critically depended on environmental stimulation for overall development.
- Exposure to a rich language environment is crucial for the child to develop good language skills.
- Neglect, abuse and other forms of maltreatment have serious negative consequences for children's brain development and cause subsequent psychological problems.
- Early experiences, particularly parent-child relationship play a critical role in brain development.
- Children differ in their vulnerability and resilience to potentially harmful influences on their development.

"The child, for the full and harmonious development of his or her personality, should grow up in a family environment, and atmosphere of happiness, love, and understanding."

CHILD REARING PRACTICES

Child rearing normally means '*socialization*' – the process by which a child is born into a given society, and becomes a social being. Further, it refers to all the interactions between the parents and their children. The interaction includes the parent's expression of attitudes, values, interests and beliefs as well as their care-taking and training behaviour (Sears, 1957). It includes the overall care, socialisation and training of the growing child in a particular culture. Thus, it may be viewed as the tasks that aid meeting the needs of the growing child, of various stages of the life cycle.

Parents bear the primary responsibility for meeting their children's physical, emotional, and intellectual needs and for providing moral guidance and direction.

The family influence is of paramount importance during early childhood years, as the interactions of the child is entirely confined to the family members and the child internalises whatever he perceives around him. The child considers his parents as models for his behaviour and adjustments to life. The child develops patterns of social behaviour similar to those of his parents or other adults/care takers around him. Child rearing includes much more than providing a child food, shelter, and clothing which are the basics for growth and development. The growing child has to be provided opportunities (stimulization) for the realisation of his potentialities with love and affection. Numerous studies conducted independently have proved the importance of love, and care and the undesirable effect of deprivations. It has been observed that, lack of love can hamper the physical, mental and emotional growth of the child and sometimes develop deviant behaviours. Child-rearing aims to develop in the child the capacity for adjustments as prescribed by the cultural system to which the child belongs. The purpose of child rearing is of two folds:

1. To help the child achieve a personal state of well-being.
2. To assist the child in becoming a productive and well socialised member of the society.

The various aspects of child rearing are as follows:

- Child birth and after.
- Diet of the mother.
- Feeding and weaning of the child.
- Bathing and clothing of the child.
- Toilet training of the child.
- Sleeping habits of the child.
- Medical care of the child.

- Play activities and discipline.
- Schooling.
- Love and affection.
- Parent-child relationship.

There is growing evidence that responsive parenting can have lifetime effects on all aspects of children's development including their health, nutrition, learning and protection.

Dimensions of Child Rearing Practices

Parents create the environment in which their children grow. They organize the daily routines that govern children's lives. As children grow, they pass through identifiable stages. Parents must be aware of these transitions and be prepared to respond to children in new ways appropriate to their changing needs. Parents disciplinary practices have frequently been conceptualised in terms of the interaction between two dimensions of parental behaviour. The first deals with the emotional relationship with the child and ranges from accepting, responsive, child centred behaviour to rejecting, unresponsive behaviour focussed on the needs and wishes of the parents. The second dimension deals with parental control and varies from restrictive, demanding behaviour to a permissive, undemanding parental style in which few restraints are placed on the child's behaviour.

Table 3.1: Two Dimensional Classification of Parenting Styles

Emotion/ Control	Responsive Child – Centred	Unresponsive Parent – Centred
Controlling/ Demanding	Authoritative Parent	Authoritarian Parent
Low in Control/ Undemanding	Permissive Parent	Uninvolved parent

Source: Maccoby and Martin, 1983.

These two parenting dimensions sum up basic differences in how parents carry out the task of socialisation. From Table 3.1 various combinations of control and responsiveness yield four types of parents or parenting practices. Each parenting pattern predicts important aspects of child development.

1. *The Authoritative Child-Rearing Practices*: Parents using authoritative style of child rearing practices are controlling

and demanding in nature. They have high expectations for mature behaviour and firmly enforces commands and use strict punishments for disobedience on the part of the children. At the same time, they are warm, nurturing, listen patiently and sensitive to their children's view. They also encourage their children to participate in the family decision-making process. These authoritative parents use a rational, democratic approach to child rearing in which the rights of both parents and children are recognised and respected.

- *effect on child's development:* the effect of authoritative parenting create children, who were zestful, content in mood, self-reliant in their mastery of new tasks, self-controlled in their ability to show sustained effort and refrain from engaging in disruptive behaviour. Study by Baumrind (1971) revealed that, independent, achievement oriented behaviour among girls and friendly, co-operative social behaviour among boys showed especially strong associations with authoritative parenting Moreover, few other researchers indicated that the authoritative style continues to predict a variety of dimensions of competence during middle childhood and adolescence, including high self-esteem, internalised moral standard, and superior academic performance in high school (Dornbusch *et al.* 1987; Hoffman, 1970).

2. *The Authoritarian Child-Rearing Practices*: In this style of parenting, parents are demanding, controlling, place high value on conformity and obedience on the part of the children. They are unresponsive, even outright rejecting, when children assert opposing opinions and beliefs. Consequently, very little communication and sharing take place between the parents and children. Rather, children are expected to accept their parent's word for what is right in an unquestioning manner. If they do not, authoritarian parents resort to forceful, punitive measures to curb the child's will. The authoritarian style of parenting is clearly biased in favour of parent's needs, with little room accorded to child's independent self-expression.
   - *effect on child's development*: Baumrind's (1967) research indicates that the pre-schoolers with authoritarian parents

are withdrawn and unhappy. They appeared anxious and insecure when interacting with peers and tend to react with hostility when frustrated. In subsequent research, girls who were products of authoritarian child rearing were dependent, lack exploration and achievement motivation, while some boys showed high rate of anger and defiance. Moreover, authoritarian and power assertive discipline is negatively related to internalisation of moral prohibitions and self-esteem in children.

3. *The Permissive Child Rearing Practices*: Permissive parents are nurturant, communicative and accepting, but they avoid asserting their authority or imposing control of any kind. They are overly tolerant and permit children to make virtually all of their own decisions. For example – children of permissive parents eat meals and go to bed when they feel like it, watch as much television as they want, play whenever they want for any longer period of time, no restrictions about going out late night etc. Some permissive parents believe that a relaxed style of child rearing is good for children, while many others lack confidence even in their ability to influence their youngster's behaviour and are disorganized and ineffective in running their households.
   - *effect on child's development*: the children of permissive parents are highly immature, and find difficulty in controlling their impulses, were overly dependent and demanding of adults, and show less sustained involvement in classroom activities than children of parents who exerted more control. Moreover, they are usually disobedient, explosive, and reactive which comes against their momentary desires. Study by Baumrind (1971) indicated that the link between permissive parenting and passive, dependent, non-achieving behaviour for boys were found but not for girls.

4. *The Un-involved pattern of Child Rearing Practices:* At the time when undemanding parenting is combined with indifferent or rejecting behaviour, it falls within the category of uninvolved child – rearing practices. In this approach, parents display little commitment to their roles as caregivers and socialising agents beyond the minimum efforts required

to maintain the child as a member of the household. Often daily pressures and stress in their lives overwhelm these parents, and they have very little time and energy to spare for their children. As a result, they cope with the requirements of parenting by keeping the child at a distance and are strongly oriented towards avoiding inconvenience. They may respond to the child's immediate demands for food and easily accessible objects. However, any efforts that have to do with long-term goals, such as: establishing and enforcing rules about homework or setting standards for acceptable social behaviour the parents attempts very little to get the child to conform (Maccoby and Martin, 1983).

- *effect on child development:* Martin (1981) reported that uninvolved mothers as opposed to responsive counterparts had pre-schoolers who were non-complaining, demanding, and interfering in their behaviour. Pulkkinen (1982) found that parents who rarely had conversations with their adolescents, took little interest in their life at school, and were seldom aware of their whereabouts and activities. These adolescents were found to be low in frustration, tolerance and emotional control, lacked long term goals, and more often had records of delinquent acts than adolescents of involved parents. Other longitudinal findings support an association between a distant, indifferent, and unconcerned parenting style and impulsive, under controlled behaviour throughout the childhood and adolescent years (Block, 1971).

As children get older, effective parents adjust their level of involvement to fit with the child's changing capacity for independent, autonomous functioning. While too little parental involvement is associated with serious developmental difficulties, too much can be overbearing and intrusive. A gradual lessening of parental monitoring and vigilance as children gets older supports their movement towards a mature, responsible behaviour, as long as it continues to be built on high parental commitment and a warm, openly communicative relationship (Maccoby and Martin, 1983).

Table 3.2: Major Parental Behaviours and Children's Characteristics

	Parental Behaviours		
	Authoritarian	**Authoritative**	**Permissive**
Children's Characteristics	1. Withdrawn	1. Self-assertive	1. Impulsive
	2. Lack of Enthusiasm	2. Independent	2. Low Self Reliance
	3. Shy (Girls)	3. Friendly	3. Low Self Control
	4. Hostile (Boys)	4. Co-operative	4. Low Maturity
	5. Low Need Achievement	5. High Need Achievement	5. Aggressive
	6. Low Competence	6. High Competence	6. Lack of Responsibility

Source: Dacy and Travers (1996). Human Development: Across the Life Span.

- *effective parenting style:* The repeated association of authoritative parenting with social, emotional, and intellectual maturity led Baumrind to conclude that the authoritative style plays a causal role in children's superior development. According to Lewis (1981), parents of well-socialized children use firm, demanding tactics because their children happen to have co-operative, obedient dispositions, not because firm control is an essential ingredient of effective parenting. Baumrind (1983) has countered Lewis's challenge by pointing out that many children of authoritative parents do not submit willingly to adult authority. Disciplinary conflicts occurred often in the authoritative homes, but parents handled it firmly, patiently, and rationally. They neither gave in to children's unreasonable demands nor responded in a harsh, arbitrary fashion. Baumrind emphasized that it is not the exercise of firm control per se, but rather the rational and reasonable use of firm control that has positive consequences for children's development.

Children's characteristics contribute to the ease with which parents are able to implement an authoritative pattern. When children react negatively, some parents respond inconsistently by giving into the child's unruly behaviour, thereby rewarding it and increasing the chances that it will occur again. Children of parents who go back and forth between authoritarian and passive, indifferent child-rearing styles have especially impulsive, aggressive, and irresponsible youngsters, who do very poorly in school (Dornbusch *et al.* 1987). Maccoby and Martin (1983) point out the direction of influence between parenting practices and children's characteristics which goes both ways. Impulsive and difficult children make it harder for parents to remain firm as well as democratically involved, but parenting practices can either sustain or reduce children's difficult behaviour.

Evidences from behaviour-genetic research and epidemiological studies shows that, parenting practices have major influence on various domains of children's development (Collins *et al.* 2000). Lack of warm, positive relationship with parents, insecure attachment and inadequate supervision of and involvement with children are strongly associated with children's increased risk for behavioural and emotional problems (Patterson *et al.* 1992; Shaw *et.al.* 1996). Even harsh and inconsistent discipline in early childhood years interference with children developing good social skill and self control.

In the process of Child-rearing, the training and values parents inculcate in their children exert a profound influence on a child's attitude – his thinking, feeling and the way he behaves.

Factors Influencing Child Rearing Practices

Child rearing practices do not exist in isolation but are usually related to a broader constellation of environmental events. Child rearing practices are considered as a product of ideas, beliefs and attitudes prevalent in a community on how to bring up children. These ideas are bound to change as a result of global environmental changes. Moreover, the process of child rearing is greatly influenced by the characteristic ways of thinking, feeling and acting prevalent in the cultural group to which the family belongs.

India is a vast country with many sets of culture, and sub-groups within each cultural group. Therefore, regardless of how child rearing is viewed, important aspects of cultural differences between groups make the dimensions of considerations rather wide. In addition, every society has some set of rules that the growing infant is required to conform. Each group in turn also differs in techniques that are used for enforcing and reinforcing conformity. However, the major factors affecting the child-rearing practices in general are as follows:

- *Culture:* Child rearing practices differ from culture to culture, and also among different groups within the same culture. They are influenced among other things, by the educational level, economic condition and traditional value system of the family and caste or sub-caste group. The different dimensions of parenting that underlie the child-rearing styles (authoritarian, authoritative permissive and uninvolved parenting) apply to a wide range of cultures around the world. Rohner and Rohner (1981) rated descriptions of parental behaviour and found that children everywhere seem to experience differing degrees of control and nurturance involved from parents and other major caregivers. Although cross-cultural variability does exist, the most common pattern of child-rearing in the cultures studied by the Rohners was a style that is warm and controlling, but neither very relaxed nor very restrictive, much like Baumrind's authoritative pattern. However, in majority of western culture, healthy psychosocial development of children is promoted most effectively by love with at least moderate parental control.
- *Social Class:* There exist social-class differences in child rearing practices in all most all cultures/countries. When asked about qualities they would like to encourage in their children, parents who work in semiskilled and skilled manual occupations such as: mechanics, drivers etc., place high value on external characteristics such as: obedience, neatness and cleanliness. In contrast, white collar and professional parents more often emphasise internal psychological dispositions, such as: curiosity, happiness, and self-control. These differences in child-rearing values are reflected in social class variations in parenting behaviours. Middle-class parents use more explanations, verbal praise, and inductive disciplinary techniques. In case of low-income and working class householders, command such as: you will do that because I told you to as well as criticism and physical punishment. These coercive practices are verbally restricted, and they do not encourage children to compare and evaluate alternative courses of action. Consequently, they contribute to the cognitively less enriching home environment among low-income families. Moreover, social class variations in child-

rearing practices can be understood in terms of a number of differences in life conditions that exist between low-income and middle-income families.

Low-income parents often feel a sense of powerlessness and lack of confidence in their relationships with institutions beyond the family, a factor that has consequences for the way they rear their children. For example: several theorists suggests that because lower-class parents are continually subjected to the rules and authorities of others in the workplace, their parent-child interaction duplicates their own experiences, only with them in the authoritative roles. Middle-class occupation on the other hand allows more room for self-direction and place greater emphasis on the manipulation of ideas and symbols. Moreover, the values and behaviour required for success in the world of work are thought to affect parent's ideas about characteristics importance to train their children, who are expected to enter similar work roles in the future. Social class differences in educational attainment may also affect these child-rearing variations. Middle-class parent's concern with nurturing their children's internal psychological characteristics is probably facilitated by years of higher education, during which the parents learned to think about abstract, subjective ideas.

Furthermore, the greater economic security of middle class parents free them from the burden of having to worry about making ends meet on a daily basis. As a result, they can devote more energy and attention in thinking about and encouraging the inner characteristics of themselves and their children (Hoffman, 1984). The constant stresses that affect many low-income families constitute an additional factor that contributes to social-class differences in child-rearing patterns, such as: poor health, no money, no food, no medicines etc., when daily crisis arise, parental irritability, child behaviour problems and coercive interactions within the household increases (Compas *et al.* 1989). These outcomes are especially severe in families experiencing chronically depressed living conditions, such as: poor housing and dangerous neighbourhoods that make day-to-day existence even more difficult (McLoyd, 1990). Nevertheless, within single social class there is considerable variation in factors that affect the child rearing style. The family structure and customs of some ethnic groups buffer the stress and disorganization that result from living in poverty. Moreover, variations in child-rearing methods are found within different social groups. Parents from rural areas are on the whole, more authoritarian in their methods than urban parents.

- *Types and Size of the Family:* In general, the trend towards a smaller family has favourable consequences for parent-child interaction and in turn, for variety of aspects of child development. Studies show that parental attitude and treatment towards children change systematically as more and more children are added to the household. More children mean less time that husband and wife have to devote to one another as well as to each youngster's activities, school work, and other concerns. As a result, parents of large families tend to feel less satisfied with their marital relationships and parenting roles. Disciplinary practices become more authoritarian and punitive as family size increases and parents try to keep large numbers of youngsters 'in line'. Investigators believe that children who grow up in large families have somewhat lower intelligence scores, poorer school achievements, and lower self-esteem. Forms of child maladjustment also vary with family size. Anti-social behaviour and delinquency appear more often among children and adolescents with many siblings.

In the Indian setting, the family has a major role in the child's socialisation. However, it is not the only possible agent, as the process which, though begins in the home, does not end there. The outside world also makes significant impact on the child as he is exposed to a succession of persons, groups and institutions. Each of which imposes its own expectations, rewards and punishments on the child and contributes in shaping the development of his skills, values and pattern of behaviour through positive and negative reinforcement.

- *Parental Attitudes, Beliefs, Behaviour and Parenting Styles:* Many studies shows that parental attitudes and treatment of children change systematically depending on their own beliefs, values, temperament etc. Parental behaviour can be organized along two dimensions – control and responsiveness – that when combined, yield four parenting styles: *(i)* authoritative, *(ii)* authoritarian, *(iii)* permissive and *(iv)* uninvolved parents. Children of authoritarian parenting appeared to be anxious, insecure, tend to react hostility when frustrated. They usually lack achievement motivation and have high rate of anger and defiance etc. Authoritarian, power assertive discipline is negatively related to internalisation of moral prohibitions and self-esteem.

In case of authoritative parenting the children are zestful, content in mood, and self-reliant in their mastery of new tasks, self-controlled in their ability. They show sustained effort and refrain from engaging in disruptive behaviour. Children of authoritative parenting are the most socially and cognitively competent. On the other hand, children being brought up by the permissive parents are highly immature, difficulty in controlling their impulses, overtly dependent and demanding of adults. They usually show less sustained involvement in classroom activities, are disobedient, explosive and reactive.

A study on the attitude of the Adivasi (tribal) and non-Adivasi (non-tribal) mothers towards child-rearing practices showed that the attitudes of the adivasi mothers and the non-adivasi mothers were not so much affected by their cultural background as by their educational level. Joshi (1982) studied educational problems of the scheduled castes and scheduled tribes of Baroda district and found that the parents of the scheduled caste and scheduled tribe students had a positive attitude towards education but were doubtful about the capabilities of their children. They complained about their inability to take interest in the day-to-day home work given by the school for their children because of their own limitation. Thus the positive attitude becomes ineffective in bringing about the expected results. Grover (1977) studied parental aspirations as related to personality and school achievements of children in Chandigarh, Punjab state and found that there was a very high and significant correlation between fathers and mother's aspirations for their sons. There was a positive and significant correlation between parents' aspirations and self-concept of their sons. High aspirations of parents led to low dominance in sons. The school achievements of sons of low aspirant parents were better than the sons of both average aspiring parents and high aspiring parents.

Sharma (1981) conducted a study on child rearing practices and child growth in Indian urban families. It was reported that 60 per cent of mothers thought it very important that children should do well in school. Most of the mothers mentioned Precise vocational targets and firm aspirations for their children. The aspirations are mostly doctor, engineer and scientists. One-third of the mothers cherish aspirations dependent on child's abilities and inclinations. However, mothers of only child tend to expect that her child would fulfil parent's expectations. Nine out of ten mothers who had only one child expected their children to be so.

- *Caste:* There was difference in the patterns of socialisation for higher caste and low caste families in India. Parental attitudes, beliefs and interactional patters differ in case of higher and low caste group. It is the caste upbringing, which are very strongly rooted affects the child rearing patterns. The higher cast group gave more importance to girl's education then the low-caste group. The study by Yardi (1972) revealed that sex difference existed in certain aspects of socialisation, but the patterns of socialisation did not vary much with the type of family and caste.

NUTRITIONAL AND HEALTH CARE OF PRESCHOOL CHILDREN

Children are the most precious assets of any nation. The future of any society depends on the attention that is provided at any given moment to its children. A happy child is a symbol of the developed country and the progress made by mankind. Thus, a happy childhood is the basis for a stable and strong adulthood. The survival and upliftment of children in a developing country like India is a great challenge. Hence, right type of both physical and psychological care, guidance, assistance and opportunities are required for their well-being and proper growth. Although the physical growth rate declines by the time the child is one year old, but the foundation of good health is laid during the pre-school age. In India about 20 per cent of the total deaths occur among toddlers in the age group of 1 to 4 years. A child who has failed to grow during this crucial period may not make up the loss in growth even with an excellent diet in later life.

The brain develops most rapidly before birth and during the first two years of life. Proper nutrition and good health are important during this time.

Significance of Nutritional Requirement

Nutrition plays a dominant role in early childhood development. During this critical period from birth to three years of age, children are at-risk/vulnerable to permanent effects of stunting and negative cognitive outcome leading to malnutrition. A child's brain undergoes rapid growth between conception to eight years of age with demand for energy and protein requirement, which has direct effect on child's future mental abilities. Micronutrients like: iron and iodine play an important role in developmental outcomes in developing countries as in India. On the whole good nutrition during early years does have positive impact on the academic performance throughout childhood and beyond.

Energy requirement varies according to age, sex, activity, climate, and the growth pattern. Proportionately, a child requires more calories per kilogram of body weight as compared to an adult person. This is mainly due to the high basal metabolic activities, extra physical activities of the child and extra energy needed for growth. The pre-school age is a period of rapid growth and development and nutritional requirements are high per unit body weight, as compared to the older child. There is an increased need for all nutrients, but the pattern of requirement varies for different nutrients in relation to their role in growth of specific tissues. Nutrients should be well balanced between the meals. There should be adequate energy and good quality protein in the diet. Since childhood is the age of rapid growth, proteins of high biological value must be included in the diet. Iron deficiency is quiet common during this period, leading to iron deficiency anaemia. Moreover, protein energy malnutrition is the most widespread form of malnutrition among pre-school children. Children often become victims of traditional beliefs, food fads and due to that many essential food items are forbidden to them.

Hence a balanced diet rich in calories and protein with adequate vitamins as A, D, C and B-complex along with minerals as iron and calcium is highly recommended for a pre-school child.

Balanced Diet for a Pre-school Child

The pre-school children's meal pattern should meet all the nutrients, which most children require. Protein allowances for children of 1 to 3 years is 1.83 gms/kgs or 22 gms. For 4 to 6 years old, 1.56 gms/kg or 29 gms to ideal weight is recommended.

Table 3.3: ICMR Recommended Dietary Allowance for Pre-school Children

Nutrients	1 - 3 Years	4 - 6 Years
Weight per (Kg)	12.2	19
Energy (Kcal)	1240	1690
Protein (Gram)	22	30
Fat (Gram)	25	25
Calcium (Mg)	400	400
Iron (Mg)	12	18
Retinol (Mcg)	400	400
Beta-carotene (Mcg)	1600	1600
Thiamine (Mg)	0.6	0.9
Riboflavin (Mg)	0.7	1.0
Nicotinic Acid (Mg)	08	11
Pyridoxine (Mg)	0.9	0.9
Ascorbic Acid (Mg)	40	40
Folic Acid (Mcg)	30	40
Vitamin B12 (Mcg)	0.2 -1.0	0.2 -1.0
Magnesium (Mg)	50	70
Zinc (Mg)	05	07

Source: Srilaxmi, B (2011). Dietetics, New age International (PVT), New Delhi.

All these nutrients are required for maintaining health and well-being of the growing child. A study on pre-school children has shown that average per head intake of leafy vegetables is 4 gms against the recommendation of 40-59 gms per day. Intake of other vegetables is 14 gms instead of 30 to 50 gms. A pre-schooler consumes only 7 gms of fruits as against a recommendation of 60 gms per day. For proteins 40 to 50 gms of pulses are recommended, but the average consumption is only 14 gms, 80 ml of milk is generally consumed instead of 200 ml of milk or milk products per day. Thus our pre-school children are exposed to an inadequate diet which is the major cause of malnutrition in India. The children often become victims of traditional beliefs and food fads. Thus, many essential food items are forbidden to them. To an extent, malnutrition results from this. Cereals, pulses, other vegetables leafy vegetables and cheap fruits are essential to provide enough of energy, proteins and vitamins to the child. Milk is a must for pre-school children; however it can be substituted by giving other forms of milk like groundnut or soybean milk, in case animal milk is not available. Composition of a balanced diet for a pre-school child is given below.

Table 3.4: Food Requirements for Pre-school Children (Per Day)

Age Group	Cereals	Pulses	Leafy Vegetables	Other Vegetables	Roots & Tubers	Milk	Fats & Oil	Sugar & Jaggery	Fruits	Egg	Meat or Fish
1-3 yrs.	175 gm	35 gm	40 gm	20 gm	10 gm	300 ml	15 gm	30 gm	60 gm	1 gm	30 gm
3-6 yrs.	270 gm	35 gm	50 gm	30 gm	20 gm	250 ml	25 gm	40 gm	60 gm	1 gm	30 gm

If the balanced diet is provided as per the requirement of the pre-school child, it will be reflected in the normal growth pattern. A pre-school child gains an average of 12.4 cms height and 2.5 Kgs weight during 1 to 2 years. The growth pattern of a pre-school child of 2 to 3 years is 8.9 cm height and 2.1 Kgs weight per year. During 3 to 4 years there is a slight decline in the growth pattern, that is 7.3 cms height and 2 Kgs weight per year. Height gain of a pre-schooler of 4 to 5 years per year is only 5.6 cms and the weight is 1.8 kgs. Even though there are different factors, which affect the height and weight gain of a child, the proportionate rate has a pattern and marked variation in it must be taken seriously.

Dietary Patterns and Food Selection

Meeting the nutritional requirements is important for a pre-school child, so that satisfactory growth and development is not hindered. Ideal dietary pattern and right food selection for pre-school children should be as follows, which initiates the development of good food habits in future.

- Small frequent meals should be provided at regular intervals as the pre-schooler has a small appetite and short attention span for eating.
- Child should never be forced to eat more than he can take.
- Foods, full of nutrients should be selected as per requirements – Adequate in terms of quality and quantity (selected from the Basic Five Groups).

- A packed snack, if required for the school going pre-schoolers, should be nutritionally adequate and easy to handle.
- Food preferences of the child should be taken in to consideration.
- Regularity in meal time is essential.
- New foods should be gradually introduced into the diet of the child, so that the child gets used to a wide variety of foods.
- New foods should be introduced when the child is hungry.
- Food selection should ensure variety in colour, texture and flavour to ensure better acceptance.
- Small frequent meals should be provided at regular intervals as the pre-schooler has a small appetite and short attention span for eating.
- Bland flavours are better accepted and excessive use of spices, condiments and oils should be avoided. Foods should be easily digestible.
- Excessive use of fried foods and very sweet foods should be avoided as these may cause irritation of the gastro-intestinal tract and the latter predispose to dental caries.
- Proper elimination is usually maintained by a daily diet of fruits, vegetables and whole grain products.

Table 3.5: A Sample Menu for a Pre-School Child (3 - 6 Years)

Time	Meal	Menu
6.30 A.M.	Early Morning	A glass of Milk
7.30 A.M.	Breakfast	Semolina Upma/Halwa/Stuffed Chappati/Parathas
9.00 A.M.	Mid-	Soybean Milk
11.00 A.M.	morning	Biscuits and Fruits (Banana/Apple/Orange)
12.30 P.M.	Lunch	Rice, Dal, Mixed Vegetable curry, Curd, salad.
3.00 P.M.		Mango/Orange Juice/Lassi
5.00 P.M.	Evening Snacks	Milk, Idli/Upma/Bread Sandwich/Egg custard
8.00 P.M.	Dinner	Chappatis, Dal and Vegetables stew, Carrot Khir
9.30 P.M.		A glass of Milk

Developing Healthy Food Habits

Over and above the points discussed earlier, the mealtime should be a happy occasion, when children and adults can enjoy each other's company and at the same time relish the food properly. The dinning environment can affect the whole experience to a greater extent. If possible, the area should be large enough to permit children to sit in groups, especially with the family members. Children during this period need to be allowed ample time to eat by themselves. Moreover, parental food habits are mostly reflected on their children or in other words, children learn good/bad food habits from their parents. Food for the children should be well prepared and attractively served to draw the attention of the children to eat. During this period, children by nature are very curious to know about everything. Hence, parents while giving food to the child need to explain the significance and advantages of taking the particular types of food and if not taken, what will be the consequences. So that, children learn about selecting healthy food items and develop habit of taking it regularly. Simultaneously, as a part of the healthy food habits regime children should be trained to maintain hygiene, while taking the food, such as: keeping the nails and teeth clean, washing hands before and after meals and develop the aptitude of self-care and clean living.

Causes of Rejecting Foods by the Pre-school Child

- At the time, when the child is unwell.
- More engaged or diverted to play activities.
- When the child is sleepy or too tired.
- Due to warm infestation (hook warm).
- When the child is psychologically upset, due to the absent of mother/attachment figure/stress in school/Birth of sibling/ shifting to a new place.
- Less time for eating.
- Lack of variety in the diet.
- Food not palatable/attractive, and in preferred consistency.
- Less apatite or food taken before regular meal, so do not feel hungry.
- Lack of peer group influences the mood of the child, thereby accepting or rejecting the food intake.

Nutritional Problems during Early Childhood

According to the Report of the United Nations (2007) 46 per cent of children under the age of five suffer from under nutrition and 35 per cent of the undernourished children live in India. Further, 50 per cent of deaths in children are caused due to malnutrition

from adversity, learn new skills, and develop creative ways of coping and becoming stronger. The American Psychological Association (APA) defined resilience as the ability to adapt well to adversity, trauma, tragedy, threats, or even significant sources of stress (APA 2011). All the definitions of resiliency stated by researchers hold a common view that, *Resiliency is the ability or capacity to cope with life threatening circumstances in a creative way ensuring positive developmental outcomes.* Therefore, Resiliency is an inner capacity that when nurtured, facilitated, and supported by others empowers children, youth, and families to successfully meet life's challenges with a sense of self-determination, mastery and hope (Resiliency Leadership Ohio, 2008).

A number of researchers have identified specific factors such as: trusting relationships, emotional support outside the family, self-esteem, encouragement of autonomy, hope, responsible risk taking, a sense of being lovable, school achievement, belief in God and morality, unconditional love for someone. A child's own genetic make-up and temperament are fundamental to whether he or she will be resilient. That is, a child's vulnerability to anxiety, challenges, stress or unfamiliarity determines his or her self-perception, how he or she interacts with others, and how he or she addresses adversities.

Importance of Resilience in Children

Everyone faces adversities in life, no one is exempted. With resilience, children can triumph over trauma; without it, trauma (adversity) triumphs. The crises children face both within their families and in their communities can overwhelm them. According to Edith Grotberg, a developmental psychologist, Resilience is important because it is the human capacity to face, overcome and be strengthened by or even transformed by the adversities of life (1995). Developing this capacity relies on protective factors within individuals as well as in the family and community. While outside help is essential in times of trouble, it is insufficient. Along with food and shelter, children need love and trust, hope and autonomy. Along with safe havens, they need safe relationships that can foster friendships and commitment. They need the loving support and self-confidence, the faith in themselves and their world, all of which builds resilience.

Characteristics of Resilient Children

> *"The resilient child is one who 'works well, plays well, loves well and expects well."*
>
> ***(Bernard, 1997)***

Several Research Studies have identified the characteristics of resilient children are as follows:

- Easy temperament – Active, affectionate, cuddly, good-natured and easy to deal with.
- Alert, easy to soothe, and able to elicit support from a nurturing family member.
- Autonomy – self-awareness, sense of identity, ability to act independently, ability to exert control over the external environment, self-efficacy and an internal locus of control.
- Increased sense of self-worth and mastery.
- Good communication skills and ask for help when needed.
- Heightened sensory awareness, high positive expectations.
- A clear and developing understanding of one's strengths relating to accomplishment.
- Sense of humor.
- Good self-regulation of emotional arousal and impulses, and attention controls.
- High IQ with problem-solving skills.
- High Social competence – emotional responsiveness, flexibility, empathy and caring.
- Academic and social successes – less risk of developing behavioural disorders.
- Good decision-making, assertiveness, impulse control, and problem-solving skill.
- Personal faith in something greater – spirituality.
- Creative.
- Capacity for and connection to learning.
- Self-motivating.
- Is 'good at something'/personal competence.
- They have talents that are valued by self and society.

Protective Factors for Fostering Resilience in Children

Resilience generally has been viewed as the protective factors, processes, and mechanisms that contribute to good outcomes despite experiences with stressors (or risks) that can lead to poor outcomes. It a dynamic developmental process that is best measured by the presence/absence and strength of risk (factors that contribute to poor outcomes) and protection (factors that buffer against risk). These factors exist at the individual, peer, family, school, neighbourhood, community, and societal/cultural levels. The protective factors are:

Table 3.6: Protective factors within the Child, Family and Community

I - Protective Factors within the Child
• *Positive Temperament*: active, affectionate, Good natured, responsive to other people. • Social competence, high orientation to social environment. • *Problem-solving skills*: flexible coping strategies, ability to use available resources effectively. • Autonomy and self-reliance but with the ability to obtain assistance from adults when it is needed. • *High Sense of Initiatives*: strong involvement in play, tendency to initiate activities, desire for novelty. • Self-regulation skills: planning, goal setting. • Sense of purpose and future.
II - Protective Factors within the Family
• Nurturing Relationship and strong attachment to a parent, grandparent, older siblings, or alternate caregiver. • High parental expectations for children's success. • Households that stress independence risk-taking and an absence of over protection (especially for girls). • Household that stress structure rules and supervision (especially for boys). • Home responsibilities and Household chores. • Sense of faith, a belief that adversity can be overcome.
III - Protective Factors within the Community
• Nurturant and responsive school atmosphere: effective feedback and praise. • Strong relationship with a favorite teacher or other adult. • Strong social network. • Opportunity to participate in socially and/or economical useful tasks. • Presence of resources in health care, child care, housing, recreation. • Community norms valuing and supporting children. • Community norms discouraging abuse of alcohol, smoking, drugs etc.

Source: Werner, E (1990): *Protective factors and individual resilience.* In S. J. Meisels and J. P. Shonkoll (eds) Handbook of Early Childhood Intervention. Cambridge University Press.

Ways to Foster Resilience in Children

Research has emphasized the importance of early childhood as a time for promoting resilience (Masten and Gewirtz 2006). Children need to become resilient to overcome the adversities they face and will face in life. They cannot do it alone. They need adults who know how to promote resilience. To a large degree, fostering resiliency occurs by integrating certain attitudes and behaviours with kids into the interactions they already have with them. This is because fostering resiliency is a process that occurs first and foremost in relationships. Parents and other care givers promote resilience in children through their words, actions, and the environment they provide. Adults who promote resilience make family and institutional supports available to children. They encourage children to become increasingly autonomous, independent, responsible, empathic, and altruistic and to approach people and situations with hope, faith, and trust. They teach them how to communicate with others, solve-problems, and successfully handle negative thoughts, feelings, and behaviours. Children themselves increasingly become active in promoting their own resilience. Children need these abilities and resources to face many common – and some not common adversities of life. Researchers found out various ways to foster resiliency in young children are as follows:

- Remove or reduce risk factors (unsafe environments, exposure to violence, bullying behaviours).
- Provide prenatal care.
- Include high quality of care in infancy (Nutritional programmes, Home nurse visiting programmes, Infant stimulation programmes).
- Counteract the negative effects of poverty and abuse/neglect.
- Provide early childhood education – school-readiness programmes and bolster protective factors.
- Provide adequate medical care on an ongoing basis.
- Provide good integrative schools with higher SES students.
- Create a motivational climate that fosters learning for learning's sake and reduces student competitiveness.
- Increase parents' involvement in their children's education.
- Provide opportunities for developing and maintaining relationships.

- Improve the quality of attachment relationships by providing caring and supportive relationships. This caring does not necessarily have to come from biological family members – though that is ideal.
- Promote competencies, coping skills and general life skills – Co-operation, healthy conflict resolution, resistance and assertiveness skills, communication skills and healthy stress management.
- Increase sense of belonging or bonding to school and achievement.
- Set clear and consistent boundaries. This involves the development and consistent implementation of family rules and norms, school policies and procedures. Also convey clear expectations about acceptable behaviours and nurture constructive use of time.
- Enhance social competencies, positive values and identities, and commitment to learning.
- Help students learn problem-solving skills and decision-making skills.
- Use peer-teaching methods. Nurture contact with pro social peers, and positive adult role models. Help students find social supports.
- Provide second chance opportunities or help children to engage in niche seeking behaviours such as: leaving deviant peer groups, engage in athletic, artistic or other activities that provide contact with pro-social adult mentors and peers.
- Provide opportunities for meaningful participation. This strategy means providing opportunities for problem-solving, decision-making, planning, goal setting, and helping others, and involves adults sharing power in real ways with children.
- Respect and nurture cultural identities and help enhance self-esteem.

Suggested Activities to Promote Resiliency in Young Children

The following list of selected resiliency-building activities is intended to offer healthy development of children in schools, and families. Important criteria for activities to foster resiliency include making sure that they are developmentally appropriate, culturally relevant, non-stigmatizing, and accessible to all Children. Suggested activities include:

- Engaged in healthy behaviours as eating, sleeping, habit formation, pro-social activities.
- Engaged in sharing and helping activities.
- Playgroups activities provide opportunities for joy, fun, friendship and happy relationships.
- Peer support activities.
- Structured after-school programmes.
- Service-learning.
- Cross-Age mentoring.
- Art, music, dance, and other creative activities.
- Sports and other recreational/outdoor experiences.
- Enforce rules and use removal of privileges and other forms of discipline that set limits to behaviour and some consequences, without crushing the child's spirit.
- Improving everyday interactions and relationships in the home in simple ways.
- Caregivers to talk to children, to listen and engage.

EMERGING CONCEPT OF CHILD CARE SERVICES IN INDIA

India is proud of its social and cultural heritage of having joint family system, where the utmost 'Care is provided to young children in its natural setting by multiple caretaking figures within the family and outside. Children are reared and taken care of by parents, older siblings, grandparents, extended kith and kin, neighbours or other community members. Later on, early childhood education (ECE) programmes were introduced in the form of nurseries, kindergarten, play school, preparatory school, balwadies, and crèches, which had its only focus on education of children', often a part of primary school. Understanding the importance of care' during early childhood, the component of care (included care and early stimulation) was introduced to the thrust ECE and the nomenclature was redefined as Early Childhood Care and Education (ECCE). Then, concepts as Early Childhood Development (ECD) and Early Childhood Care and Development (ECCD) were introduced as integrated concepts which focused on the holistic-all round development of children starting from conception to eight years of age. These programmes aimed at addressing development of children to its fullest level aligning all areas of care and development – health, nutrition, play, early learning, within a protective, enriching and stimulating environment. Further, programmes of ECCD or ECD in India have taken a life cycle approach, as in Integrated Child Development Services (ICDS) targeting not only the child, even the pregnant and lactating mothers and adolescent girls. ECCD has a lasting impact on early childhood development in the most effective way to break the inter-generational cycle of multiple disadvantages and remove inequity leading to long term social and economic benefits. In addition, children of working mothers are provided with care by the implementation of new crèche scheme as Rajiv Gandhi National Crèche Scheme for children of working mothers with effects from 2006.

Thus, Child Care has become a global theme as there is a growing realisation among nations that action in one part of the world has repercussions, either direct or indirect, everywhere. There is a need for concerted efforts to find solutions to child care problems on a universal basis.

SUMMARY OF CHAPTER

Meaning and Definitions of Child Care

- Care is universally acknowledged as fulfilment of children's need, exercising their rights in an enriching and stimulating environment.
- Caring and rearing of pre-school children are of utmost importance, considering the fact that these years are of greatest significance in a child's life.
- Care of the pre-school children includes both physical and psychological care within safe and secure environment.

Benefits of Child Care

- Early childhood years lays the foundation of later years.
- It is acknowledged as the most critical' period for the development of several cognitive, social and psychomotor competencies', which contribute to later success in life.
- If not taken care of or supported by a stimulating, enriching physical and psychosocial environment, and the chances of child's brain development to its fullest potential is hindered.
- Early childhood stage is even more crucial as the foundation for inculcating of social and personal values, habits, behaviour and attitudes gets developed and that too lasts a life time.

Importance of Children's Environment

- The current situation reflects the growing realisation among policy-makers of the need for a supportive environment for healthy and happy childhood.
- Environment exerts strong influence on children's visual system, language development and healthy brain development.

Child Rearing Practices

- Child rearing includes the overall care, socialisation and training of the growing child in a particular culture.
- Various dimensions of child-rearing practices are authoritative, authoritarian, permissive and uninvolved parenting.
- The factors affecting child-rearing practices in India are culture, social class, types and size of the family, parental attitudes, beliefs, behaviour and parenting styles, caste and religion.

Nutritional and Health Care

- Physical care includes the child rearing practices as well as nutritional and health care.
- Nutritional and health care of the pre-school children is of great significance, as a child who has failed to grow during this crucial period may not make up the loss in growth even with an excellent diet in later life.
- Energy, protein, vitamin-A, B-complex, iron are important nutrients during early childhood to prevent deficiency diseases.
- Developing good habits during these years is required for which nutrition education on the part of the parents, teachers and community in general are necessary.

Psychological Care of Young Children

- Psychological care for young children means, a stimulating home and school environment; well planned and consistent disciplinary practices; parental love, affection for the child, a general atmosphere of happiness in the home and acceptance by siblings and playmates.
- Relationship within and outside the family play an important role in providing psychological care to the children such as: parent-child relationship; sibling relationship, peer interactions, relationship with the grandparents and/or other care givers.

Developing Creativity in Children

- Providing creative and conducive environment to the children during these years is important.
- Creativity provides opportunities to children for self-expression and give utmost satisfaction.
- Creative children usually have greater divergent thinking, highly imaginative, talented and risk taking behaviour.
- The talent of creativity needs proper nurturing which can only be fostered by congenial stimulating environment – both at home and at school.
- Both parents and teachers can play significant role in developing creativity among children.

Promoting Resilience in Young Children

- Resilience is important because it is the human capacity to face, overcome and be strengthened by or even transformed by the adversities of life.
- Developing this capacity relies on protective factors within individuals as well as in the family and community.
- Resilience generally has been viewed as the protective factors, processes, and mechanisms that contribute to good outcomes despite experiences with stressors (or risks) that can lead to poor outcomes.
- These factors exist at the individual, peer, family, school, neighborhood, community, and societal/cultural levels.
- Fostering resiliency occurs by integrating certain attitudes and behaviours with kids into the interactions they already have with them.
- Parents and other care givers promote resilience in children through their words, actions, and the environment they provide.
- Everyday young children face different form of stresses or trauma in their lives. These life events cause young children to feel vulnerable, worried, fearful, sad, frustrated, or lonely.
- Efforts of sensitive parents, early childhood educators, and other adults can keep children safe by preventing stress and trauma through promoting resilience in young children by fostering protective factors that can buffer the negative effects of stress and trauma.

Emerging Concepts of Early Childhood Care in India

- Child Care in India has emerged as one of the central concept in developmental policies and programmes concerning with the welfare, progress and empowerment of the individual (child), family and the community.
- Child Care services in India reveal a gloomy picture. Few good quality childhood programmes are being initiated, yet understanding the importance of early childhood years is very much required.

Education for Pre-School Children

MEANING, SIGNIFICANCE AND OBJECTIVES OF PRE-SCHOOL EDUCATION

"Education is to contribute to the fullest development of the human personality, peace and human rights".

Meaning of Pre-School Education

Recognition of educational programmes for young children as an essential part of continuous education has developed gradually in the whole world. However, today a large group of both parents and educators know the significance of the child's early experiences for his educational foundation. Recent research has confirmed what many people have believed regarding the importance of a good programme in early childhood education for children. Moreover, this realisation of the importance of human resource development for the future of a country has generated immense interest and creative thinking in the field of child development. The age of the children before they enter into class first or primary education is generally called pre-school age. Thus, education to the children, prior to the schooling is known as 'pre-school education'.

Pre-school education is informal education of the child between the age group of 3 to 6 years, carried out in formal institutions before the child joins the primary classes. It aims at the development of all the faculties of the child before joining the school at the age of six. It intends preparing the child for the life ahead. It rather gives the child a good head start, which helps him to face the later years with more confidence and ease. Pre-school education has been called by the psychologists, educationists and policy-makers by variety of names such as: nursery school education, kindergarten education, pre-primary education etc. The group settings in which pre-school education is provided to children are known by variety of names such as: nursery school, play-school, kindergarten schools, pre-primary school and so on. These settings are specially designed to provide care, supervision, stimulation and education to pre-school children outside their homes. These settings are included under the general term entitled 'Pre-school education' that serves children before entry into primary schools or formal schools.

Significance of Pre-School Education

The children of today need to be prepared for the vastly complex and rapidly changing world of tomorrow. This calls for an integrated, meaningful, educational system. Nearly forty per cent (40%) of the total population of India are children below 12 years and there are 61.9 million children belong to the age group of 3 to 4 years (Gupta and Sharma, 1990). Our nation's future, its prosperity or poverty, strength or weakness depends on the care with which we build up the character, and habits of our children. The Planning Commission of the India in their Sixth Five-year Plan sates "...The pre-school years of the child is the period of its maximum learning and intellectual development and hence of gross potential educational significance". The Indian Association for Pre-school Education (1972) in a National seminar on integrated approach to pre-school children, and urged that investment in human resource development must begin during the early years. Hence, the pre-school education is of greater significance mainly due to the following reasons.

- The pre-school age is the most impressionable age in one's life. Whatever is learnt at this age gets so deeply embedded in a child that it becomes difficult to change later on. It is, therefore, the duty of the adults to provide rich experiences to the child and help him develop good habits, proper attitudes and a questioning mind.
- The rate of growth and development during pre-school age is so rapid that the child is able to take in almost anything if it is

given to him in a form in which he can understand it. The more experiences/exposures we give the child at this age, richer is the dividend. At no other stage is he able to benefit as much from an enriching environment as he can at the pre-school stage.

- Due to economics pressure, women's education and social duties many mothers are away from the home during the day time for career and to supplement the family income. As a result of urbanisation, joint families are breaking up and it is a problem for working mothers to leave their children at home and go out to work. So establishment of pre-school is also a social necessity these days, where young children can be looked after properly.
- The tremendous wastage and stagnation that are seen in grade I and II can be reduced and avoided if the children who join these classes are prepared in advance for formal schooling. Since, a child who has had pre-school experience before joining the primary school adjust himself easily and successfully in primary classes because of his early preparations. It is through better emotional control, developing proper habits and attitudes.

Such preparation in the pre-school helps him considerably in his subsequent education. So, pre-school education prepares a sound base for primary education.

- With urbanisation and industrialisation, people are moving to cities, hence the living space is becoming limited day-by-day. There is hardly any space for a child to move about, run and play. There is no scope for the child to investigate and experiment, both of which are necessary for the child s optimum development. Hence, pre-schools with enough and enriching space for free movement and proper play equipment with are perhaps the more positive answer for such children of today.
- The pre-school year is the period of socialisation. Children love to play with other children, which they do not get at home. More so, during these years the peer group becomes increasingly important to them. In a pre-school, a child gets the opportunity of playing with other children and thus learns to share, wait for his turn and co-operate with others.

- Among the educated mothers very few are there to understand the significance of early childhood years. Since, in India many mothers are uneducated, are unable to guide their children properly, the homes environment may not be fully satisfying and challenging for the optimum growth of the children. In this case, at least pre-school teachers are better trained, equipped and experienced enough in guiding and providing better environment to the young children once they are in pre-school.
- Early stimulation and educational enrichment can promote creativity in young children. It was felt that early educational intervention providing stimulation and instruction during the pre-school years – would make a difference in the children s school experiences.

Objectives of Pre-School Education

The aim of Early Childhood Care and Education is to facilitate optimum development of the child s full potential and lay the foundation for all round development and lifelong learning. While parents and home have the main responsibility of the welfare of the child, a strong partnership between the community and the ECCE centres is important for the well-being of the child and in achieving the following objectives. The broad objectives of pre-school education as drawn by the National Council of Educational Research and Training (NCERT) New Delhi, India and later approved and incorporated in the report of the Education Commission of India are as follows:

1. To develop in the child a good physique, adequate muscular co-ordination and basic motor skills, through the various activities of the pre-schools.
2. To develop in the child good health habits and to build up basic skills necessary for personal adjustment, such as: in dressing, toilet, eating, washing, cleaning etc.
3. To develop desirable social attitudes and manners, to encourage healthy group participation and to make the child sensitive to the rights and privileges of others.
4. To develop emotional maturity by guiding the child to express, understand, accept and control his feeling and emotions.
5. To encourage and stimulate aesthetic appreciation.

6. To stimulate intellectual curiosity and to help him understand the world in which he lives and to foster new interacts through giving opportunities to explore, investigate and experiment.
7. To encourage independence and creativity by providing the child with sufficient opportunities for self-expression.
8. To develop the child's ability to express his thoughts and feelings in fluent, correct, clear speech.
9. To develop moral values such as: faith in God respect to elders and younger, promotes civics concept and other human values.

Hence, broadly the objective of Early Childhood Care and Education (ECCE), in which pre-school education is included, is total development of the young child. National Policy on Education (2013) viewed ECCE as an important programme in its own right, as it:

- Prepares children for primary schools.
- Supports services for girls in under privileged area.
- Supports services for working mothers in all the income groups.

According to V. Kaul, Early Childhood Education Programme, NCERT, Early Childhood Education is what it is and what it is not described as follows:

Early Childhood Education is ....

- A balanced play based programme of language, cognitive, creative and psychomotor activities.
- A child centred programme catering to individual children's learning and emotional needs through individual, small and large group activities and one to one communication.
- A school readiness programme which readies children for learning to read, write and do arithmetic later.
- A programme which indirectly promotes self-control and thereby inner discipline in children through interactions.

Early Childhood Education is Not ....

- A syllabus bound programme for teaching 3R s nor a song and a rhyme and go home approach.
- A teacher centered programme that follows formal class-room approach as in school.
- A programme for formally teaching reading, writing and arithmetic, which is to be done in primary.
- Not a programme which demands unquestioning obedience or exercise strict classroom discipline.

PRINCIPLES OF LEARNING DURING PRE-SCHOOL YEARS

There is increased recognition of the social consequences of neglecting development throughout childhood and the major qualitative improvements needed in primary schooling and parental education. This perspective is strengthen by an increasing recognition of the need to ensure the sustainability of recent gains in child survival by empowering parents with knowledge and skills about child survival and development.

The period between the ages of three and six is also one of rapid physical and mental development. Children gain confidence in their bodies, strive for independence by doing things on their own, and experiment with objects in the surrounding environment. They show a livelier curiosity at what is going on about them, enjoy the company of other children, and seek to imitate adult behaviour. They learn to assert themselves as individuals and begin to acquire self-control and discipline. During this period, children s intellectual and social development proceeds apace, as illustrated by their acquiring sophisticated language skills and adopting culturally acceptable behaviours. While the health needs of children in this age-group still require constant attention, it is essential that they be provided with challenges that responds to their enormous thirst for learning and be prepared for symbolic and logical thinking, required in formal schooling. Some of the basic principle characterising how young children learn includes:

- *Children Construct Knowledge:* From infancy children are mentally and physically active, struggling to make sense of the world. Children construct their own knowledge or working models through repeated interactions with people and materials. Throughout childhood, these mental constructions are continually reshaped, expanded and recognised by new experiences.
- *Children Learn through Social Interaction with Adults and other Children:* The development of higher-order mental functions, such as: conceptualisation, begins in social interaction and then is internalised psychologically. The principle of learning is that children can do things first in a supportive context and then later independently and in a variety of contexts. The support of adults and more competent peers provides the necessary assistance or 'scaffold' that enables the child to move to the next level of independent functioning.

- *Children s Learning Reflects a Recurring Cycle that Begins in Awareness and Moves to Exploration, to Inquiry, and Finally, to Utilisation:* Any new learning by children begins with awareness, which is generated from their experiences with objects, events, or people. In the next step in the cycle, if children are to really know about and understand something, they must explore, using whatever means possible, usually employing the various senses. Through enquiry, children analyse and compare their own behaviours or concepts to what is observed in society and make closer approximations to the conventional patterns of the culture. The final aspects of the cycle of learning is utilisation, where children are able to use what they have learnt for multiple purposes and apply their learning to new situations.
- *Children Learn through Play*: Children s spontaneous play provides opportunities for exploration, experimentation, and manipulation that are essential for constructing knowledge. Play contributes to the development of representational thought. A child expresses and represents ideas, thoughts, and feelings when engaged in symbolic play. During play a child learns to deal with feelings, to interact with others to resolve conflicts, and to gain a sense of competence. It is through play that children develop and express their imaginations and creativity.
- *Children s Interests and 'need to know' Motivate Learning:* Children have an inherent need or inner push to exercise their emerging mental abilities and to make sense of their experience. Parents and teachers need to identify content that intrigues children and arouses in them a need and desire to figure something out. In short, caregivers and teachers create awareness and foster interest in children, by planning the environments and introducing new and stimulating objects, people and experiences.
- *Child Development and Learning are Characterised by Individual Variations:* Each has an individual pattern and timing of growth and development as well as individual styles of learning. Children's personal family experiences and cultural backgrounds also vary. Recognition that individual variation is not only normal but also valuable requires that decisions about programmes and assessment be as

individualised as possible. Learning environments that incorporate these principles enable a child to develop a positive concept of self and seek, establish and maintain supportive relationships that continue to produce successful outcomes. The cycle of success can be as perpetuating as the cycle of failure. Access to adequate environments, which are capable of responding and enhancing the basic universal needs, are indeed the rights of young children.

The Knowledge of How to Learn

Special characteristics related to learning in pre-school on the part of the pre-children are as follows:

- *Confidence*: A sense of control and mastery of one s body, behaviour and world's the child sense that he or she is more likely than not to succeed at what he or she undertakes, and that adults will be helpful.
- *Curiosity*: The sense that finding out about things is positive and leads to pleasure.
- *Intentionally:* The wish and capacity to have an impact, and to act upon that with persistence. This is clearly related to a sense of competence, of being effective.
- *Relatedness*: The ability to engage with others based on the sense of being understood by and understanding others.
- *Capacity to Communicate*: The wish and ability to verbally exchange ideas, feelings and concepts with others. This is related to a sense of trust in others and of pleasure in engaging with others, including adults.
- *Co-operativeness:* The ability to balance one s needs with those of others in a group activity.

These characteristics equip children with a school literacy more basic than knowledge of numbers and letters.

CONTRIBUTION OF THE PHILOSOPHERS TOWARDS PRE-SCHOOL EDUCATION

The care and education of young children outside the home is not a modern idea. Plato proposed it centuries ago. More recently, during seventeenth to nineteenth centuries, Rousseau, Pestalozi, Frobel, Lock, Dewey and Montessori visualised schools of early childhood as one of the means of improving social condition. The guiding principles and methods advocated by these reformers were coloured by their own philosophical beliefs and had laid the foundation of early childhood education.

John Locke (1632-1704)

The idea that early experience could have a profound effect on adult life was experienced forcefully in the writings of physician and philosopher John Lock. In his essay concerning human understanding and some thoughts concerning education, Locke opposed the idea that children are innately sinful. He proposed that the newborn child is like a blank slate upon which experience would write its story. Contact with adults and the outside world would establish the character and mental ability that would be the child s unique gift or curse throughout life. Locke believed that because childhood shaped later behaviour and was the period during which life long habits are formed; it deserved a great deal of attention. If the parents took the time to guide children into the path of reason, to teach them socially desirable habits, to help them to confront their appetite and impulses, they would surely see the fruits of their labour as their children grew rational and responsible members of society.

In Locke s view, children could become rational only if they lowered to express their curiosity. Hence, parents need to encourage children s curiosity. Parents could also provide encouragement by answering their children s question with attentiveness and respect. If parents behaved in the eminently rational fashion Locke described, they would automatically command the child s respect, attention, and affection. Locke rejected the idea of innate knowledge, which had been much discussed in the 17th Century.

Jean-Jacques Rousseau (1712-1778)

Rousseau is the champion of modern education, who did not get any formal education by himself. Rousseau ideas on childhood education, principles of curriculum, methods of teaching etc., have been well presented in his immortal work 'Emile'. According to him children s interests are the basis of all his education and make a strong plea for giving full freedom to children. He believes that, children must learn from their own experiences and should not be spoon-fed. Further, Rousseau believed in the importance and uniqueness of childhood. He regarded children as qualitatively different from adults, not merely as in complete adults, or uniformed students. Children must be understood and valued for what they are rather than for what they will become. They are born as physical and psychological individuals, and adults need to respect to this individuality rather than levelling it to suit his or her individual interests.

According to Rousseau, children should be allowed to be educated with his/her natural environment. Education is a lifelong process and in Rousseau s views only through experience, child will able to learn. He emphasises on direct experiences, practical activity, and learning by doing and no verbal lessons. To him children do not pay little heed to verbal explanation, nor do they remember them. In short, Rousseau's philosophy on pre-school education centres round the following main ideas, such as:

- Education must be child centred.
- Education through doing (hands-on-experiences).
- Teaching through things and articles.
- Use of very little books.
- Sense training.
- Play-way education.

Johann Heinrich Pestalozzi (1746-1827)

The concept of early childhood education was brought into focus as the nineteenth century began, by a man possessed of a unique combination of talent, courage, and devotion. Johann Pestalozzi s work with young children is Switzerland spanned a thirty years period. Through his theorising, writing, and teaching he became one of the most famous and influential champions of early childhood education in Europe. Pestalozzi was born in the year 1746 in the city of Zurich in Switzerland. His father was a doctor, who died at an early age and his widow mother, who had greatly influenced his ideology, was rearing Pestalozzi. According to Pestalozzi "home is the real school, where the child gets love, and learns co-operation". He has given family love and care an important place in the life and education of the child.

Pestalozzi has been immensely influenced by the educational doctrine of Rousseau and has a hatred for verbalisation. According to him, all words learned without thinking produce almost hopeless confusion in the minds of the children. Whereas, if learned through direct actions (hands-on-experience), it may be clearly understood by the child in meaningful ways and thus remembers for longer period. His philosophy of pre-school education may be summed up as follows:

- Education in natural atmosphere with the care of parents – Like Rousseau, Pestalozzi believed that, the children should be educated under the care, guidance and patronage of the parents. Equally important in the love, affection, sympathy and encouragement for better learning.
- Minimum experience of objects and direct observation on the part of the children are required where the senses are used and learning is clear and definite.
- Innate tendencies of intellectual and mental faculties should form the basis of education. Pestalozzi was of the view that the child, when born brings with him certain innate tendencies and therefore he should be provided with such an education, which should be based on these innate tendencies. Such an education shall be in accordance with the requirement of a developing child.
- Unchecked growth of innate power – According to Pestalozzi, "education is a natural, harmonious and progressive development of man s innate powers". The pre-school teacher should therefore, try to see that the innate powers of the child should be allowed to develop properly. Hence, the education should be such, which should be based on the interest, attitude, and limitations of the child. It should also be planned according to the various psychological developments during various stages of child s life.
- Education is the best agency for social and individual reform – The door of the progress of the society can be opened only through education. Therefore, Pestalozzi suggested that the education should have the capacity to fulfil all these requirements, needed for the individuals proper development in the society.
- Pestalozzi believes in obedience and disciplining the children. However, discipline should be based on love and understanding. He therefore says, 'without it there is no education possible'. The child must obey the teacher or parent, learn to respect; but only in case of necessity must an order be given". Thus, in Pestalozzian education there is balanced quantity of freedom and obedience of children.

Friendrich Wilhelm Froebel (1782-1852)

By opening the first kindergarten in 1837, Froebel, a German, created a profound change within the emerging field of early childhood education. Like Pestalozzi and so many others before him, Froebel was deeply concerned about children. Froebel considered himself 'an educator of mankind' and believed that education must begin in early childhood. 'Come, let us live for Children' was the epitaph on the tombstone of Froebel, the Father of Kindergarten. According to him, *"we should live for children, because children will live for us and they are the future of the mankind"*.

Froebel s thinking concerning the education of young children was extremely progressive. For example, he believed, as do many psychologists, that a child s experiences have a profound effect upon the development of an adult personality. He further believed that, childhood has value in itself, and is not just something as all pass through on the way to adulthood. According to Froebel, children deserve the same rights and respect as adults and must be treated as individuals passing through a unique phase of life. He felt that excessive interference in the child s spontaneous discovery of the world about him could be detrimental. Parents and teachers must be patient and understanding. Froebel understood, as did Pestalozzi, that the emotional quality of a child s life is important, and that the child s emotional life is heavily affected by the quality of parental love. He realised that individual differences in interests and capabilities should be considered in devising a curriculum, and that any educational curriculum had to be related to the child s own experience. Finally, he proposed that play is a most important activity for the optimum development of a child. All of these are ideas that still permeate early childhood educational thought.

Unlike Rousseau, Froebel believed, that the child should properly develop only in the society. He insists on group activities in home, school and community, which enable the child to discover his own individuality and to develop his personality. The child s capacity can be fully developed through co-operation and joint activities. Moreover, the child gets pleasure in constructive work through which his ideas find concrete expression. Nature study occupies an important place in the child s curriculum as devised by Froebel. It provides different opportunities for his learning experiences through numerous activities. Materials for reading writing, language, number and constructive works are all provided by nature study. The main features of Froebel s philosophy on pre-school education are as follows:

- *Self-Activity*: Froebel believed that the growth of the child is directed by his inner force. He regarded self-activity as a process by which the individual realises his own nature and builds up his own world and then unite and harmonise the two.
- *Play – According to Froebel*, "play is the purest, most spiritual activity of man at this stage......It gives therefore, joy, freedom, contentment, inner rest and peace in the world. It holds the source of all that is good". Froebel recognised that play needs to be organised and controlled on definite materials, so that it may not degenerate into aimless play.
- *Songs, Gestures and Constructions:* Froebel saw an organic relationship between songs, gestures and construction. He regarded these as three co-ordinate forms of expression in the child. What is to be learnt by the child is first expressed in a song, then it is dramatised or expressed in gesture movement and lastly illustrated through some constructive work such as: paper, clay modelling, drawing or painting. Thus, a balanced development of the mind, the speech organs and the hands is aimed at. These three activities provide exercise to the senses, limbs and muscles of the child.
- *Gifts and Occupations*: To provide constructive activities and engagements, Froebel devised to produce suitable materials known as gifts. The gifts suggest some forms of activity and occupations are the activities suggested by gifts. These have been carefully graded and possess all the novelty of playthings. The order of gift is devised in such a way as it leads the child from the activities and thought of one stage to another.
- *Role of Teacher* – According to Froebel, the teacher is not to remain passive and required to demonstrate certain activities to children to learn and follow. He/she has to inculcate values like love, sympathy, humility, co-operation and obedience to elders and avoid any punishment for the children.

John Dewey (1859 – 1952)

John Dewey is one of the greatest philosophical thinkers that the United States of America has produced. He has been universally accepted as a great humanist and a great educator. He regards education as an indispensable social progress. To him society cannot progress without the help of education. Moreover, Dewey says that, education is a process by which civilisation is preserved and developed further. It is not something that the child begins at school entrance, but a process that begins at birth and proceeds throughout life. Thus, education proceeds by remaking experience, and it is this reconstruction that gives an aim to education. There is in reality no end to education because as long as the individual is making adjustments to his environment he is learning. Education according to Dewey has two sides: the psychological and the social.

(a) *Education is Psychological:* The nature of the child is dynamic, reconstructing and reorganising. Education, therefore, should start with the psychological nature of the child. The teacher must utilise the activities springing from the nature and make it coincide with his efforts.

(b) *Social Efficacy*: The aim of education according to Dewey is social efficacy. He considered school as a social institution, where teacher must be familiar with the social situation. John Dewey formulated 'social efficacy' as the aim of education in view of the charged tenure of society. Moreover, he believed the school to be a fundamental modem of social progress and reform. Through education, society can formulate its own purposes, organise its means of attainments, and shape itself in the direction it wishes to go. It is therefore, essential that the school should include both the social and individual goal.

Dewey along with Rousseau emphasised greatly the role of direct experiences – concrete meaningful experiences – in the education of the child. Not only are concrete situations necessary to learning, but all learning should come to the child as a bi-product of activity, never as something learned directly for his own sake.

Maria Montessori (1870-1952)

Maria Montessori achieved a universal reputation for her unique contributions to the early childhood education. Unlike Froebel she saw no value in play and made no provision in the daily experiences of the children with whom she worked. She did recognise, however, the need for children to participate in the work of the school, and children in her school were given a part in the house keeping activities. This provided them with their only opportunity to work together in-groups, because most of the work of the school did not lend itself group endeavour. She believes in the system of education as a joyful process of 'self-discovery' and 'self-realisation'. She at first worked for the deficient children and then for the younger children under six in kindergarten where she tried out her own ideas.

Montessori emphasised the importance of structure in the learning environment of her students. Accordingly, the Montessori environment tends to be highly organised on the child s level. Much of the curriculum is composed of work with self-correcting didactic materials. Those didactic materials, according to Montessori, must be relatively simple, inherently interesting, and self-correcting. They emphasise the interaction between sensory-motor activity and cognitive development. Thus, many of them involve puzzles, stacking blocks, and cards containing numbers and letters, which the child arranges in prescribed ways. One example involves 'sand letters' or large letters of the alphabet with rough surfaces. By running her hands over these textured letters the child learns the essential movement involved in reproducing the letters.

An essential part of the Montessori programme is that these materials be used in certain 'prescribed ways' only. In other words, the child is not encouraged to explore the materials and play with them any way she wishes. To the contrary, the goal of the programme is to have the child learn to use these materials in the prescribed manner. *First*, the teacher, whose role is also highly structured, will demonstrate how the materials are to be used. Then she or he watched the children as they try the materials, and notes their progress. Montessori believed that self-esteem would naturally follow, as the child became more independent and accomplished. Furthermore, the Montessori materials encourage sensorimotor development, eye-hand co-ordination, and the development of concepts. Children in Montessori programmes are encouraged to learn letters, numbers and many learn to read as well. Moreover, Montessori laid stress on the social development of children who learn healthy habits and social behaviours in their 'Children s Houses'. Children are trained in clearing the rooms and arranging seats for meals. Montessori was aware of children s social needs and their roles in improving the society.

Physical education is an important part of Montessori method. Montessori emphasised the motor and muscular development of children and believes that efficiency in these promote improvement in other activities like: writing, drawing, walking, running etc. Therefore, physical growth and development is given due importance in the early childhood education of Montessori. Educational principles underlying the philosophy of Maria Montessori are as follows:

- *Development from Within:* Like Froebel, Montessori believed that, education of a child is from within (must be from inside). It must help the child to unfold his/her individuality, potentiality and ability. Thus, suitable environment must be provided for developing and growing naturally and normally.
- *The Doctrine of Liberty:* She believes that the freedom is the birth right of every individual child. Hence, she supports the spontaneous development of the child through full liberty. She strongly disagree with putting restraints on the children, as she thinks that these may 'mar or stifle the innate power of the child'.
- *No Material Rewards and Punishments:* Montessori believed that incentives or rewards are unnatural. Accordingly, any forced efforts for development through reward or punishment are not normal and is not sustainable also.
- *Principles of Individual Development:* She believes that every child is unique. He/she progress and develops in his/her speed and rate. Thus, collective method of teaching may crush his/her individuality. She treats each and every child as a separate individual and recommends that, he/she must be helped and guided in a manner that helps him/her in optimum growth and development.
- *Principle of Self-Education or Auto-Education:* Montessori has shifted the emphasis from teaching to learning. She believes that, self-education or auto-education is the only true education for the child. She has devised the didactic apparatus, which attracts the attention of the children, keeps them busy spontaneously, leads them to learn the power of movements, reading, writing and arithmetic etc.
- *Principle of Sense Training:* Montessori asserts that our senses are the gateway of knowledge. The training and development of senses depends the acquisition of knowledge throughout life. She pointed out that the senses are very active between the ages of three and seven and that a lot of learning takes place during this period. Thus, she advocates that the sensory training is the key to intellectual development.

- *Role of Teachers:* For Montessori, the role of teacher is very important, as she believes that function of a teacher is to direct and not to teach, for which she replaces the word 'teacher by' directress.
- *No Place for Fairy Tales:* For Montessori, fairy tales has no place in the curriculum of young children. As she believes that, fairy tales confuses children, their thinking become unrealistic and the children are far from developing true understanding. Further, it hinders them in the process of adjusting themselves to the real world.

Montessori Teaching Materials

The Montessori approach offers a broad vision of education as an aid to life... Montessori classrooms provide a prepared environment where children are free to respond to their natural drive to work and learn. The children's inherent love of learning is encouraged by giving them opportunities to engage in spontaneous, meaningful activities under the guidance of a trained adult. Through their work, the children develop concentration, motivation, persistence, and discipline. Within this framework of order, children progress at their own pace and rhythm, according to their individual capabilities, during the crucial years of development.

Montessori Method is based on the spontaneous activity of the child which is aroused precisely by the interest the child takes in the material. Montessori materials for younger children are roughly divided into six subject areas: botany, geography, math, language, practical, and sensorial. Not surprisingly (to ourselves, anyway), we were quite drawn to the sensorial materials. There's something viscerally pleasing about these objects that makes us want to purge all other playthings from our house and rebuild our inventory from scratch, Montessori-style.

Mahatma Gandhi (1869-1948)

According to Mahatma Gandhi, "The real education begins from conception as the mother begins to take up the responsibility of the child. If a mother is correctly instructed and prepared for her coming responsibility, then that will be the education of the child as well". Basic education, which was once regarded as the national education of India, was called as Gandhi s 'brain child'. Gandhi was a great advocate of child-centred education like Rousseau, Comenious, Pestalozzie and Froebel. He pointed out that education

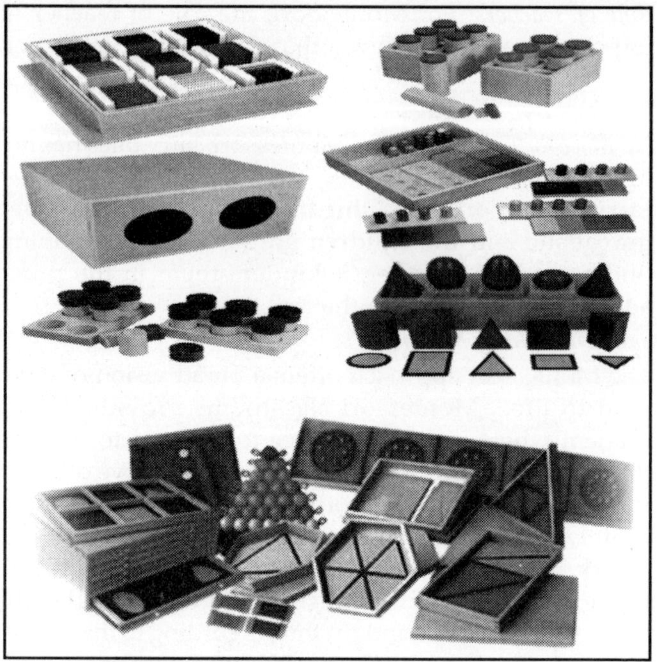

Fig. 4. 1: Montessori Teaching Materials

should fit the child rather than the vice versa. The child s ability, interests and need should be taken into consideration in determining the programmes and practices in schools. Learning experiences need be provided according to the individual differences.

Gandhi laid great stress on the character development of the child in education. He held that education of 3 H s, *i.e.* – Hand, Head and Heart rather than 3R s should be emphasised in the childhood education. He suggested for refinement of emotions and impulses through training in schools. Tender feelings of love, sympathy, fellow feeling, co-operation etc. are to be developed properly through suitable education. Moral virtues should be cultivated in the children providing adequate educational facilities. Moreover, he introduced craft as the centre of the teaching, learning process and tried to train the man in all aspects of this body, mind and spirit. The craft chosen according to the local needs and conditions should be productive and partly supportive.

Mother tongue has an important place in Gandhian pedagogy and it is used as the medium of instruction. Gandhiji observed that good knowledge of mother tongue is necessary for developing proper thought. Without the capacity to speak effectively and to read and write correctly and lucidly no one can develop precision of thought or clarity of ideas. Moreover, it is a means of introducing the child to the rich heritage of his people s ideas, emotion and aspiration, and can, therefore, be made valuable means of social education. Gandhian education visualised democratic citizenship to be developed among children who should be trained in the rights and duties of citizens. Hence, according to Gandhi, schools should be shaped as democratic societies and civic virtues like co-operation, sympathy, equality and dignity of individuals should be inculcated in the children for making them good citizens in future.

Sri Aurobindo (1872 – 1950)

According to Sri Aurbondo, "Education is not training merely the mind but of the whole human system, all the faculties of life. Mere stuffing the mind with information is no education. All the knowledge is within and has to be evolved by education rather than instilled from outside". Sri Aurobindo was of view that both matter and spirit are necessary for the well-being of the mankind, and education should help in bringing about a balanced development of both. He professed Integral Education, which should emphasise the psychic, physical and mental aspects, which constitute four disciplines, *e.g.*, Beauty, Power, Knowledge and Love.

According to him three to six years (pre-school years) are an age of play. Hence the system of education should be through educational games. Along with well-equipped playing facilities, there should be provision of sound health and nutrition services. Painting, photography, singing, dancing, playing musical instruments and dramatic performances should be inseparable part of the educational system. He believes that the secret of child s successes lies in their training from the nursery stage and only 'self-regulation', 'self-discipline' and 'self-education' can bring out the best. In his book 'A System of National Education' Sri Aurobindo has enunciated three principles of teaching, such as:

(a) Teacher is not to transmit knowledge to the child, rather to help and guide him in his pursuit of knowledge. That is, all knowledge is within one s self and is revealed through the

process of 'Swadharama' and 'Swabhab'. Understanding the self or knowing the inner aptitude and aspirations of the child is the main task of the teacher.

(b) Nothing should be imposed on the child from outside, but should start from within. Therefore, education has to be provided not only according to individual s needs, but also according to his will.

(c) *Thirdly,* the child should be led from near to far. That the child should be taught from known to unknown this emphasises experience as the basis of all learning. All the new knowledge must be built around his daily experiences directly connected with the environment. The audio-visual materials are usual according to this principle in the sense that they aid in getting real or stimulated experiences.

These three principles determine the method of teaching to be followed for children. Aurobindo tried out this educational idea in the original Ashram School, which was developed in the 'International Centre of Education' at Pondichery. He brought out a synthesis of Eastern as well as Western culture. In spite of his extreme nationalism and love for the Indian culture, he had no disliking for Western culture and people. His writings showed great vision, comprehensive and spiritual approach to education.

FUNCTIONS OF PRE-SCHOOLS

The demand for pre-schools is increasing day-by-day everywhere in India. To cater to this need, a large number of pre/nursery schools are coming up these days. But unfortunately only few of these institutions understand the significance of pre-school education. A large majority of these schools are run on the same pattern as the primary schools. This is rather unfortunate as the needs of these young children are very different and an entirely different approach is necessary if we want to stimulate their optimum development. Hence, quality child-care at the pre-school has five major functions: it serves as an extension of the family; it aids children s development; it is a way for society to intervene constructively when families and children need help; it acts as compensatory education; and it provides developmental care to the children between two to six years of age.

Pre-school as an Extension of the Family

A good pre-school provides positive experiences that most families try to give their children. It extends and supplements the parent s care in a way consistent with the values and goals of the child s family and culture. It strengthens the child s basic attachment to his parents and sustains them as the major force in his personal development. Pre-schools are more successful when parents are deeply involved in them. In many communities, pre-school as an extension of the family will encounter problems of ethnic relevance. Children achieve dignity and self-respect with the help of positive images of themselves, their parents, and their communities and pre-schools provide the atmosphere for it.

Pre-School as an Aid to Child Development

The years from three to six are an optimal period for mastering certain developmental tasks. Pre-school developmental care presents many opportunities to help a child to master such tasks as:

- Developing a sense of self, personal identity and a sense of autonomy.
- Developing a healthy personal hygiene.
- Developing concepts of morals and personal rights.
- Dealing with certain psychological impulses as with guilt, anxiety, and shame.
- Learning how to get along with others.
- Mastering language and using it to produce desired results.
- Learning more about the symbols and concepts of culture (for example, numbers and letters, drawing 'realistically').
- Acquiring concepts of space, time, and objects.

Pre-school as Child Care Intervention

A normal and happy family can, with luck, fulfil all the conditions required for normal development of the children, but most families fail to do so for one reason or another. No institution can fully meet all the child s requirements, but the families in trouble can find the help they need by taking elements from a variety institution, including family care, foster care, residential care and pre-school. Even destitute families would function better if pre-school came to their permanent help. Pre-school, then, can function as one component of a system of supports to the family, together with such components as social service programmes, health programmes, and programs to increase employment. The intervention function of pre-school is particularly important for three groups of children:

- *Children who are Vulnerable:* Vulnerable children are those whose development is at risk. Through special circumstances of birth, physical endowment, or difficult life experiences, some children are particularly unable to measure up to developmental takes and problems. They have special needs for the continuity of care, stimulation, affection, stability, and thoughtfulness of a quality pre-school programme.
- *Children who are Handicapped or Disabled*: Handicapped or disabled children include those who suffer from such afflictions as severe mental retardation, physical handicaps, or a childhood psychosis. The care of these children can be too much for even the most affluent family. Parents who must care for such a child 24 hours a day, 7 days a week will be overloaded with responsibility. It will be a strain for the whole family, and the child s development will suffer. Hence, in this case, pre-school can relieve such parents of a portion of their care giving burden.
- *Children from Families who live in Poverty:* Children from families in poverty are the third and by far the largest group for whom intervention may be important. Not all poor families need pre-school, but many of their children lack the healthy and developmentally sound environment that pre-school can provide.

A quality pre-school programme can identify the children of a community and assess their needs, can help make services available to them, and can involve the parents and help to strengthen the family.

Pre-school as Compensatory Education

Compensatory education is a special programme for children with special needs, arising out of a cultural or economic difference from the surrounding community. The essential idea of compensatory education is that it should make up for some special disadvantage, providing disadvantaged children with the basic attitudes and skills which most other children acquire naturally during the pre-school years. This education has definite clearly defined goals and objectives chosen to prepare the child for what society will expect of him/her.

Pre-school as Developmental Care

Developmental care is also called as 'quality care', which provides security and warmth, together with a range of developmental opportunities that parents normally provide when they have the necessary time and resources. These opportunities further include the chance to be with other children: individual attention to each child s strengths and needs, and activities designed to promote physical, social, emotional, and intellectual development. To ensure that these opportunities are provided, pre-schools are need to follow a carefully planned curriculum, using the services of consultants in health, education, nutrition, and other fields, and encourage parents interest and involvement in all aspects of the programme.

Thus, pre-school is the place from where the children derive maximum benefits other than their homes. Hence, its physical set up, site, surroundings, plan and programmes are of greater significance in achieving the goals of pre-school education.

PHYSICAL SET-UP OF PRE-SCHOOL

For the first time the child is brought away from home when he enters the pre-school. It is up to the pre-school to reduce the tension and anxiety of the child by making the environment and teaching-learning process pleasant and appealing to the child. The pre-schools need to be a supplement to the home and not a substitute. Along with the home, the pre-school gradually introduces the child to a large group and helps him to learn to meet its demands. It is a process of vital importance as the child s attitude towards the society outside the home in general and school in particular depends, to a large extent, upon the kind of experiences he gains at this stage especially in a pre-school. It therefore is important to make careful planning with regards to the physical set up, programme planning, curriculum, personnel etc., while planning to set up a pre-school for the young children.

The Pre-school Building

The pre-school is the living place for an organic community of growing children, primarily interested in educating them the 'gracious art of living' and not a place of formal learning where the main purpose is to communicate a certain prescribed quantum of knowledge. The pre-school environment thus helps or hinders the realisation of these goals. The building which houses the pre-school may be stimulating or stifling and may be conducive or inhabiting to the development of children.

Hence, the first basic requirement is a clean, pleasant and well-maintained building. Children spend most of their time during the day in pre-school rooms or grounds. Hence, the surroundings and environment of the pre-school are bound to exert a far-reaching influence on their growth, development and general health. Moreover, it has its significant influence on the behaviour of the children. Therefore, the school building, its situation, design, lighting, ventilation and general environment all has important role to play in the behaviour and welfare of the children. Although, the physical setting of a pre-school is the product of compromises and adjustments, yet it must aim at providing the utmost to the children. The essentials of a good pre-school are the surroundings the site and the plan.

The Surroundings

The surroundings greatly influence a child's health, attitudes and development of personality. It can be so designed to be comfortable, safe, and stimulating for children and to serve as a catalyst in enhancing contact between children and the pre-school personnel. The psychological basis for providing wholesome surroundings is the unconscious response of children to aesthetic stimuli. Hence, the pre-school building must be located amidst desirable surroundings. Ugly and unclean surroundings act directly on the subconscious mind, and bring about adverse effects on character formation. Researchers have found out that, there is a world of difference between the outlook of a persons raised in clean, healthy and adequate surrounding and one who had spent his childhood in crowded, dirty and unclean surroundings.

Site of Pre-School

The site of the pre-school includes proper location, soil, the aspect and elevation. The ideal location of pre-school is in the neighbourhood of the children served; as far as possible. The pre-school may be located away from the crowded areas of the city/ town, burial ground and main traffic areas for the purpose of children's safety. The vicinity must be such as: to permit any future expansion. Proximity to a garden or a public park permits direct play of sunlight even in the remotest corner of the school building for the greater part of the day. It will also add to the influence of the pre-school on children's appreciation of beauty.

Site of the pre-school also includes the soil on which the building is built, which is also needed to be taken care of. Soil makes the school building strong, safe, congenial and educational. The points to be considered in selecting the site with regard to soil conditions are a raised area, dry and have natural drainage free from water logging. Another important aspect of site selection for the pre-school is aspect and elevation. The site should allow the construction of the school building to face south, verandas should be planned on only one side of the rooms for free access of light. Moreover, planting of trees on the other side will help to serve as sun-breakers especially in places which are very hot most of the year.

The Plan of a Pre-School Building

The plans for the pre-school buildings would vary with the needs and available resources. However, the basic desirable elements needs to be considered while planning for a pre-school building, such as:

- The building should be planned the confirm strictly to the laws of sanitation, hygiene, ventilation and lighting.
- A single-storey building is preferable for convenience and safety for the small children.
- The building should fulfil the minimum requirements of playrooms, lavatories and wash rooms.
- There must be some open space for the outdoor play activities around the school building.

Keeping the requirements in view, a plan for the pre-school building can be consider with minimum requirements of space met. It consists of two playrooms measuring 20" x 25", a kitchen room 14" x 14", and toilet and washing 15" x 18" and an outdoor area of 1000 sq.m. If the fund does not permit, then it can be reduced to one playroom instead of two and size of the kitchen space and play area can be reduced.

In a pre-school equally important are the factors to be taken care of with regards to the rooms, floors, walls, windows and doors, sanitary facilities, ventilation, storage space and outdoor play areas.

- *Rooms:* Rectangular playrooms lend themselves more readily to activities of the children then square ones. It provides enough space for children to live and work together freely without regimentation for space. The workspace should be adaptable, flexible, liveable and home like. The amount of space should be adequate in relation to the number of children to move about freely at 1.5 square meters per child.

Table 4.1: Detail Estimation of Space and Cost of a Pre-school

Types	Size (Feet)	Cost (Rs.)
Pre-school with Two play rooms		
(a) Room (each)	20″ x 25″	2, 00.000
(b) Kitchen	14″ x 14″	1,00.000
(c) Toilet and Wash	15″ x 18″	60,000
(d) Outdoor play area	1000 Sqft.	
(e) Open Space	500 Sqft	
Pre-school with a single play room		
(a) Play Room	25″ X 30″	3,00.000
(b) Kitchen	12″ X 12″	80,000
(c) Toilet and Wash	12″ X 14″	50.000
(d) Outdoor Space	800 Sqft.	
(e) Open Space	200 Sqft.	

The room should be free from hidden areas to facilitate supervision. Walls with a variety of pleasant colours can add beauty and a feeling of spaciousness if properly selected from primary colours such as: red, blue and yellow. All the rooms should be provided with an outlet and inlet, but should avoid opening to each other.

Spaces can be adopted and arranged quite easily. With low dividers – such as: equipment, storage shelves, or erected partitions – a large, airy room can also include spaces for small groups and individual activity. In a small room, elevated platforms will increase the usable square footage and can function as stages or interest areas, while space beneath can be used for storage or games. Dust-free cross ventilation through open windows is desirable, depending upon the climatic conditions of the given area. Hence, a skilful use of paints often helps in making dark areas brighter and softens the areas which are too bright.

- *Walls:* The wall space should be functional and lend itself to promote activities. Enough of space for pinning the pictures, posters etc., at the eye level of the child is desirable in order to have picture boards. The arrangement of windows and doors should allow large spaces for bulletin boards, for attaching things to pull on and for black boards. The walls should be coated with a suitable washable, porous material to stop noises coming in or going out. Walls with variety of pleasant colours can add beauty and a feeling of spaciousness, if selected properly. Moreover, the walls of the pre-school can be painted with attractive pictures and posters for the children. Uses of bright colours are desirable as children like it very much.

- *Floors:* The floors are better to be cemented as the children may have at times to draw some pictures on the floor. It should be of such material that can be cleaned easily and maintained in a good sanitary condition. Since, many of the child s activities are conducted on the floor, it is necessary that warmth, and freedom from dusts are ensured.
- *Windows and Doors:* The doors and windows are equally important in providing conducive learning environment for the young children. Therefore, their placements need careful consideration. The windows should be low enough to enable a child to lookout for better understanding of the outside world in different seasons, different time of the day and in different occasions. Moreover, windows should have the facilities for easy operation by the children, whenever required. All windows need to be fitted with guards, screens or both. At the same time, all doors should be light in weight so that children can handle them easily. The heights of door knobs should be within easy reach of the children and of such type that they can easily use it without much difficulty.
- *Sanitary Facilities:* Water facilities are essential for the cleaning up activities in the pre-school. The toilet and washing facilities should be easily accessible from both the indoors and outdoors. One toilet for every ten children is essential. The toilet floor should be washable but not of slippery tiles. Toilet fixtures with seats varying at heights from 25-30 cm from the floor are desirable. The sizes must suite to the size of the children who will be using them. Fixtures of the suitable size for keeping the hand towels etc., assists in the development of routine habits and also promotes self-confidence and independence in the child. Care must be taken to see that sinks and toilets are equipped with disposal drains.
- *Storage Space:* Storage space is necessary in the pre-school for keeping play equipments, linen, books, teaching aids and

records. There must be space for large toys, blocks, as well as for the smaller articles. Both open and closed shelves, cupboards can be built according to the specific plans for use. It should be low in height, so that children can take the required things from the shelves or cup boards and again keep it back in its place properly. This enables the children to take care and manage the things independently. All storage space should be well ventilated and kept free from insects and cobwebs.

- *Outdoor Play Areas:* A nursery school must have a playground close to the building. Outdoor play space should stimulate imaginative play and allow children to exercise large muscles and to play together in-groups or individually. According to the mood of the weather, many indoor activities can be moved outside: large scale painting makes little mess outdoors: housekeeping and dramatic play can benefit from a setting of bushes and trees; while outdoor music, dancing, marching, or storytelling – or even a nap under a shady tree – can be a new and rewarding experience for many children.

A minimum area of two square meter of play space per child is desirable. If several groups of children use the area and the space is limited, a schedule for using the playground should be provided so that all children are not outdoors at the same time. The play area should be marked by the balance of space in the sun and shade, which can be used as required by the children. Moreover, the outdoor play area should include – hard surface area where wheel toys can be used and balls bounced, grass plot for playing, running and jumping, spot for pets, gardens and digging. A space for sandpit for sand play and manipulative activities, and also some space for water play will be ideal for giving opportunity to the children for more exploration.

The outdoor area needs to be regular in outline, so that outdoor play can be supervised satisfactorily. It should be securely fenced with a non-splintering material at least 4 feet high and kept in good repair, with a gate that can be locked. All outdoor play space should be free from nails, rocks, broken parts, and edges, and glass pieces. The area should be well drained, and surface material should be appropriate for the activities in the area. The proportionate relationship between indoor and outdoor space will not only differ according to the school's location and situation, but also in terms of the budget, other infrastructure and programmes to be developed.

CURRICULUM FOR THE PRE-SCHOOL

'Curriculum' has two different uses in Pre-schools. The word conventionally means a carefully planned set of lessons to be taught and learned or a set of learning opportunities to be presented in a certain way. A curriculum in this sense is usually spelled out in detail, with clear goals, concrete and measurable objectives, a set of requirements for teacher training, a rationalised educational philosophy, and a method for evaluation. In a broader sense, 'curriculum' means all the developmental experiences that are planned for the whole programme. In this sense, the word includes the entire day's activities; the care giving style, the degree of freedom or control for both children and caregivers; the relative emphasis on cognitive, emotional, or social values; and even the choice of whether to accept and use unplanned events as developmental experiences.

Hence, "a curriculum, encompasses the entire range of school experiences and opportunities for learning, designed by the teachers, the administrators and planners for the total and integrated development of children" (Educational Planning Group, 1995). A curriculum becomes rich and wholesome when we take into consideration the following aspects:

1. Developmental needs and abilities of the child at a particular age.
2. Goals, aims and objectives of Pre-schools, which direct the experiences and activities for a particular age.
3. Schedule/time table planned for a particular age.
4. Teaching strategies adopted and practised to suit that age level.
5. Topics selected for learning, related to the real life experiences and developmental level.
6. Teacher as a person.
7. School climate in the form of relationships, attitudes and beliefs, practices, norms, rules and regulations.
8. Parents attitudes, values, beliefs and rearing practice.

Major Goal's of a Pre-School Curriculum

The major goals of a pre-school curriculum are to:

1. Safe-guard the child s physical and mental health.

2. Stabilise the child s emotional status and adjust the child to the school environment.
3. Provide experiences for acquiring meaningful concepts.
4. Foster readiness in all areas of learning.
5. Help the child face reality and to learn to solve his problems.
6. Bring the child through his daily contacts with children to a clear understanding of the type of behaviour that is generally acceptable.
7. Give the child a start in the development of acceptable social behaviour.
8. Develop the Child s aesthetic appreciation.
9. Help the child to build a philosophy of living.

Types of Pre-School Curriculum

For practical planning purposes, curricula can be divided into three types, which reflect the experiences of the children in the programme, the philosophies of the parents, and the orientations of trained staff members:

(a) *Teacher – Controlled Curricula:* This type of curricula is the most authoritarian and most fully programmed of the three types. The teacher directs the child's activities following clearly defined directions which tell him or her which materials to use, what to teach, when to teach it, and how to respond to the child's success or failure. In this way, the teacher's activities are as programmed or directed as the child's. This type of curriculum often has two advantages. Since the goals are clearly spelled out, teachers can see the value of the curriculum and can readily acquire a sense of commitment and involvement. Since the teacher is taught exactly what to do, step-by-step, with the children, she or he may learn to be effective and confident in a matter of months. The child, however, tends to lose the benefits of spontaneity and self-directed exploration. This curriculum may be academically effective in the short run but may constrict the child's development in social and emotional areas and may negatively affect his self-reliance and initiative.

(b) *Child Controlled Curricula:* This type of curricula leaves most of the initiative to the child. The teacher's job is to respond sensitively and intuitively with learning experiences which meet the child s interest and which are based on the teacher understanding of children's developmental needs and strengths. Child-controlled curriculum at its best can introduce the child to the joy of learning and can help him acquire the discipline of self-directed work. But there are problems for both children and teachers. Many pre-school children have not learned to handle such a high degree of freedom. And even a sensitive adult may require years to learn how to respond constructively to the initiatives of children. A teacher has to be trained for more programmed curricula like this. In the western countries pre-schools such type of programme is commonly seen. One such programme is known as 'High – Scope' programme enabling the children full freedom in plan-do-review situation.

(c) *Teacher and Child Mutually Controlled Curricula:* This type of curricula combine both approaches, permitting the child to exercise his initiative and the teacher to respond within a relatively controlled and clearly defined structure. This type of curricula offers advantages of both extremes and minimises their disadvantages. Much more than a compromise, the mutually controlled curriculum has outstanding advantages of its own and may well be the best choice in most pre-schools.

Factors Determining the Effectiveness of the Curriculum

The factors which determine the effectiveness of the pre-school curriculum are:

- The thoroughness of the teacher's education and preparation to use the curriculum.
- The planning of activities to achieve particular goals. In order to maintain a high level quality, a pre-school must have clearly defined goals and objectives.
- The quality of supervision. A pre-school programme with several caregivers needs supervisors who have a clear understanding of both pre-school development and the chosen curriculum and who can provide guidance, consultation, and evaluation of the caregivers performance.

Schematically the factors that make up a wholesome curriculum are given as follows, adopted from the Educational Planning Group, Government of India (1995).

It is needless to emphasise that a curriculum, however, well planned may be, may not be universally recommended. Particularly

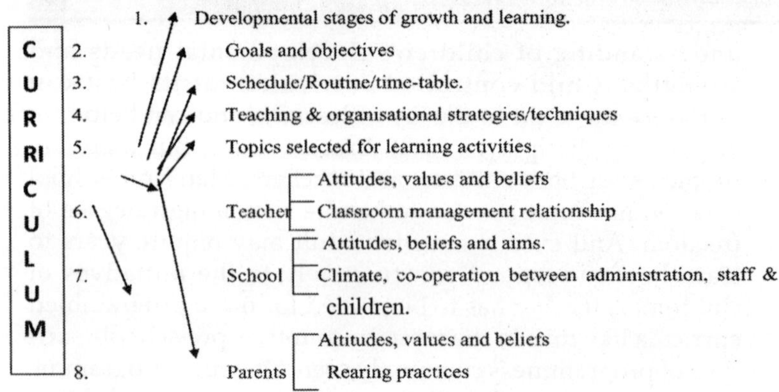

Fig. 4.2: Factors affecting Curriculum Development

a curriculum for very young children, like those of pre-school stage, need be designed looking to the social and economic condition of the community, learning materials available in the locality and the experience and expertise of the teachers. It is always desirable that the teachers, looking to all the above aspects, should plan their own curriculum as per the objectives set for the all round growth and development of the young children.

PRE-SCHOOL PROGRAMME

The programme of pre-school needs to be drawn up that it meets the objectives of pre-school education. The pre-school/ nursery school education aims at the all round development of the child such as: – Physical, social, emotional and intellectual. It helps the child to develop good health habits, proper attitudes and desirable social skills. It leads to better adjustment to groups and increased emotional maturity on the part of the child. It develops in the child a questioning mind and scientific outlook, and thus stimulates the total development of the child.

Principles of Pre-school Programme

While planning the pre-school programme it is important to remember the following principles for achieving the goals of pre-school education.

(a) *Take into Account the Developmental Level and Needs of the Children:* A child is ready for certain activities only at a particular age. If these activities are introduced to the child before he is ready for them, it becomes difficult for the child to master them and then requires a lot of trial and error. Sometimes it may even make the child avoid the activity as such. On the other hand, if it is introduced at the proper time, when the child is ready for it, then the child masters it with ease and enjoyment.

(b) *Cater to All-round Development:* A pre-school programme should be able to cater to all aspects of child's development, *i.e.* Physical, motor, language, cognitive and social development etc.

(c) *Be Flexible to Serve the Needs of the Children:* The type and duration of the activities in the pre-school should depend on the interests of the children for whom it is being designed. The teacher s plan should be a tentative plan, which may be modified according to the needs, interest and situation in which the children are being brought up. For example – on a rainy day, children may like to play with the rain water making paper boats, throwing small stones etc. In this case the teacher may have to change her scheduled plan and give the children an opportunity to play according to their interests. The programme of the nursery school should never be rigid at all.

(d) *Be Balanced between Individual and Group Activities:* In a pre-school, there are varied type of activities provided during the free play period, and the children are free to choose any activities they make like. However, it is the duty of a teacher to ensure that each child gets an opportunity for individual as well as group work, for developing better interaction with other children and for growing himself/herself. If the teacher finds that a child indulges in only solitary play, she gradually brings him to a group, and similarly if she finds that a few children are always clustered in a group, she tries to divert them at times to individual work. Making balance between these two types of activities is essential on the part of the pre-school programme for achieving its main objectives.

(e) *Be Balanced between Free Play and Guided Activity:* A balance between the free play and guided activity is also very necessary in the pre-school programme. Each day for a certain amount of time the children should be allowed to play on their own without interference from the teachers. It gives them an opportunity to explore, investigate and find out different possibilities of using different types of play materials. They learn from self-chosen and self initiated play. The free play periods should involve both indoor and outdoor play. A certain amount of time is also allocated for the guided play in which the teacher takes the initiative to introduce the activity. This period need not be for more than 10-15 minutes for the younger age group and 15-20 minutes for the older age group. The guided activity is the teacher-initiated activity, where the teacher plans some activities and presents them to the whole group either to provide some specific learning experiences to the children or to cater to some needs of the group.

(*f*) Alternate *between Active Play and Quiet Play:* The pre-school programme should be such, which needs to alternate between active play and quite play. If the children are taken outdoors for play that involve too much physical activity, then this activity should be followed by some quiet activity at indoors. Too much physical activity makes the children exhausted and so it is necessary to provide some restful activity (pause), after a spell of active play. Similarly, passive or quite play should be followed by active play, as it will be difficult for children to remain quiet for a long period of time.

(*g*) *Be Functional and Meaningful*: In a pre-school, the teacher should ways have a clear idea in her mind as to why she wants to have a particular activity, otherwise it may become meaningless. For example – If the teacher wants to take the children to the garden, she should know why she wants them in the garden. Similarly, the pre-school programme should be related to the community life and society, and should inculcate social values and skills in children.

(*h*) *Satisfy the Needs of Each Individual Child and the Group:* Each individual child is unique and his/her needs, requirements and interests are different. So does the need of one group of children differ from another group of children. The needs of urban children may be different from the needs of rural children. For example – for rural children training on health, hygiene and mannerism is adequately required than the urban children. Moreover, providing opportunities for clay, sand and water play is more necessary for the urban children than the rural children. For rural children there are many opportunities for play with water, mud, and clay. The pre-school programme should also cater to the needs of the individual child. The teacher should not assume that all the children in a group are alike. For instance, it is likely that a particular child may need more attention from her, perhaps because of a setback he received at home. Or another child, the teacher may feel, is not yet ready for group work and should have more individual activities.

(i) *Provide Concrete First-hand Experiences:* During pre-school stage, the child's understanding is at a sensory perceptual level. A verbal explanation or description does not make much sense to him. Whereas, he understands a thing, which he can see, hear and feel and learns by doing things. He understands the world around him through the medium of play. So the teacher should try to develop concept in him through play and giving him an opportunity to explore, compare, classify and handle a variety of objects. Hence, firsthand experience on the part of the children during this stage is essential and effective as well.

(j) *The Theme Should be from the Children's Environment:* The themes of the pre-school programme content should be selected from the children s environment and should be able to evoke their interest. Some suggested themes for the schools are as follows:

- self and family;
- animals;
- birds and Insects;
- homes;
- vegetables and fruits;
- plants;
- modes of transport;
- community helpers – postman, police man, milkman, doctors;
- air;
- water;
- cleanliness;
- safety;
- colours;
- festivals;
- seasons;
- foods etc;
- size;
- shape;
- texture;

(k) *Programmes should be Age Appropriate:* Separate activities should be planned, as far as feasible for 3 to 4 years and 4 to 5 years old. These can be done with the children by dividing them into smaller groups according to their ages or developmental levels and giving them activities by rotation. For some activities like sorting, placing pebbles on outlines etc., it is sometimes also useful to put one older child with each group of 3 to 4 years old, to enhance the learning of the younger group children.

Types of Pre-school Programme

Planning programme for pre-school calls for both long-term and short-term planning to achieve the objectives of pre-school education.

- *Long-term Planning:* Long-term planning is chalking out a programme for the whole year in advances with regard to learning experiences, teaching aids, budget, and materials and play equipment. In planning the learning experiences, the teacher should have a clear idea of the specific developmental objectives and plan the different steps accordingly. As regards the equipment and play materials, repair and replacements will be necessary and some new equipment will have to be procured. The teacher needs to plan the budget accordingly and devise a long-range plan for the acquisition of all these requirements. Moreover appointments of the new staff and allotment of specific responsibility of the teachers needs to be planned for the whole year for carrying out the programme successfully. The full year s plan should then be split into term/quarter wise plans and then into monthly plans.
- *Short-term Planning:* For effective functioning of the pre-school it is necessary that the programme for the whole year be divided into smaller units, terms/month-wise. Certain experiences like drawing and painting are provided to children right from the beginning of the year, but there are other experiences such as: field trips, which are not done during the first term. They can be started only when the children are adjusted to the school and have become familiar with its environment. The experiences provided differ also according to the age of the children. Hence, such type of short-term planning is essential for pre-school programme.
- *Weekly Planning:* Weekly planning includes chalking out the activities to be undertaken during the week. It includes

details of the arrangements needed, collecting the aids and materials, and contacts and approaches to be made with the parents. So that the pre-school teacher will know, what, how and when she is to carry out the various activities in the school. It makes her feel confident and can able to successfully achieve the pre-school goals.

- *Daily Planning:* Daily planning is also an essential part of the pre-school programme. In her daily plans the teacher should chalk-out the activities that she is going to take up, the special arrangements that she must make and the method that she is going to follow. It may be necessary to change the daily plans according to the needs of the individual children and the group as a whole. For some unavoidable reason also, the daily planning may get changed.
- *Evaluation:* Mere planning is not adequate. Every teacher should evaluate the programme critically to see whether she has been able to do what she planned to do with the children and whether the children have benefited by the programme. Evaluation needs to be based on informal evaluation techniques like observations, structured interviews, analysis of children s products/work and play way techniques like group games, quiz etc. She should make a note of the points, which she has, not able to put across and plan the next year s programme based on the experiences gained in the present years.

The evaluation should be continuous and should cover all aspects of development. It should be based on the objectives spelt out for each aspect of development for a particular age group. For example, motor development should be evaluated in terms of gross motor skills and fine motor skills including eye-hand co-ordination.

Evaluation of children should include both feed forward and feedback dimensions. By feed forward is meant evaluating children's previous knowledge/skills with respect to a topic, setting or activity before introducing it. Feedback refers to evaluation after conducting the activity to judge the extent of learning that has occurred. Both types of evaluation are very important to ensure that the programme is being transacted in an effective way.

Table 4.2: Example of Behavioural Indicators of Evaluation

Motor Development
• Can the child throw a ball in a given direction? • Can the child catch the ball with his hands? • Can the child balance his body well while walking? • Can the child copy a given pattern?
Language Development:
Listening Skill: Is the child attentive while listening to stories? Does the child understand and follow instruction? *Speaking Skill:* Can the child describe things in a picture? Can the child narrate an incident or a story? Does the child speak in full sentences? *Reading Readiness:* Can the child distinguished between different shapes? Can the child discriminate the beginning sounds of words? Can the child discriminate and sound of words?
Cognitive Development
Concept Formation: Does the child recognise basic colours? Can the child arrange objects of a colour from light to dark? Is the child able to differentiate a 'big' object from a 'small' one? Can the child arrange objects from biggest to smallest, heaviest to lightest etc.? Can the child describe events in a correct sequence? Can the child complete a given pattern Can the child complete a two/three piece puzzle?
Social Development
• Does the child like to join other children in-group activities? • Does the child share things easily? • Can the child wait for his turn? • Does the child enjoy coming to the pre-school? • Does the child talk with other children?

PLAY AND PLAY EQUIPMENT FOR THE PRE-SCHOOLERS

"The right to play is truly a basic right for each child, whatever the social or economic situation may be. Indeed fostering of play is clearly part of preventive medicine". Play is important to children, whatever their circumstances.

Play, as described by Piaget (1951), is the repeated responses purely for functional pleasure of the child. It consists of some rules and regulations, which are imposed by players for their own convenience. Play is also described as any activity in which the child is engaged for enjoyment. Thus, any sort of pleasure giving activity of the child is called play. It is part and parcel of a child s life. Play is fun. 'Children without fun, children without play, are children without a childhood'. Play is a mirror of society. It reflects its basic values and transmits these to the child. It is one of the major educational influences, helping the child to acquire the technical knowledge, the roles and the values that will be required in adult life. Exploring, talking, constructing and negotiating are all features of young children's play. Further, children's social and cultural world also shapes opportunities for play. Active play supports children s growing understanding and can be a foundation for school learning.

Despite the centrality of play to the health, well-being and development of children, it is rarely taken seriously by governments. Either by omission (neglecting to protect and invest in the creation of spaces and opportunities for play) or commission (the imposition of excessive constraints on children's lives), many children all over the world are unable to fully realize their right to play. These concerns prompted the UNCRC to produce a General Comment focusing on Article 31 of the UN *Convention on the Rights of the Child,* in order to provide guidance for governments on how to fulfill their obligations to children. *General Comment No. 17* highlights the fundamental importance of recognizing and facilitating this right for girls and boys of all ages. It emphasizes the role of play in providing opportunities for the expression of creativity, imagination, self-confidence, self-efficacy, and for the development of physical, social cognitive and emotional strength and skills. It further highlights that, through play, children explore and experience the world around them, experiment with new ideas, roles and experiences, and in so doing learn to better understand and construct their social position within the world. The General Comment stresses that play is essential for the realization of other rights. For example, Article 31 itself recognizes the interrelationships between play, recreation, leisure, rest and participation in cultural life and the arts. Play is also a key dimension of education, necessary to achieve the best possible health, integral to the child s optimum development, and a valuable route to recovery and reintegration after trauma, loss, neglect or violence.

Although children have a spontaneous urge to play and will seek out opportunities to do so in the most unfavorable environments, the Committee recognizes that certain conditions need to be assured if the right to play is to be fully realized. Children need to be free from harmful stress, violence, discrimination and physical dangers. They require appropriate time and space. They need access to natural environments, material resources and other children. They also need the key adults around them to recognize the importance and legitimacy of play, as well as support children in play activities. Governments must therefore act to promote and protect these conditions.

An individual learns throughout his life span. Especially in early childhood, intellectual development is very rapid and about eighty (80%) per cent of brain growth appears to be completed by the time a child is six years old. During the impressionable stage of pre-school years, when child's development is fastest, environment creates the deepest impact on him. Hence, this crucial stage demands provision of the right type of play environment for learning. A properly planned play provides the child with dynamic experiences and opportunities for learning and expresses him.

Values of Play

Play is a truly universal phenomenon. It exists in some form in every human society and dates back to prehistoric times. It provides tremendous benefits for children with regards to all round growth and developments. Moreover, it has preventive, therapeutic and creative values for those requiring special care and attention (*e.g.,* Handicapped Children). The most significant values of play are:

(i) *Physical Value:* At the time of play different parts of the body of the child are activated. Due to these activity muscles, glands and body cells are properly developed. Play also serves as an outlet for surplus energy. If the energy is not spent properly it could have made the child irritable and nervous. Specially, outdoor play gives scope for exercises in the fresh air and thereby improves health and strength. Moreover, the development of the large and small muscles of the body is not a wholly natural occurrence, and through specific play activities proportional muscular development can be attained.

(ii) *Social Value:* Play aids children to co-operate with others and develop friendly relationship. He learns social manners, behaviours and how to solve-problems from his friends while playing. Moreover, he learns competitions, tolerance, the give and take, coming with the contact of his peers. He gets maximum social contact in the play, which he may not get either at home or in the school. He also learns sex-role identification and how to behave in the society with the same sex group as well as opposite sex group.

(iii) *Cognitive Value:* Cognitive process is a dynamic and continuous process beginning with sensory reception, and then passing through perceptual organisation on (in visual, auditory, tactile, gustatory, and olfactory sensory modalities), short-term and long-term memory, language-reception, comprehension, expression, and vocabulary development, problem-solving, imagination and creativity. All these can be greatly enhanced by play as it help the children to observe, concentrate, experiment and gives them ample opportunities for exploration and sense of achievement. Play helps children to observe, concentrate and experiment.

(iv) *Moral Value:* The child learns what is right and what is wrong, how to respect elders, and how to behave with younger from his playmates. He gets moral training while playing from his friends. It helps him to learn to be honest, to lose with equanimity with team spirit.

(v) *Therapeutic Value:* Through play the preserved tension or emotions are released. The shy child can learn to enjoy himself with others; the aggressive child can learn to take his turn; the child who seems to take a sense of security can gain self-respect and the respect of his classmates through the skill he may show in a game. The eager child has an opportunity to learn to be patient, and the over competitive child can learn to accept his losses with good grace. Play therapy is a set of techniques used to help children with emotional problems.

(vi) *Recreational Value:* Play and games have recreational value once the necessary play skills have been learned and have become part of one s experience. Great enjoyment and relaxation can be had from play activities. Play gives children emotional satisfaction and keeps them occupied and prevents boredom. Toys help to keep a child happy and to reduce his anxieties.

(vii) *Educational Value:* Through the use of toys in the pre-school the child learns about the colour, size, shape of the object. The child who has problems of writing, he can learn it through drawing, painting, pasting and collage work during the play activities session in the pre-school.

There are some parents and teachers who believe that play is a fun and is waste of time and energy. But truly speaking, play involves greater social interaction in the child. It develops physical, motor skills, language, emotional and intellectual abilities in children during pre-school years.

Types of Play in the Pre-School

Different types of play can be organised in the pre-school so as to ensure the over-all integrated development of the children. These are as follows:

(a) *Free and Structured Play:* In case of free or spontaneous play, the child is allowed to play the way he wants without any specific guidance from the teacher, except motivating and initiating play activities. There is no direct involvement on the part of the teacher. Structural play or guided play on the other hand is the activities planned by the teacher to meet specific objectives. For example, if development of motor skills is the objective, the teacher devises play activities, which foster this aspect of development.

In a pre-school programme there must have always be a balance between the free play and structured play. The pre-school teacher sees to it that sufficient time is set apart for spontaneous play so that the children s interest and initiative are sustained. Yet, to make the programme a complete one and foster the total development of the child, she also structures some of the play to meet specific objectives. With very young children, the time set apart for free play is much more but as the children grow older, there is a proportionate increase in time for structured play. However, right through the pre-school years, the time given for free play should always be more than the time for structured play.

Structured play is found to be particularly useful for socially disadvantaged children. Since experiences with play materials have been limited for those children they are at a loss regarding how to use them or how to initiate play activities. For example – in a pre-school, where blocks were made available for children, there was a scramble for them and each child got a block or two. They then held on the blocks and did not proceed any further. It took quite some time for the children to get used to the idea that with a large number of blocks, one could make varieties of constructions and devise different types of play activities. In such cases, both structuring the activity and the teacher's joining into motivate the children, to become important. As experiences increase, children then become able to initiate their own play activities.

(b) *Individual and Group Play:* During pre-school years, the young child is just learning to be a member of a group. His skills in this aspect are not perfected and very often he goes back to individual activities. He is still not able to play in a big group but he certainly can play in small groups for a limited time. The teacher, therefore, sees to it that the programme is so devised that children do not always remain alone but learn to participate in group play. Most of the children enjoy it but in every group there may be a handful of children who may have to be coaxed.

In a pre-school, group play activities are by and large supervised. This is because children are still very young and are not in a position to follow the rules of the game without adult support. Yet, they follow some basic rules on their own. After a few minutes of play, there is invariably a difference of opinion and the group breaks up. This is because the children are still learning to control their own emotions or to accommodate the wishes of the group. The pre-school teacher needs to makes it a point to keep a balance between individual and group play. During early years, individual play is preferable. As children grow older, the time allotted for group play gradually increases.

(c) *Vigorous and Quiet Play:* Children love vigorous/active play activities and are quiet likely to tired themselves out if the adults do not intervene. Hence, a pre-school teacher, after a spell of vigorous activity, gets children to relax by introducing some restful activities. For example, after such active play as running, climbing, hopping and so on, the teacher introduces quiet play activities such as: playing with blocks, threading beads, drawing, painting etc. Such an interchange of active and quiet play is worked out right through the day's programme so that the children do not get restless, sitting quietly at one place for a long time nor do they get over-tried by too much activity.

(d) *Outdoor and Indoor Play:* The same balance is also useful regarding outdoor and indoor play activities in a pre-school. A resourceful pre-school teacher alternates indoor and outdoor play. The percentage of time spent indoors or outdoors, however, depends to a great extent on the weather. On hot summer days, except for the early morning hours, it may be too hot to play outside. So, after a spell of outdoor play in the morning, by and large, it may be necessary to keep the children inside. On the other hand, during winter days, it will be much more pleasant to have a large share of play activities planned outdoors. However, in places where there is no such climatic variation, a fair balance must be kept between the two types of play is necessary for optimum results.

Play Materials and Equipments for Children

High quality early learning and child care programmes provide safe, stimulating environments that are warm, comfortable and aesthetically pleasing for the children. Children are active learners who use the physical environment in a direct, hands-on manner. Hence, the play materials and equipment are part of a child s learning experience. Just as any good workman needs the tools best suited for his/her work, so children need play equipments and materials suited to their age, strength and interests. The role of play equipments and materials cannot be underestimated. These are children s friends and aids to enable the children learn various concepts, to explore, manipulate, communicate, observe, release surplus energy, exercise the whole body, teach adjustment with peers and adults, learn to share and co-operate, give vent to their emotions and develop sense of responsibility and leadership among young children.

Play equipment helps children to release their energies, reveals their talents and give expression to their creative urges. Thus, while selecting the toys or play equipment's for the children, parents, pre-school teachers and other adult care takers must bear in mind the following points:

1. The price or the cost of the play equipments should be proportional to the value of play and to the expected life of the play equipment.

2. They should be suitable to the age and maturity of the child, although developmental stages among children of the same age can vary. However, knowledge of the child s age growth patterns, muscular development and interests should be taken into consideration.
3. The size of the play equipment must be proportionate to the control, competence and safety of the child.
4. Play equipments for the children should be build from a durable material to last long.
5. Safety of the use of the play equipment is of great importance. Reasonable precautions should be taken to avoid dangerous play materials. It should not be too small that they can be inhaled or swallowed. Neither they should be made of up easily flammable materials, nor having point or sharp edges, which may cause injury.
6. Simple play equipment usually holds more challenge than the complicated ones and has more different uses. The construction and the mechanism of the toy must be easy to understand and to manipulate.
7. While selecting the play materials for children, attention should be given to those play materials having multiple benefits and use such as: that involve the use of both gross and finer motor skills, things that stimulate imagination, creativity and concentration. These play equipments lend themselves to a variety of uses, allow the child to work out his own ideas and develop independence and self-confidence.
8. There should be variety in the selection of play equipments, since at the pre-school stage an ever-increasing range of objects interest the child. Children like variety and versatility.
9. Depending upon the number of children to be admitted in a pre-school, sufficient number of play equipments must be provided to give them satisfaction and enjoyment.
10. The play materials should be such having greater objects from the real world, enabling the children to have wider and deeper experience regarding the world in which he lives. For example – if a child has not visited a town, can do little with a model of a car.
11. The play materials for the children need to be in accordance with the local conditions with regards to its adaptability and

suitability. Moreover, children from different socio-economic levels have different play needs. A child from an urban area will differ from the sub-urban youngster just as the child from a rural or a tribal area will differ from them both.

12. The area, storage space, type of housing and architecture play an important role in determining the selection and use of play equipments for the young children.
13. The materials/texture of which the play equipment is made, is of significance. Warmth and grasp ability is the reason why most toys for the young children should be of wood or fabric. Offering equipment of a variety of textures can provide rich sensory experience.
14. Children love colourful play materials. Hence, different forms of toys, colourful preferably primary colours – red, yellow and blue) play equipment s should be provided to the children to attract and create interest in them. Moreover, it forms a basis for the development of sensitivity to different colours.
15. As much as possible the play equipments are of creative in nature, which gives a real picture of the particular things.
16. Low coast, indigenous play equipments in the pre-schools should be used. A teacher needs to be good collector of materials, she can create a number of play materials which would form a great wealth for the school.
17. The teacher must always, consider the health of the children while selecting the play equipments for the children. The under-right, physically handicapped, and the very strong are after within the same class. Hence, according to each child's requirement it can be chosen.
18. The teacher must have a thorough knowledge of all types of games and play method quiet, active, rhythmic – to be able to suit the needs and interests of different age groups.
19. During the impressionable stage of pre-school years when child s development is fastest, environment creates the deepest impact on him. This crucial stage demands provision of the right type of material and equipment for learning. Properly planned play provides the child with dynamic experiences and opportunities for learning and expresses him.

Low-Cost Play Equipments

While play equipments are so significant in a child s life, it is disheartening to find that the equipment and materials available in the country today are neither suitable nor adequate to meet the requirements of young pre-schoolers. A very large number of Anganwadis, particularly in the remote and backward areas, have been unable to obtain even the basic items required for the use of children. Even very few pre-schools in our country can afford to have expensive play equipment and materials. Instead of selecting sophisticated and expensive equipment in pre-school teacher should always go in for sturdy and easily replaceable play things. Much depends on the imagination, resourcefulness and creativity of the teacher. If resourceful, she can have a good collection of equipment and work materials for children's activities from the things in the environment. She should be constantly is search of indigenous materials that will challenge the children. Without much cost the indigenous low-cost materials would facilitate the advancement of pre-school education in our country.

Moreover, proper placement and arrangement of play equipment would facilitate their use. All the play materials should be arranged attractively in the room and placed on low open shelves, so that children may take out the play materials themselves whenever needed. In this way, children will also learn that, there are fixed places for things to be kept and that they make take out any material they like from the storage places but they should put it back in its place when the play is over. This in turn will help the children to learn to use and care for the equipment and materials by themselves.

Play Equipments/Materials for Physical and Motor Development

While children are playing and exercising their bodies they are at the same time acquiring knowledge about themselves and their environment. There are a few common list of play equipments are given below, which help in the physical development of the children in a pre-school.

- Swing.
- Climbing frame
- Rope Ladder.
- Balancing Frame.
- Building Materials.

- Water.
- Balancing Board.
- Sliding Objects.
- Rocking object (Boat, Horse, Stands).
- Tyres.
- Balls.
- Ropes.
- Tricycle.
- Pushing Trolley.
- Empty barrel
- Jumping board.
- Spade.
- Watering cans.
- Bucket.
- Blocks.
- Peg Board.
- Star dice board.
- Threading Board.
- Threading disc and blocks.
- Build in set.

Play Equipment's/Materials for Intellectual Development

There are many games and activities that can help the children to introduce to new concepts and enable them to develop thinking skills. There are no specific play materials for developing intellectual development, but the use of most simple materials available all around on the part of a pre-school teacher is important. It is worthwhile to make a collection of objects which can be used to enhance/develop intellectual abilities through play, especially when children have to count, match arrange, divide, make a pattern etc. For this following simple materials can be of great use:

- Twigs.
- Shells.
- Sticks.
- Beads.
- Leaves.
- Stones.
- Seeds.

- Mosaic bricks.
- Puzzles.
- Problems-solving toys.
- Cards.
- Constructional sets.
- Match boxes/cigarette packets.
- Bottle-tops.
- Buttons.
- Marbles.
- Painting materials.
- Drawing materials.
- Dice.
- Picture cards.
- Coloured arches.
- Assembly toys.
- Number stand.
- Number board.
- Number chain.
- Number pegs.
- Form stand.
- Form board.
- Form plates.
- Gradation tubes.
- Paper chart materials.
- Blocks of all sizes.

Play Equipments/Materials for Languages Development

Children learn language by listening, imitating, repetition and practice of conversation, appreciation and encouragement by others. In the pre-school, children are allowed individually and in a group to interact with each other inside and outside the play room. Moreover, during music/rhyme session with the help of the musical instruments, children are given the opportunity to learn different words, languages etc. The simple musical instruments for the pre school children are:

- Drum.
- Daphli.
- Damru.

- Bells.
- Story books.
- Puppets.
- Flute.
- Ghunguru.
- Pipe.
- Ektara.
- Picture books.
- Charts.
- Tambourine.
- Jalra.
- Rattlers.
- Pictures.
- Picture.
- Cards.

Play Equipments/Materials for Science Activity

- Magnifying glass.
- Magnet.
- Balance.
- Measuring utensils.
- Clock.
- Torch.
- Bulb.
- Rubber tube.
- Jars.

Play Activities for Pre-school Children

For the healthy growth and development of body and mind, children need many essentials, for instance, good food, enough rest and sleep and attention to health. Children also need clean surroundings, plenty of fresh air and exercise so that all their muscles, large and small, develop properly. Children need to be active – do not except them to sit still in one place for a long time. Children need practice – in exercise such as: running, jumping, crawling, skipping and balancing which will make their bodies strong and skilful indifferent ways. A child also needs to learn – while playing games which provide enjoyment several habits are acquired, for instance, children learn to listen, to watch, to follow directions, to obey to wait and to co-operate.

There are some typical activities a pre-school child likes to do which can well be provided in a pre-school for satisfying his all round requirements of the body and mind. In order to provide these activities in a pre-school a teacher needs to look for the materials around or has to depend on the available materials in the environment.

1. *Creative Activities:* Children love to create with their hands. As they work with their, hands, they are also exploring with their senses, gaining new experiences and using the imagination. They express their thoughts and feelings when they make something; they are also practising skills with their hands and fingers and are co-ordinating and controlling their muscles. Creative activities like free painting, drawing, painting, pasting college work, paper craft, modelling, weaving, clay work and printing not only allows good exercise to the free muscles but specific organised activities enhance co-ordination between muscles and brain. It can be done on plain paper or even old newspapers. To conduct organised creative activities, children can be encouraged to fill the various forms and shapes with coloured pencils and crayons. They can also be taught to learn to print different figures with the help of cut vegetables like ladyfinger with natural colours. Paper craft can be done with the help of old news papers.
2. *Story Telling*: Children love listening to stories, and while they listen they learn (new words) as well. They learn new words but also new ideas, feelings and experiences. Story telling also inculcates imagination in children. When a story is told to children it exposes them to sequence of happenings around a theme that sparkles imagination in them. Such exposures enable them to further make their own stories. Given a picture or situation, children gradually are able to frame their own stories. So opportunities should be provided to enhance this aspect of learning.
3. *Science Experiences*: Children learn from their environment all the time. They are curious and so they observe, and having observed, they wonder. Pre-school can help them to learn from these observations in simple ways. Children can be encouraged to sharpen their senses, their minds and their reasons; thereby becoming more alert, more observant and

more thoughtful. In this process children will be prepared for school where lesson will be taught through science. Science is a way of learning, which is learning by inquiry, by discovery.

A very important factor in a child s mental growth is curiosity. Encourage the child to be curious; stimulate curiosity with questions. Another important factor is learning from experience. Teach the child to use every part of the environment. Trees, leaves, plants, animals, stones, sun, shade, water, air, mud, light, sand and household articles are sufficient. A third important factor in learning is discussion. Let the children talk freely and encourage them to ask questions. Every experience leads to new questions, new experiments and now activities – all of which leads to development for children.

4. *Rhythm, Music and Movement*: Children love rhythm, music and movement. Music brings pleasure to children and offers avenue of expression to children, which closely relates to that of language. A simple song accompanied by music brings children to happy state of mind and engages them more and more specially in rhythmic activities. It also helps the children to memorise the words and tone etc. The songs are to be short and in local mother tongue, so that children can learn easily. To produce music and rhythm, simple, low-cost play equipment s can be used. There are many ways to make rounds and rhythms that increase children s enjoyment, from the available waste materials.
5. *Dramatisation*: Children like to play freely, pretending to be various people and acting out different experiences. Pre-school can provide a few simple settings to create the right atmosphere. For example, a house or shop etc., where children will create their own story and act it out, enabling them for self-expression.
6. *Outdoor Play:* For healthy growth and development of body and mind, apart from the basic needs, children also need clean surroundings, plenty of fresh air, and exercise so that all their muscles, large and small, develop properly. Children need to be active running, jumping, crawling, skipping and balancing. Hence, enough out-door play facilities should be available in a pre-school. By providing some outdoors spaces and play materials. Children can be encouraged to spend time outside the pre-school building. There must be place for keeping the

pet animals and sandpit for providing some new experiences to these children. A small garden in a pre-school will have added advantages for young children. Providing sand-pit and water will certainly attract children to do the outdoor play activities. Variety of activities can be arranged with sand and water for the children which they love to do.

7. *Field Trips and Excursions*: The children need to be taken out at least once a week to observe and explore the environment around them. Some of the common interests of the children at this stage are observing animals, trees, flowers, birds, and other beauties of nature. They can also be taken to visit the people who work for them like: doctor, postman, grocer, washer man etc. Also to places like: markets, bus stand, railway station, post office, police station and cinema theatre etc., from where children will get first hand ideas and experience to develop proper understandings. The purposes of an excursion or field trip for young children are to:
   (*a*) help the children learn about the world in which they live, through first-hand experience at their development level;
   (*b*) help them to have a group experience and build good relationships with other children and adults;
   (*c*) increase and clarify existing concepts;
   (*d*) have fun and enjoyment;
   (*e*) help them become more aware of the things around them through guided observations;
   (*f*) increase their frame of reference.

These play-way readiness activities strengthen and promote various faculties and provide pre-school children the confidence to face the challenges of the school system in general.

PRE-SCHOOL STAFF AND PERSONNEL

The staff is the most important element in a pre-school. Teaches and other caregivers influence the development of children more than any specific curriculum or educational methodology. Obviously, selection of staffing deserves thoughtful attention with regards to their competencies and number of staff members.

The Pre-School Teachers

The head teacher of a pre-school must have a basic knowledge of child development and care. She must know how to run a pre-school, its requirements for safety and health, nutrition and mental health service. Moreover, she should be able to recruit and guide the other staff; work with parents and maintain their involvement; and collaborate with other community agencies. The job obviously requires a person of ability and experience and one whose professional training should includes an academic degree in a field such as: early childhood education or child development, or whose experiences and competencies are equivalent to such formal training. The pre-school teachers are those responsible for immediate, face to face care of the children. They are the principal staffing concern, since the effectiveness of the programme depends on the quality of their interaction with the children. There are several basic requirements for the pre-school teachers, such as:

- Should be at least 18 years old – mature enough to handle the young children.
- Should be healthy enough to perform all duties safely and should have no disease that could be communicated to the children.
- Must be willing and able to carry out the activities required by the curriculum.
- Must be able to work with children without using physical or psychological punishment; be able to praise and encourage children; be able to provide them with learning and social experiences appropriate to their ages; be able to recognise physical hazards and either eliminate them or take precautions against them.
- Be willing and able to increase her skills and competence through experiences, training, and supervision.
- Be very progressive and enthusiastic always to work for the development and welfare of the children.
- Be academically well trained and qualified. Preferably training in early childhood education or child development or child psychology.
- Preferably women to deal with the young children with their soft and motherly affection.
- Be a good 'house keeper' both indoors and outdoors so that the school is always clean and attractive.
- Be enthusiastic and enjoy being with the children – Relax and smile.

The crucial role of leadership the pre-school teacher plays in shaping the attitudes, skills and learning of children makes her the key to the successful programme in the pre-school. She needs to be sensitive to the needs of young people, respect the dignity of the individual, and recognise the existence of individual differences in human personalities and human capacities. She should also think of education in terms of lives, problems as people face them today. A good pre-school teacher gives human orientation and social direction to her teaching. She endeavours to emphasise the best of the culture heritage with the ever-expanding fund of knowledge in order to provide learning experiences relevant to the demands of contemporary society.

Other Personnel for the Pre-School

There is necessary for one or two pre-school assistants for housekeeping services like: cleaning, washing the linen and care of the grounds, putting up new sheets on the bulletin and easel board, putting on and taking of the equipment and mending etc. They need to be the persons, who must not become irritated by noise or confusion. Since, children spend much of the time on the floor, the floors must be cleaned daily to be without dust and they must be free of broken equipment, glass pieces, loose nails and other hazards. The assistants need to be on duty in the toilet room and washing area as well helping the children and the teachers to handle the situations effectively.

A physician is desirable to be the staff of a pre-school as a part-time worker. He or she can be responsible for the physical examination of the children and for the morning inspection too. Moreover he/she can also be of great help in case of accidents or emergencies, preferably a paediatrics doctor who has the training to deal with the children s problems. In case of a whole day pre-school, a cook is a must to get the appointment. The pre-school teacher plans menu supervises the preparation and serving of food. However, a cook should be there to take directions from the teacher, and prepare nutritious, tasteful food on time for the young children. Moreover, she should be well trained to prepare food according to the taste and create homely atmosphere while serving children.

Staff: Child Ratio

The ratio of staff members in a pre-school to child is an indicator of the amount of individual attention available to each child. The number of the staff member is influenced by the programme, finance, fees, plan of building, provision of equipment, the age group, and number of the children enrolled, characteristics of children, abilities of the teacher and the training and experience of the teachers. The amount of individual attention needed by each child varies but is related to developmental level. However, it is generally agreed in our Indian condition that there should be one adult for every 15 children (1:15). In case of younger age children (2+ to 3+) ratio may be little less, as they require significantly more individual attention, as compared to the older children (4 + to 5 + years).

PRE-SCHOOL RECORDS AND REPORTS

Records and reports are of great value in guiding the behaviour and planning the education for the individual child and in achieving the objectives of the pre-school education. Through the records the teacher knows the child s family background, home environment, developmental history, health records, needs and abilities, in order to stimulate the child to achieve growth. The teacher, therefore, collects the required information from a variety of sources and keeps it in a folder to which she adds her own observation of the progress made by the child in the school. Records of various types are also valuable for parent education as basis for discussion and to keep the parents inform of behaviour and progress of their child at school. As the child leaves the nursery/pre-school and joins the primary school, these records may be passed on to the primary school teacher. This detailed information will help the pre-school teacher to get full understanding and work with the child in a better manner.

Significance of Reports and Record Keeping in Pre-schools

Reports and record keeping in pre-schools is of great importance because of the following reasons:

(a) *Understanding the Individual Child:* Keeping records and reports in pre-schools help the teacher to understand the individual child better. The teacher collects most of the information such as: child s family background, home environment, developmental history, health status, needs, abilities and problems, (if any) from the parents. She can supplement it with her own observations of the child and his family. By doing so the teacher gets the perception of the whole child in a meaningful way. On the basis of her estimate and understanding about the child, she plans to provide such experiences as and when necessary for the child for his optimum development.

(b) *Assessing the Child's Rate of Development:* A regular recording of a child's development helps the teacher to assess the pattern of development better. As the teacher keeps regular observation on a particular child, she makes a note of the progress that he/she has made. At times, it may so happen that the teacher finds that, instead of showing progress, the child actually regresses in certain aspects of development. Then the teacher will have to find out the causes for it and take necessary steps to overcome the setback.

(c) *Curriculum Planning:* Proper maintenance of records and reports in a pre-school is very useful for purpose of curriculum planning. The curriculum of the pre-school needs to be based on the needs, interests and abilities of the children in order to be effective for the young children. Hence, the teacher should provide such experiences to the children which are meaningful, interesting and functional for them and which are in accordance with their developmental level. This is possible only when the teacher keeps detail records of the children.

(d) *Determine the Readiness of the Children:* The records help the teacher to determine the readiness of the children for school. The information about the child s physical, emotional, intellectual and social development should help the teacher to determine whether a particular child is ready for particular activity or not. The satisfactory progress in primary classes depends to a great extent on the readiness of the child for schooling.

(e) *Guiding the Teacher in Achieving the Goals of pre-school Education:* Keeping records and reports of the pre-school children enable the teacher to know where how, what she is doing. It certainly helps her as guiding principle in achieving the objectives of pre-school education in the long-run.

(f) *Valuable Resource for the Researchers:* Carefully kept records are also valuable from the point of view of researchers. In India, we have hardly any systematic data on the pattern of child development. Hence, these records on pre-school children s growth, development and behavioural pattern will certainly yield a great deal of research material for studies in child development. Practical use of these records is of significant importance for the researches, teachers as well as the parents those are concern and responsible for the young children.

Type of Records

There are different types of records maintained in a pre-school to keep all the information concerning the children and their background. They are:

(a) *Personal Record of the Child*: This record will include the name of the child, sex, date of birth, place of birth, ordinal position, religion, mother tongue and detail address etc.

(b) *Home Background of the Child:* Detailed information about the parents or guardian of the child, such as: their age, educational qualifications, occupations, income etc. Information about siblings, type of family (single and joint), information about relatives staying at home, facilities at home, etc., are also included in this record.

(c) *Health Records*: Results of the medical check-up and recommendations, including height, weight and body measurement of the child are taken at the time of admission. Moreover in the health record, height and weight measurements are to be taken once a month, in order to have general index of child s nutritional health status.

(d) *Attendance Record*: It is very much required by a pre-school to keep a record about the number of days the child attends the school in a month. A bound record or register is better for keeping the record intact. Names of the children are usually entered alphabetically. Moreover, the reasons for absenteeism can be studied towards taking remedial measures and the impact of the school assessed in relation to attendance.

(e) *Stock Register*: For every pre-school, a general stock register is must, as adequate details about the stock maintained will help to know what is essential in the present and future. A stock register contains detail list of all the articles and other items such as: accessories, toys, equipment, furniture etc., in an inventory register with proper headings.

(f) *House Visits Records:* Keeping records of house visits by the pre-school teachers are equally important in terms of date of visit, purpose of each visit, information elicited, response of the parents and specific observations made. Before making the visit, the teacher should inform the parents about the date and time of visit. The house visit records should elicits detailed information regarding the habits of the child and his history of illness, mannerisms, toilet habits, sleeping habits, eating habits and interaction with the family members. Moreover, the record must have certain information about the child rearing practices, especially the disciplinary methods the parents adopt, parental interest and altitudes towards childcare etc. All these details give a clear picture of the child and his family. Accordingly, the teacher will try to understand the behaviour of the child. On subsequent visits, she records only the changes if there are any, in the different aspects of development.

(g) *Parents - Teachers Meeting Records:* Parents and teachers meeting at school is very important for co-ordinating the overall growth and development of the children. Keeping records of these meeting aims to determine how much the parents participate in the school programme. In this record various activities in which parents take part at school, the nature of their participation and frequency of participation are noted down. Moreover, this record show whether or not the parents are interested in and aware of the school programme. Accordingly, the pre-school teacher will try to contact the parents regarding the child s development. Reports about discussion in the parent s meetings, suggestions, interchange of ideas and above all decisions reached by both the parents and teachers can also be included in it. By doing so, both teachers and parents play an equal role in the overall development of the young children.

(h) *Records of Admission Forms:* This form is given to the parents, at the time of admission in the school. Following information are required which are recorded properly in the school admission register also.

Personal Record

Name of the child:

Age:

Sex:

Father's name:
Number of Brother/Sister:
Mother's Name:
Their age and Sex:
Father's Educational Qualification:
Mother's education and occupation: Family Income: Rs.
Full Address:

Apart from this the parents are to give information regarding the immunisation record of the child. The date of registration and number on the waiting list at the time of registration is recorded. Moreover the roll numbers are also entered. Similarly, at the time of withdrawal of the child from the school, the date, age, reasons for withdrawal are recorded in this form.

(i) *Progress Report of the Children*: The teacher rates children s progress in different aspects of development, such as: emotional, personal, social, language and intellectual, from time to time. Moreover, she also checks against the factors that interfere with his development, his special interests, abilities and his special problems. By doing so, it can be well analysed whether the child is progressing in normal rate or regressing. Accordingly, the teacher can modify her techniques, while working with particular child, and if required can provide special help and support.

HOME-SCHOOL RELATIONS

The age group of 2½ to 6 years is the most important period of the child s life when the vital foundation for a better future life is laid. Family, home and surroundings are the factors, which influence the child's life most strongly during these formative years. It sets the stage for the development of many proper and improper characteristics, habits, behaviour both within and outside the family, most importantly, the school. Parents are the first socialising agents for the child inside the family and teachers at school in early days of life. The home is the smallest world the child is fully acquainted with, but during pre-school stage, when the child steps into the pre-school for the first time, his world becomes much wider. In the school the child finds himself surrounded by unknown children of his own age, and teachers whom he/she may not know earlier at all. The search for emotional support used to be there all the times, but gradually starts playing with the children, develops skills, and finds outlets for his hidden talents. Thus, teacher in the school plays a very significant role in a child life, like his/her parents. Home and school are the two worlds for pre-school children, where total developments take place. Therefore, home and school need to work together for proper understanding of each other, guiding the children co-operatively for better welfare of the children. The teacher may not able to know the child s interests, needs and motivation without an intimate contact with the parents. Only when the teacher works through parents, she can create a healthy, secure and favourable environment for the child in the pre-school. Hence, home and school relationship must always exit for the best interest of children.

The home-school relationship aims at creating better environment (both physical and psychological) for the children to enable them to grow properly to the fullest. Hence, teachers and parents need an understanding of and skills in the enabling aspects of communication. There are three aspects of this enabling process are as follows:

1. *Strategies*: It needs to be viewed within a three dimensional framework such as: beliefs, perspectives and action.
2. *Techniques*: These are the ways parents and teachers can actualise their communication needs.
3. *Styles*: It provides the basic system by which the teacher in the pre-school conveys her sense of meaning of events and things to the parents regarding their children.

Significance of Home-School Relations

The home school or parent teacher relations help to create:

(a) A better understanding between parents and teachers concerning what children are like.

(b) A better understanding with regard to what is pre-school education.

(c) An opportunity for parents to meet other parents and learn from their experiences.

(d) Understanding of the new techniques of child-rearing and training practices.

In order to achieve these goals, the teachers should help the parents to gain confidence in them to play the role of parenthood effectively, and to learn more about their children and child development. Moreover, home school relations promote a bond between home experiences and the educational programme. It also engage parents in assessing, implementing, and evaluating their child's growth. In order to make the home-school relations effective or in other words for successful parent-teacher communication, following points need to be stressed upon, on the part of a pre-school teacher.

1. Understand the needs, feelings and expectations of each parent.
2. Be receptive and encourage the parent to share their ideas and feelings.
3. Be attentive, let parents know you are indeed paying attention to their message.
4. Create a truly responsive environment for listening.
5. Cater to the individual needs of the parents regarding their children and achieve good co-operation from them.
6. Be more positive and less critical of children.
7. Encourage reflective listening in you and in the parents.
8. Respect the parents for what they are.
9. Avoid nasty conclusions and remarks.
10. Be very impartial and not compare children.
11. Be very comfortable, free and friendly with the parents.
12. Have the attitude of learning from the parents as well.
13. Avoid boasting and dominating on parents.
14. Convey the fact that the teacher is interested in the welfare of the child and seek co-operation of the parents to do her duty more efficiently.
15. Accept the parent s suggestions to maximum possible extent.
16. Avoid discussing about the child in his presence with his parents.
17. Use positive reframing of messages to help parents see the positive aspects of sensitive issues.

For sound and effective home school relations, a forum for parent education should be organised. The methods and contents used in this session will depend upon the objectives of the particular school, socio-economic status, and educational level of the parents, financial conditions of the school, the community and the interests and the abilities of the teachers.

Ways of Developing Home School Relations

There are various ways, by which home school relationship and parent education regarding child development can easily be achieved. They are:

- *Home Visits:* The affairs of home and surroundings affect the child directly, it becomes imperative for the teacher to study them. Home and personal visit have proven to be among the most effective of communication practices. Perhaps the most substantive aspect of this technique is its nurturance of the parent and family perspective. As Osborn (1991) notes, home visiting has been a successful part of educational and family support efforts for centuries. The basic premise of the home visit is that parents are an integral force in their children s lives and thus need to be engaged in empowering activities (Swick, 1993). Functions of Home Visit include:
  1. helping teacher gain more sensitive insight into parent and family needs, strengths, and perspectives. For example, if, after a home visit, the teacher feels that they child does not get proper attention from the mother of home, the teacher tries to give extra attention and love to the child in the school;
  2. providing parents opportunities to share their learning experiences with teachers;
  3. opening up parents and teachers to the many dimensions of home and school learning;
  4. allowing parents and teachers to share their knowledge of child development and learning;
  5. a friendly social visit will make the child and parents feel comfortable as well as important;
  6. parents develop confidence that the teacher takes good care of their children.
- *Parent s Interviews or Individual Meetings:* An interview with the parents gives the teachers and the parents a chance to talk freely about the child, and understand the child even better than before. Many parents who are shy, never talk in a meeting, may freely express their views to the teacher when they are alone. Some parents may not like to talk about the problems of their children, but if they are given the opportunity to discuss with the teacher, they may benefit.

The interview or meeting with the parent(s) can be planned or casual. Informally they can have the meeting when they come to the school to leave their children in the morning and at the time of taking back the children in the evening. Moreover, the teacher can also take advantage of such situations to inform the parents anything about the child. If anything serious to be taken care of regarding the child, the teacher can request the parent(s) to meet her, whenever it is convenient for both of them.

- *Parents and Teachers Meeting:* Parent s meetings in the pre-school is an integral part of the school curriculum. It helps to establish contacts with the teacher and the pre-school itself. It also gives the parents opportunities to meet with other parents, discuss, and exchange ideals about their children. By such interactions, parents enriched themselves in child rearing and care and may also modify their own ideas and behaviour towards their children for better results. All parents are very much concerned about their own children's development and given the scope of learning better child care obviously interest them.

However, the role of teacher in arranging parent s meeting is of great significance. The teacher needs to plan properly to impress upon the parents the need for and the purposes of regular parent s meetings. While planning, the interest and needs of the parents are to be considered to ensure effective parents participation. Besides the informal discussions in such meetings, demonstrations, films, lectures and displays can give additional information. The frequency of the parent s meetings may be decided in the beginning of the each academic year. It will be more practical and realistic on the part of the pre-school teacher to chalk out the programme for the parent s meetings for the whole year with the help of enthusiastic parents. She may form a parent s programme committee with a few willing parents, and entrust the work to that committee. The teacher may guide, co-ordinate and help the committee work. The ultimate aim of this meetings however, is that the parents should derive maximum benefit regarding childcare and parenting.

- *Parent's Participation in School Programmes:* Another aspect of home-school relationship is the parent s participation in school programmes with their children. This will enable them to know that, almost all the children are alike in their needs and behaviour. Moreover, parents are quite aware about the different programmes of the pre-school and will try to prepare their children accordingly. Organisation of children s festivals is an important part of the parent s programme. On such occasions, samples of children's work can be exhibited and a short programme of half an hour s duration by the children, and games for parents can entertain both the parents and children. Parents can also be invited to join the picnics and outdoor trips. By doing so, many willing parents may lend a helping hand to the staff in arranging the transportation or fulfilling any other requirements.

- *Materials for Parents:* Along with the various meetings, programmes in the pre-school to develop the home school relations, maintaining written diary for each child to communicate with the parents is essential. Any message or information regarding the child s progress in the school to be given to the parents can be written in the diary and sent home with the children. The parents can return the diaries noting the information.

Moreover, newsletter is excellent for keeping the parents. Informed about child development child-rearing practices new trends in education of young children, new songs and stories will help the parents to guide their children better. It also provides information about what is happening in the classroom and for sharing of family oriented material (such as: special radio T.V. programmes, daily news cuttings etc). Moreover, it may include the forthcoming classroom activities, special events, parent-teacher meetings and other important information. Parent s enjoy and use newsletters, especially those that have items of concern to them and their children. Effective newsletters involve parents in the design and content, include items about what the children are accomplishing, one attractive, and are easily posted in the home. Some suggestions for making the newsletter technique effective are:

- involve parents and children in their development and distribution;
- make these newsletters personable, attractive, and readable;

- include 'two-way' communication items in the newsletter, where parents can respond to items by invitation;
- include children s work in each issue of the newsletter;
- have a parent s corner where parents can share concerns and issues;
- each issue of the newsletter should include some 'should learning activity' for parents and children to do together;
- have parents and children evaluated the newsletter each year.

- *Parent s Counselling by Pre-School Teacher:* Not all parents have the knowledge regarding the special needs and requirements of young children during this period. A pre-school teacher is to identify these needs and help parents to develop an awareness, understanding and requirements for normal and natural growth and development of young children. Usually parents lack understanding regarding children's developmental needs and, thus here comes the role of parental counselling. A pre-school teacher with proper education and training of child care and development plays a vital role of a counsellor for the parents. She can assist the parents in understanding the early intervention in preventing later educational deficits. Further, she may be of great support for parents to develop realistic expectations from their child. Through discussion, exchange of ideas and interactions with parents, pre-school teacher can enhance and equip parents with parental abilities and skills to manage their children. Further, pre-school teacher may provide parents with an opportunity to share both positive as well as negative experiences to develop mutual (parents and child) problem-solving skills.

Thus, together, parents and teachers need to conceive of their partnership as growth oriented experiences in which they seek to nurture each other toward becoming full partners in their support of children's learning and development. Hence, home-school relationship is a vital aspect of the pre-school programme. The schools, however efficient, cannot stimulate optimum development of children, unless they work in close, co-operation with the parents. Parents are now becoming more aware of the new trends in education of children and like to know more about their duties to bring up healthy and well-adjusted children.

Therefore, the task of the pre-school teacher extends beyond guiding the children, in educating the parents also. Hence, every pre-school has to integrate its educational programme with the child s education at home. Getting the full co-operation of the parents is a great challenge and the teacher must accept it.

VALUES OF PRE-SCHOOL EDUCATION: The Research Experiences

Research evidences shows that children having early childhood education/pre-school education are at an advantage position in a lot of socio-emotional and cognitive variables. A 'Happy Child' makes a better school going child, than one under stress and pressure to learn too much and too fast. Contemporary research has revealed that children s emotions are deeply affected by their attitude to learning as also their ability to learn. The whole idea of pre-school education is to provide the child with wholesome learning environment, where he can learn through play; and get an opportunity for all round development for children between 2½ years to 5½ years old. Between this age group, a child s cognitive, psychomotor and sensory controls are best developed through the medium of play and creative activities rather than through formal teaching of subjects. However, instead of an upward extension of the play way method, what is to be seen is a downward extension of formal academies. Some research evidence collected from the studies done in the Indian context are presented here to show the significance or effect of pre-school education/early childhood education for the all round development of the child.

Developmental Studies on Urban and Rural Children

A study of adaptive, language, personal-social and motor development of children in the age group of 2½ to 5 years was conducted in the urban, rural and industrial areas, in seven different centres of the country. Only the urban samples were drawn from the pre-schools. The study was done both longitudinally and cross-sectionally and the sample comprised of more than 7,000 children. The results showed that in language development rural children showed late development by 1 to 1½ years in almost all tasks as compared to urban children. Children from the industrial areas were found to be faster than rural children but slower than their urban counterparts. The language tests included naming and identification of pictures, use of objects, comprehension, concepts of time, right and left, and ability to give one s own name, age and address, action against test, humour, following directions, following preposition, naming parts of the body, responding to picture cards and responding to picture books.

In adaptive development the pre-school going urban sample was found to be faster than the rural children or children from the industrial areas. The tests included blocks, play, form adaptation, drawing, form discrimination, number concept, colour identification, immediate memory, comparative judgement and problem-solving. The differences were striking in the entire drawing task, in number concept and in colour identification. In these tests rural children were for behind the urban ones. In motor development, too, the urban children were found to be faster than the children from the other two areas. The tests included ball play, standing, walking and running, ascending and descending steps, and skipping, hopping and jumping and hand skills such as: threading beads and cutting. In case of personal and social development, the trend is the same as that seen in the other aspects of development. In majority of tasks given to assess the personal and social development, the urban children were faster. It was studied by using interview schedules with mothers and other caretakers. The schedules covered behaviours of eating, sleeping, elimination, dressing, personal hygiene, communication, play and developmental detachment.

Critical Analysis: The above findings certainly favour the pre-school education, but implication of this evidence is serious. In almost all tasks, the urban pre-school going children were found to be better than the rural children or children from the industrial area. The differences are striking particularly in all tests connected with school, such as: all paper and pencil tests, number tests, picture vocabulary tests etc. Rural children were found to be having trouble in all these tests. It implies that rural children, who form the majority of children in India, enter school without having had any kind of preparation for schooling. The primary school, on the other hand, is formal and rigid and does not give much scope to children for helping them to adjust to the demands of school. The process of schooling therefore becomes too difficult for them and as such many of them either have to repeat the class or leave school altogether. This is partly the reason for the high rate of wastage and stagnation in the early primary classes.

Effect on the Language and Intellectual Development of Under-Privileged Children

In order to study the effect of pre-school education on the language and intellectual development of under privileged children, the sample consisted of children of semi-skilled and unskilled workers. The experimental group consisted of 14 children who were doing their final term in the pre-school and had a mean age of 5 years 11 months. The control group was drawn from class-I of a primary school and consisted of 15 children with a mean age of 6 years 6 months, none of whom had pre-schooling but did have five months of schooling in class-I. The tests used were story narration for language and drawn-a-man for intelligence. The results showed in no uncertain terms than the pre-school group is at an advantage in both language and intellectual development, in spite of the fact that they were chronologically younger than the primary school group.

Effect on the School Readiness of Under-Privilege Children

This study was an investigation into the effect of pre-school education as given by a public agency with its limitations of space, play equipment and inadequate funds on a group of under-privileged children entering primary school. The sample consisted of 252 five-year old children from 27 Municipal Corporation Primary Schools. All children belonged to the low and lower middle class families, the average income of which was Rs. 200 per month. Children (n=109) in the experimental group had received pre-school education in corporation pre-schools before coming to class I, whereas children in the control group (n=143) came to Class-I without any pre-school education. Children were tested immediately after they were admitted in class-I. The tests consisted of reading and number readiness tests. The components of the reading readiness test were word meaning, sentence meaning, visual perception, and auditory discrimination. The results showed that the group with pre-school education performed significantly better than the group without pre-school education. The crucial points of the study were that children under study were underprivileged and the nursery schools which gave these children the 'head start' were not fancy ones – they were poorly equipped with toys, had limited play space but yet were able to produce results.

Effect of Pre-school Education and Home Stimulation on Child Development

This study was done to study the difference of the effect of the regular attendance in the pre-school and home stimulation on different aspects of child development. The sample consisted of 78 nursery school children, aged between 3 and 5 years. The tools used were rating scales with an inter-rater reliability of 73. The criteria used for home stimulation were leisure time activities of the parents, quality of food, and availability of space, toys and picture books. The findings revealed that regular attendance in the pre-school made a significant difference in the intellectual development of children from high stimulation homes, whereas in motor development both groups showed improvement with regular attendance. The results imply that regular attendance in the pre-school makes a difference in both groups of children, no matter whether they receive stimulation at home or not. However, there are differences in the aspects that are more affected, the low stimulation group showing gains in intellectual growth. A possible reason for this may be that in low stimulation homes the opportunity to use social and language skills is limited. Since the pre-school lays a good deal of stress on such skills, regular attendance in the school is likely to help these children derive more benefit in these aspects. On the other hand, in the case of children of high stimulation homes, it is the intellectual development that improves with regular attendance, probably because the language and social skills are taken care of at home.

Effect on Cognitive Development of the Children

The sample consisted of 60 three to five years old children from 3 primary schools. All children belonged to low and lower – middle class family. It was seen that the children who have attended pre-schools have better cognitive style than the children those have not experienced pre-school education.

Research Comments on the Effect of Pre-school Education on Children's Development

Various researches have proved that the pre-school encourages to foster a harmonious development of child s physical well-being, social and intellectual development. To Modak (1970) pre-school develops social sense and adjustment in children. Verma (1966) states that strong research evidence and the experimental researches on the education of the disadvantaged pre-school children suggest that, the enrichment of the pre-school experience would provide a promising antidote to this cultural deprivation. Muralidharan (1970) states that one of the major causes of educational wastage particularly in Class-I is that most of the children enter school without having or developed a kind of school readiness. It has been observed by Salomy (1973) that children who have had the benefit of pre-school experience are much more receptive to formal schooling; their educational achievement tends to improve, the charges of their dropping out of school are reduced and also provide the guidance and understanding of adults and opportunity to mix with other children. Dakshayani (1970) claims that researches have also proved that, children who have been given opportunities for appropriate pre-school education stand better adjusted in primary school.

PRE-SCHOOL EDUCATION IN INDIA: Growth And Development

Pre-school education was unknown in India almost up to the end of the nineteenth century. It is around this time that the European missionaries introduced the concept of kindergarten education. In the early part of the 20th Century most of the Kindergarten schools were attached to the institutions established mostly by the missionaries. To them goes the credit of popularising the kindergartens in India. These institutions were not the typical kindergartens in India. These institutions were not the typical kindergartens as envisaged by its founder. These kindergartens were later Indianised as 'Balwadis' or 'Shishuvihars'. The Indian movement in the field of pre-school education owes much to Annie Besant and Tagore in the early part of the 20th Century. At that period, there were three types of institutions in the field of pre-school education in India, they are:

(i) Institutions run by Theosophists.

(ii) Special type of schools for children of rich families runs by Maharajas.

(iii) Schools and Centres in Gujarat and Maharashtra, run by private individuals.

Other developments which took place in the pre-school movement in India were opening of Shishu Vihar Mandal at Yeotmal in Maharashtra and Centre of Cosmic Education at Allahabad in 1951, Happy Education Society at Delhi, Nai Taim

Sangh at Wardha, Balniketan Sangh at Indore in 1941, and the Association Montessori International in India. In 1944 the Central Advisory Board of Education (ABD) gave concrete suggestions for the reorganisation of pre-school education in India. The CABE reports recommend that we should make a provision of 1,000,000 free places in many schools or classes for children in the age range of three to six years.

In 1937, Mahatma Gandhi did not have any plan for the child below seven years. But when he retired from jail in 1944 he had realised that he could not neglect the child below seven, and then he gave his views on the pre-basic education of children under seven. This education according to Gandhi should be conducted in co-operation with parents and community. The first pre-basic education school, established under Kasturaba Memorial trust, started functioning in July 1945 and Sevagram, under the guidance of Smt. Shanta Narulkar. Owing to more urgent calls on the national resources since, 1947, it was not possible to plan any comprehensive development for the education of children of pre-school age until 1951, when Indian Council for Child Education was formed with Smt. Sarladevi Sarabhai as its president. The Ministry of Education, Government of India, in their report progress of education in India 1947-52, remarked:

> *"Pre-primary education was for the most part confined to urban areas and has been the responsibility of parents. The policy of the Government in this respect has been that of assistance and encouragement. There has been a sudden expansion of this education in the middle of the century due partly to Madam Montessori's stay in India, but mainly due to organised efforts and ability of certain private bodies".*

Pre-school Education in Five-year Plans

In the *First Five-year Plan,* though the need for pre-school education was stressed but no definite financial provision was made for this purpose. As a part of the *First Five-year Plan* the Central Government set up a Central Social Welfare Board with the object especially of assisting voluntary agencies in organising welfare programmes for women and children.

In the later part of the *Second Five-year Plan* the Planning Commission made a provision for child welfare and education. This was done on the recommendation of the Child Care Committee, which was appointed by the Central Social Welfare Board. Out of

Rs. 307 crores provided for education during the second plan no special provision was made for the pre-school stage.

It was only during the *Third Five-year Plan* that the Government formally recognised the need for pre-school education. The Planning Commission had asked the Central Social Welfare Board to appoint an expert committee to survey and report on child care in the country. For the first time, pre-school education was recognised by the Government of India as the base of national system of education, and thus a national policy was to be formulated for the cause of pre-school education. The report of the expert committee, set up by the CSWB, is a landmark in the history of pre-school education as for the first time its, recommendation to the Government covered the 'total child', including education, health, nutrition and recreation. The committee pointed out that pre-schools should be self-sufficient and should be started by the voluntary agencies. Balwadis should be started both for rural and urban areas. The Community Development Departments and Central Social Welfare Board should run these pre-schools. As a result of these efforts the total number of pre-school child care centres was estimated to be 3,500, which an enrolment of about 14.5 lakhs which was 35 per cent o the total population of children between 3-5 years.

In 1964, the Indian Association of Pre-school Education (IAPE) was formed. In 1966 the Education Commission gave its suggestions for strengthening the pre-school education. The IAPE brought out a comprehensive document, which dealt with such important problems such as:

- Pre-school education for the rural and tribal children.
- Education at the training centre.
- The system of pre-school education.
- Recent trends in pre-school education.
- Voluntary efforts in pre-school education.
- Pre-school teacher education.

In 1969, the National Council of Educational Research and Training (NCERT) decided to set up the Department of Pre-Primary and Primary Education. It was suggested in the draft of the *Fourth Five-year Plan* that, "in the field of pre-school education government effort will be confirmed mainly to certain strategic areas such as: training of teachers, evolving suitable teaching techniques, production of teaching materials and teacher s guides. In the social welfare sector, however, there will be a small provision for the opening of Balwadis, both in rural and urban areas". Children below 6 constitute nearly 17 per cent of the total population of India and 15 million are being added every year. In the last two years of the Fourth Plan period, services for one million additional children belonging to weaker sections were to be launched. In addition to this training of personnel through new types of training programmes were to be launched. Therefore, Fourth Plan period was marked by these developments in pre-school education.

The *Fifth Five-year Plan* had the rural, tribal and slum areas as its target for child welfare. The plan aimed at providing integrated services – health, welfare, education, nutrition and family planning as bases to promote child welfare. During this plan, 13 million children in the age group of 0 to 6 years were to be covered by extending integrated services to 18 per cent of the total children in the weakest section of Indian society. In the Fifth Plan Rs. 25 crores were provided for the educational component and Rs. 75 crores for the social welfare plan. A national policy resolution for children was issued in 1974.

As a result to this a National Children s Board was constituted. The Integrated Child Development Scheme was introduced in 33 experimental areas, which provided supplementary nutrition, immunisation, health check, referral services, nutrition, health education and non-formal education to children in the age group of 0 to 6 years. Further 117 ICDS experimental projects were introduced during 1978-80. The focal point of the ICDS projects provided services through Anganwadies, which were run by local voluntary workers who was assisted by a helper. The work of Anganwadi workers was to be supervised by a Mukhya Sevika. For the first time the 'early childhood education' has been used in place of 'Pre-school education' as the former is intended to be more board-based and cover the entire period of crucial development upto 5 years. Special attention is to be paid to the children of underprivileged groups.

The *Sixth Five-year Plan* provides an outlay of Rs. 2524 Crore for development of education and culture. Out of this Rs. 905.37 crores, 35.87 per cent of the total outlay, have been allotted for the early childhood education which is highest amount ever allotted for this purpose.

Seventh Five-year Plan laid stress on expansion of schemes such as: services for children in need of care and protection; and crèches for the children of working/ailing mothers. Ensuring minimum standards in services at children s home and crèches through properly trained staff and adequate supervision was also emphasised. Moreover, development through programmes in different sectors, important among these being ICDS, universal immunisation, maternal and child care services, nutrition, pre-school education, protected drinking water, environmental sanitation and hygiene, and family planning. The plan also witnessed expansion of the programme of ICDS, with the sanction of 1037 projects. Implementation of the programme of Universalisation of Elementary Education was accelerated. Non-formal education programmes were promoted. Pre-school education centres were supported in the educationally backward states through grant to voluntary organisations.

Agencies Working for Pre-school Education in India

Following are the agencies which manage the pre-school education in India.

- *Private Bodies*: The private sector in India in the form of individual person, private bodies, trust voluntary organisations etc., has played a significant role for the spread of pre-school education. Most remarkable among them were the Marrie Montessori and nursery schools and training centres.
- *Government and Autonomous Organisations:* There are several national level organisations working in the field of pre-school education, including managing, controlling and evaluating the standard of it. Among them most important are:
  1. Central Social Welfare Board (CSWB);
  2. Indian Council for Child Welfare (ICCW);
  3. National Council of Educational Research and Training (NCERT);
  4. National Institute of Public Corporation and Child Development (NIPCCD);
  5. Indian Red Cross;
  6. Kasturaba Memorial Trust;

7. Indian Association of Pre-school Education (IAPE);
8. State Institute of Education (SIE);
9. Children s Education Society;
10. All India Women s Conference (AIWC);
11. National Children s Fund.

Existing Condition of Pre-School Education in India

It is not hard to comprehend that the educational development of a nation is vitally connected to all other aspects of development. More so true that, the educational situation in a given period is an inseparable part of the general socio-economic condition of that period. There is little doubt that pre-school education is a matter of critical significance from the point of improving the social milieu at macro level and the quality of life at a micro level.

Unfortunately, pre-school education in India is a neglected chapter. Ordinarily, this section presents a sorry picture with the only serious measures in the positive direction being the Compulsory Education Act and the Integrated Child Development services. There is a good deal of confusion in India regarding programmes in pre-schools. A large number of pre-schools, particularly in urban and semi-urban areas, operate as downward extensions of primary schools, making children sit in well formed rows and teaching them to read, write and count. The activities followed in such schools are mostly geared to the demands of the primary schools. This is partly because of the parent s pressure and partly due to expectations of the primary schools that the pre-schools develop formal skills of reading and writing before the children enter class one.

Out of a total of about 575, 926 villages in the country, it is estimated that about 48,566 are not served by any school at all. Approximately 4.5 million children are being offered and kind of early childhood education or pre-school education. These constitute barely 5 per cent of the population in the age group of 3 to 6 years and are mainly from the better socio-economic strata of the society. It can be said that parents truly 'want the best' for their children especially in the urban areas. Parents want their children to grow up to be happy and useful citizens, able to solve their own problems and attain some measures of economic security. They want to be sure that their children are educated efficiently in good schools. In order to give their children a head start in the rat race that will one day be their lot, parents begin pushing them in the educational gristmill when they are barely out of infancy. Anxious and worried parents, influenced by mass media and peer influence, believe that sooner the children begin learning academics, the more successful their school life as well as future life experiences will be. For this, parents try to get their children admitted to different preparatory schools. This has led to a mushroom growth of preparatory schools. A number of surveys reveal that parents feel that if their children learn before hand in preparatory school, all that which they are supposed to learn in bigger schools and this assures their admission in certain elite schools. Even to ensure their children s admissions, parents sometimes send their children for private tuitions. It seems that though parents are aware of ill-effects of sending their children to school at an early age, yet they are pushing them when they have not yet finished their toddler hood in order to get the best school for their children.

In a scathing comment on pre-school education in India, the Yash Pal Committee Report, which was accepted by the Government on July 29th, 1994, states, "Right from early childhood, many children, especially those belonging to the middle classes, are made to slog through homework, tuition and coaching classes of different kinds. Leisure has become a scarce commodity in the child's especially the urban child s life.... The committee has recommended banning admission tests, textbooks and homework for pre-primary school children. But while the centre has directed the states to implement the recommendations, little is likely to charge. An NCERT study in 1992 revealed that only 15 per cent of the nursery schools in the capital used play oriented methods: the rest focussed on reading, writing and arithmetic.

The whole idea of pre-school was to provide the child with an informal setting where he could learn through play. It was intended that such methods of learning would continue into class one and two. However, instead of upward extension of the play way method, downward extension of formal acədemies is being observed today. Parents especially in a hurry these days expect that their child should get into a 'good school' and are even prepared to push him or her to any extent. Today almost all nursery schools or pre-schools conduct admission tests of their own. They expect children of age group 2½ to 3 years to answer questions and identify familiar objects. Even some enterprising teachers have brought out a guidebook, advising parents on how to prepare their children for admission tests.

However, things are changing gradually, especially in metro cities, where the damaging pressures to learn the three "R"s - reading, writing and arithmetic too soon are being done away with for good. Hence, over the last few years experts and educationalists have called for a drastic cut in the pressure of education on young children (Yash Pal Committee Report). A Resource Centre, monitored by the NCERT has been started at the IIT Nursery School, New Delhi is organising workshops to orient teachers in the play-way readiness programme for early childhood learning, as well as offering help in planning a year's work. But it must also be noted that while the effort is on to establish a child-friendly approach in schools, there continues to be dozens of schools and parents who resist reform. So a large number of children continue to be coerced to spell, add and subtract, count backwards and memorise facts they fail to comprehend well before they are ready to learn. Hence, they are traumatised. However, the joys of learning through pre-schools and nursery schools in India need to spread faster and wider. This is only possible through good pre-schools, which prepares a 'happy child' and a better school going child. Moreover, a happy child is better off than one under stress and pressure to learn too much and too fast. It is high time that parents, teachers, educationists, psychologists, and the Government took steps to stop the abuse of pre-school education as early on possible. Dr. D. Paul Chowdhury (1991) has suggested some remedial measures in this regard are as follows:

1. No formal education should be introduced in the nature of reading, writing, and arithmetic till the age of five.
2. There should not be any admission criteria for entry to these institutions.
3. There should be plenty of open space for children to play around.
4. Pre-school centres should not have any desks for children upto the age of five.

5. The children should be encouraged to use their mother tongue at the nursery level.
6. Pre-school centres should also provide other services in the field of health, nutrition and recreation to be integrated with non-formal pre-school education.
7. There should be some opportunities for free activities for children, which again require plenty of open space.
8. There is a need for orientation and reorientation of teachers and education of the parents about the concept, scopes, principles, contents and methods of pre-school education.
9. There should be arrangements for recognition or licensing of pre-school centres on the basis of rigorous criteria.
10. Experts based on the available literature and knowledge on the subject should work out detailed minimum standards.

However, it is the duty and responsibility of each one of us to provide necessary assistance and support for the welfare of the young children of our country considering the social, economic, cultural context into account.

ROLE OF FAMILY IN PRE-SCHOOL EDUCATION

Family is the most important single influence on the development of the child. The parents are the transmitters of the cultural and social standards. Parents as the first teachers lay the foundations of the preliminary education. Most of the education at this stage is at the unconscious level. While communicating or interacting with the child, the parents unknowingly impart knowledge, develop skills and inculcate values. The ways in which the parents communicate with the child and their choice of words have a lasting impact on the personality of the child. It is the family, which teaches the child how to get along with others. The family teaches the lessons of co-operation and give and take. The major roles of family in pre-school education are through parents.

Role of Parents in Pre-School Education

Parents play a major role in the successful pre-school education through proper understanding their children and assisting them as and when required. The parents must understand that no two children are alike and therefore their approach in dealing with different children must differ. Parents can learn much more about their children if they observe them carefully. The parents must try to understand the child s natural curiosity and accordingly allow him to explore, investigate and learn freely. Parents need not be rigid or too liberal for children in case of habit formation, learning good and acceptable behaviour. Rather, they must encourage the child to communicate freely and express their feelings to them. Listening to children, talking to children and playing with children enable the parents to come closer to their children and understanding them better. Through storytelling and singing of songs parents can improve the language development of their children. Meeting the child s physical needs is of prime importance. Nutritious and balanced diet with regular eating habits needs to be developed by the parents. Along with it parent must provide ample opportunities for exercises regularly. It is essential for parents to help the child in taking decisions and choosing alternatives to solve-problems. Equally important on the part of the parents is to recognise the child s emotional needs and accordingly making his life better and richer. Accepting the child as he/she is and showering love and affection is also essential for normal growth and development. Non-fulfilment of these needs may develop later problems of maladjustment.

Apart from their role as educators at home, parents can participate in pre-school education in various ways. They can be employed as paid personnel, can have voice in decision concerning pre-school education programmes, or they may be considered as resources in the educational process. In this form of participation, parents, and more generally mothers, are given training (or information) enabling them to enhance the development of their own children. During group sessions, mothers discuss the various ways of stimulating their children so that the latter may acquire capacities and attitudes enabling them to succeed at school, and adapt themselves to living conditions. Home visits are another ways of preparing mothers for their role. Mothers learns the modest ways of bringing up their children and care for them. In sum, parent's role can be summarised as follows:

- Parents as caretakers of physical needs of the child.
- Parents as givers of love and affection.
- Parents as playmates to the child.
- Parents as models for the child to imitate.
- Parents as disciplinarians.

- Parents as teachers of attitudes, values and skills.
- Parents as providers of a stimulating environment.
- Parents as providers of comfort in times of trouble.
- Parents as admirers of child's achievements.
- Parents as stimulators of child's abilities.

SUMMARY OF CHAPTER

Meaning, Significance and Objectives of Pre-school Education

- Pre-school education is informal education of the child between the age group of three to six years, before the child joins the school in regular primary classes.
- It aims at the all round development of the children and intends preparing for the life ahead.
- The pre-school years of the child is the period of its maximum learning and intellectual development and hence of gross potential educational significance.
- Broadly the objective of Early Childhood Education (ECE), in which pre-school education is included, is total development of the young child.

Principles of Learning in the Early Years

- Principles characterising young children s learning includes: children construct knowledge, children learn through social interaction with adults and other children, children s learning reflects a recurring cycle that begins in awareness and moves to exploration, to Inquiry, and finally, to utilisation, children learn through play, children s interests and 'need to know' motivate learning, learning are characterised by Individual Variations.
- Special characteristics related to learning in pre-school on the part of the children are – Confidence, curiosity, intentionally, relatedness, capacity to communicate and co-operativeness.

Contribution of the Philosophers towards Pre-school Education

- The philosophers contributing towards pre-school education are – John Locke, Jean-Jacques Rousseau, Froebel, John Dewey, Maria Montessori, Mahatma Gandhi and Sri Aurobindo.
- The guiding principles and methods advocated by these reformers were coloured by their own philosophical beliefs and had laid the foundation of early childhood education.

The guiding principles and methods advocated by these reformers were coloured by their own philosophical beliefs and had laid the foundation of early childhood education.

Functions of Pre-schools

- The major functions of pre-schools are, it act as an extension of the family, an aid to child development, as childcare intervention, compensatory education and developmental care.
- For proper functioning and achieving the goals of pre-school education – proper arrangements with regard to its physical set up, programme planning, curriculum, personnel, equipment, evaluation etc., are of greater importance.

Physical Set-up of Pre-school

- The pre-schools need to be a supplement to the home and not a substitute.
- The child's attitude towards the society outside the home in general and school in particular depends, to a large extent, upon the kind of experiences he gains at this stage especially in a pre-school.
- It therefore is important to make careful planning with regards to the physical set up, of a pre-school for the young children such as: – The Pre-school building, surroundings, site of pre-school, plan of a pre-school building.

Curriculum for the Pre-school

- A curriculum encompasses the entire range of school experiences and opportunities to learning for the total and integrated development of children. There are three types of curriculum, such as: *(a)* teacher-controlled curricula; *(b)* Child-controlled curricula; and *(c)* Teacher- child mutually controlled curricula.
- A pre-school includes different types of activities such as: creative activities, story telling, science experiences, rhythm, music and movement, dramatization, outdoor play, field trips and excursions etc.

Pre-School Programme

- Planning programme for a pre-school calls for long-term and short-term planning to achieve the objectives of pre-school education.
- Evaluating the pre-school programmes enable the teachers to assess the level of benefits on the part of the children.

Play and Play Equipment's for the Pre-Schoolers

- Play is essential for the children and it is a truly universal phenomenon. The most significant values of plays are in terms of physical, social, cognitive, moral, therapeutic, recreational and educational nature.
- There are various play types in the pre-schools, such as: free and structured play; individual and group play; vigorous and quite play; and outdoor and indoor play.
- In order to make children's play more meaningful and effective, play equipment is of significant importance.
- Selections of play equipment for various age groups of children require lots of considerations.
- Low-cost and indigenous play equipment would facilitate the advancement of pre-school education in our country.

Pre-School Staff and Personnel

- Pre-school staff and other personnel are the most important element in a pre-school.
- They are the pre-school teachers and other care givers who influence the development of children in many more ways.
- The ratio of staff members in a pre-school to child is an indicator of the amount of individual attention available to each child.
- It is generally agreed in our Indian condition that there should be one adult for every 15 children (1:15).
- In case of younger age children (2 + to 3+) ratio may be little less, as they require significantly more individual attention, as compared to the older children (4 + to 5 + years).

Pre-school Records and Reports

- Keeping records and preparing reports are of great value in guiding the behaviour and planning the education of the individual child to achieve the objectives of the pre-school education.
- Different types of records maintained in a pre-school, such as: records for keeping information regarding child s personal, home, health, attendance, stock register, house visit and parent-teacher meeting records, admission and progress report of the children etc.

Home - School Relations

- For effective pre-schooling home-school relationship is essential, which aims at creating better environment (both physical and psychological) for the children for optimum growth and development.

- Home school relationship can be improved through home visits, parent s interviews and meetings, parent s participation in school programmes and developing materials for parents.

Values of Pre-school Education: The Research Experience

- Research evidences shows that children having early childhood education/pre-school education are at an advantage position in a lot of socio-emotional and cognitive variables.
- Contemporary research has revealed that children's emotions are deeply affected by their attitude to learning as also their ability to learn.
- Between this age group, a child's cognitive, psychomotor and sensory controls are best developed through the medium of play and creative activities rather than through formal teaching of subjects.
- Some research evidences collected from the studies done in the Indian context are explained to show the significance or effect of pre-school education/early childhood education for the all round development of the child.

Pre-School Education in India: Growth and Development

- The Indian movement in the field of pre-school education owes much to Anne Besant and Dr. Rabindra Nath Tagore in the early part of the 20th century.
- Only in the Third Five-year Plan that the Government of India formally recognized the need for pre-school education.

Role of Family in Pre-School Education

- The role of parents in pre-school education can never be underestimated. Parents as the first teachers lay the foundations of the preliminary (pre-primary) education.
- The major roles of family in pre-school education are in terms of parent s roles as – caretakers of physical needs of the child, givers of love and affection, playmates to the child, models for the child to imitate, disciplinarians, teachers of attitudes, values and skills, providers of a stimulating environment, providers of comfort in times of trouble, admirers of child s achievements, stimulators of child s abilities.

5

Welfare and Development Programmes for Young Children

MEANING OF CHILD WELFARE

"There is no trust sacred than the one the world holds with children. There is no duty more important than ensuring that their rights are respected, that their welfare is protected, that their lives are free from fear and want and that they grow up in peace."

Children are the future citizens of a country and constitute the most important segment of the human resources. They are the most vulnerable section of the population and have a right to demand for care, protection and support from the society, particularly in the absence of a family to fulfil its basic needs. India has the largest child population in the world, a tremendous bulk of 'human capital for future'. Understanding the true worth of such valuable resources in the development of a progressive nation, concerted efforts are continuously taken for the welfare and development of Children. Child welfare covers the entire spectrum of services for children in terms of care, support, nurturance, and learning. Beside normal children, care is also provided to all the categories of children: Socio-Culturally Disadvantaged (SC, ST, Tribal) children, working as labourers, living in poor families as in urban slums, street or orphaned ones, the differently abled ones (handicapped), victims of abuses, terrorism, racial attacks or migrants, etc., are included in the purview of child welfare programmes. Child welfare programmes thus seek to provide direct care and supportive services to the families of these children because one of the important responsibilities of the community and state is to assist the family in its natural obligations for the welfare of the children. Highlighting the value of Children 'as a potential asset' in a given society, all the programmes on Child Care centres around the overall development of the child to its fullest extent. However special attention is focussed mainly on three categories of children in the poverty groups: *(i)* children of working mothers; *(ii)* destitute children; and *(iii)* handicapped children. Government and non-governmental/voluntary organizations have become increasingly active during the last few years in India, to provide services which reinforce, supplement or substitute the functions that parents cannot perform. Child welfare services are provided in various facets as direct care giving, nurturance, supportive, preventive, and rehabilitative in nature.

HISTORY OF CHILD WELFARE SERVICES AND DEVELOPMENT PROGRAMMES IN INDIA

Earlier, Care of the child was the responsibility of the extended family in its own 'socio-cultural niche'. But the helpless and destitute children were looked after by certain organized religious trusts, or by philanthropic persons, or the village community and the role of the state varied from indifference to benevolent depending upon the attitude of the individual ruler.

In the pre-independence period, child welfare services were in the nature of providing institutional services to the orphans, destitute, poor and the disable children. Other non-institutional services were maternity and child welfare services as play/hobby centres, milk distribution centres, small libraries for children etc., mostly run by the voluntary agencies, who shouldered the major responsibilities for programmes and activities for the welfare and development of children. It was only after independence when the constitution was enacted that the responsibility of social welfare was taken over by the government. The constitution of India proclaimed that the state shall in particular, direct its policy towards ensuring that children of tender age are not abused, childhood and youth are protected against moral and material abandonment. So the first government initiative in this area was the setting up of a Central Social Welfare board in 1953, which started a grant – in – aid scheme for voluntary agencies.

Child welfare received its major focus, as an integral part of the development process in India from the Fourth Five-year Plan. It was then extended from the confines of only custodial and remedial functions to encompass preventive and developmental aspects. Further in this Plan, priority was given to programmes fulfilling the needs of destitute and neglected children. Importance was given to voluntary organizations and their involvement in welfare services through sponsorship and foster care, rehabilitation of handicapped children through development of institutions of blind, deaf, mentally retarded and orthopedically handicapped. Systematic surveys and research to aid planning welfare services were encouraged for improving the effectiveness of these services. Moreover, family planning programme was integrated with maternal and child health (MCH) programmes.

During the Fifth Five-year Plan, along with the launching of Integrated Child Development Service (ICDS), several other services related to child welfare began. These included child care and development programmes like crèches for children of working women/ailing mothers, services for children in need of care and protection, integrated education for the disabled, etc. It covers around two-third (2/3rd) of disadvantaged children of the country. 'Minimum Need Programme' for upliftment of underprivileged families, groups and communities to cope with social change, was introduced during this plan.

During the Sixth Five-year plan there was further expansion of ICDS projects and provisions were made for pre-school education in educationally backward states through grants in aid to voluntary organizations.

The Seventh Five-year Plan laid stress on expansion of schemes such as: *(i)* Services for children who are in need of care and protection and *(ii)* Crèches for the children of working/ailing mothers. Ensuring minimum standards in services at children's homes and crèches through properly trained staff, adequate supervision was also emphasised. Creation and opportunities for vocational training of children from these homes, self-employment, and training-cum-production centres were given importance.

In the Eighth Five-year Plan, it was proposed to phase out other government-sponsored initiatives by merging them with ICDS. The Ninth Five-years Plan addressed the issues concerning

ECE more exhaustively than previous plans. While acknowledging the first six years of life to be critical, it recommended the institution of National Charter for Children to ensure taking care of all developmental aspects of the child by the end of the Ninth Plan. This plan also emphasized the involvement of Women's groups in the management of ECE programmes, particularly under the decentralized Panchayati Raj System. The major initiatives suggested under currently run Tenth Five-year Plan include strengthening PSE component of ICDS by need based training of AWWs, provision of learning material at AWCs, setting up of Pre-School Education centres in uncovered areas, building advocacy and training of community leaders.

Hence the concept of early childhood care and education, has integrated health, nutrition education, and early stimulation aspects in the child care services. India has in this context been able to put together a fairly supportive policy framework and has launched some major initiatives for children at this stage of development. Prominent among these are some federally supported schemes such as: the Reproductive Child Health Scheme, (RCH) in the Department of Health and Family Welfare, the Integrated Child Development Services (ICDS) in the Department of Women and Child Development (DWCD) recently rechristened as Ministry of Women and Child Development (MWCD) and pre-school education provisions through some primary education programmes. As a result, there has been a noticeable progress over the last fifty years in the provision for children, be it the ICDS or the primary education services. Family planning programme was integrated with maternal child health (MCH) programme.

The provision of centre based early childhood education in India is available through three distinct channels – public, private and non-governmental. Public, government sponsored programmes are largely directed towards the disadvantaged community, particularly those residing in rural and marginalised areas. Though a number of programmes are being implemented by various departments and ministries, the more important, on which the attention is required to be focused in XI Five-year Plan are as under:

Public Initiatives

- *Integrated Child Development Services (ICDS)*: The non-formal pre-school education service under ICDS has been identified not only as a significant input for providing sound foundation for development but also as a contributing role to the universalisation of primary education, by providing to the child the necessary preparation for primary schooling and offering substitute care to the younger siblings thus freeing the older ones – especially girls to attend school. For accomplishment of this task, the AWW is expected to attend multifarious ECE tasks. These include not only organization of PSE activities for three hours a day, but also attending various peripheral activities like preparation of PSE aids using indigenous material with the help of local artisans, establishing functional links with primary school teachers, maintaining records and registers concerning attendance of children in PSE sessions, programme planning in contextualised way, creating awareness among the masses and the like.

- *Rajiv Gandhi National Crèche Scheme for Working Mothers*: Keeping in mind the need for an effective and expanded scheme for childcare facilities, a new crèche scheme named Rajiv Gandhi National Crèche Scheme has been recently launched for the children of working mothers. The scheme has been designed by merging the existing two schemes of National Crèche Fund (which was set up in 1994 to meet the growing requirements for crèches with a corpus fund made available from the social safety net adjustment credit from the World Bank) and the Scheme of Assistance to Voluntary Organizations for running crèches for children of working and ailing mothers (which was started in 1974 in pursuance of the objectives of National Plan for Children, 1974). Under this new initiative, the crèches are being allocated to the States/UTs on the basis of the proportion of child population. Uncovered districts/tribal areas under the scheme are being given highest priority so as to ensure the balanced regional coverage. The services being provided pertain not only to care aspect but pre-school education as well. Currently, 22038 crèches have been sanctioned till 31st March 2006 to run across the country.
- *Sarva Shiksha Abhiyan (SSA)*: Under SSA, which is one amongst the eight identified flagship programme of the Government of India (GOI) for universalizing elementary education and which has succeeded the DPEP, provisions have been made

not only for greater convergence of pre-school education initiatives, specially of ICDS, with that of primary schooling but also of setting up Balwadis as Pre-School Education centres in uncovered areas, training inputs for stakeholders, organizing awareness and advocacy campaigns in favour of importance of PSE and the like. Further, in order to practice any innovative activity to strengthen ECE, a financial provision of Rs. 15 lakh per annum in a district has been made available. It is the result of actualising these provisions that many states have not only opened the PSE centres (either separately or as a wing attached with the primary schools) but also have designed various state specific interventions suiting to their local relevance.

Private Initiatives

The past few decades have also witnessed an unprecedented expansion of early childhood initiatives in the country. Together with major public initiatives like: ICDS, a remarkable expansion has taken place primarily in private sector, which has played an important role in the growth of ECE in the country. Private initiative here refers to fee charging/profit-making initiatives in ECE. In the absence of available figure on unrecognised private sector initiatives (which are operating in various catchy names: like family and day care homes, nurseries, kindergartens and pre-primary classes in private primary, elementary and secondary schools), it can be roughly estimated that number of children enrolled in these initiatives comes to around 10 million (National Focus Group, 2005), or as about the same figure as the major public initiative of ICDS at that time. These private initiatives, which were mainly in the urban areas for nearly a decade ago, have now started springing up in semi urban or even rural areas also.

Voluntary and Corporate Initiatives

The ECE services, being provided by voluntary or non-governmental organizations with financial assistance of national and international aid agencies, trusts, denominational and parochial groups, also play a marginal role especially in socially and economic backward areas, special communities in difficult circumstances like tribal people, migrant labourers and for children affected by natural calamities of specific contexts like flood, earthquake etc. The various integrated services under these

NGOs run initiatives are either being provided in the name of crèches or in the name of ECE centres. Some NGO's also run mobile crèches, which move along with the construction labour from one site to another. In addition to these, some universities also have Laboratory Nursery Schools attached to them, particularly to Departments of Child Development like in M.S. University, Vadodara. Apart from this, in order to discharge their social responsibilities specially in the era of liberalization, privatization and globalization , various corporate groups like ICICI have also come forward by running pre schools, which, over a period of time, have established themselves as fairly competitive with pre-schools being operated under private initiatives.

In line with these five-year plans and Constitutional Provisions, Government of India formed National Children's Board and Indian Council for Child Welfare which was land marks towards, safeguarding the interests of children. Apart from it, several polices were adopted for children among which the National Policy for children in 1974 is a milestone. The policy recognises children as the 'Nation's supremely important assets' and declares that the Nation is responsible for their nurturing and solicitude.

CONCEPT OF EARLY CHILDHOOD CARE AND DEVELOPMENT (ECCD) IN INDIA

"Early Childhood Care and Education (ECCE) is an indispensable foundation for life-long learning and development, and have critical impact on the success at the primary stage of education. It therefore becomes imperative to accord priority attention to ECCE and invest adequately by providing commensurate resources". The term ECCD is used by International and Inter-governmental organizations, to mean programmes and activities in the area of early childhood, to bring all round development in children. However, early childhood care and development (ECCD), is a broad concept that can be defined in many ways. One useful description is:

"Early Childhood Care and Development refers not only to what is happening within the child, but also to the care the child requires in order to thrive, grow and develop to its maximum extent in normal as well as in difficult circumstances of life. For a child to develop and learn in a healthy and normal way, it is important not only to meet the basic needs for protection, food and health care, but also to meet the basic needs for interaction, and stimulation, affection, security, and learning through exploration and discovery. ECCD activities are those which support young children appropriately and seek to strengthen the environment in which they live".

Early childhood care is one of the best ways to assure the child a smooth transition into primary school. It is also a critical factor in the child's sub-sequent transition to adulthood, influencing both social skills and behavioural choices.

ECCD is seen as a lifetime programme of continuous learning and experience from birth through adolescence for children. They provide children a good start in life. ECCD activities:

- Fosters in children the natural need for discovery and curiosity; and their desire to learn which forms the basis of life-long learning. Such interest is a potential asset that stays with them for the rest of their lives and helps them to do better in later life.
- Respects and builds parents to play the pivotal role in child development.
- Supports parents in their skills as parenting, training on literacy, child rearing, health and nutrition, stimulate and create a good developmental environment for children.
- ECCD programmes go much beyond school readiness, by preparing children for life and encourage them to be open for learning and to avail life s opportunities. It also increases in children self-confidence, trust, feeling of security and assurance; enhance cognitive ability and other learning potential, improved social skills, more creative ways of thinking and problem-solving.
- Involves mostly mothers in the caring process thus builds confidence, and encourages parenting skills and becomes involved in their children s learning and development.
- Have direct impact on girls – the next generations of women and mothers. When parents see the benefits of ECCD activities for their daughters, they allow them to continue with their education, which otherwise would not have as in some cultures. Moreover, a direct consequence of this may lead to the fact that boys by observing girls having access to learning opportunities, become aware at an early age that girls have a right to learning and availing other opportunities too.

- Can reduce inequality in society by giving children from disadvantaged backgrounds a chance in life and in school.

As ECCD is concerned with the holistic development of children, it involves many people – particularly family, school, community members, local administration and policy-makers. It forms an important component of integrated development work, which has a permanent place on the agenda of the Government, International and Inter-governmental organizations and the NGOS.

Thus, Child Care has become a global theme as there is a growing realisation among nations that action in one part of the world has repercussions, either direct or indirect, everywhere. There is a need for concerted efforts to find solutions to child care problems on a universal basis.

NEED FOR CHILD WELFARE PROGRAMMES AND POLICIES

Influence of modernisation and industrialisation, has resulted in degeneration of family systems. Social and economic changes have eroded the quality of childcare. There has been an increase in social problems like: destitution, delinquency, and vagrancy. There are no statistics of the extent of such problems. It was estimated that in 1981, there were 37.59 million orphans 1.38 million juveniles involved in cognisable crimes.

India has 158.8 million children in the 0-6 years age group (Census, India 2011). The proportion of child population group of 0-6 years is 13.1 per cent. The bulk of these children in India are not only important for themselves but also for the families they live in, and the society they belong to. It is important for the child himself in the sense that he/she will be able to perform his duties well, when he/she has a healthy body, a curious mind and a good personality. His/her welfare adds to the wealth for the family, as he/she forms a part of the family as a future productive member. His/Her betterment is also the benefit of the society, as he/she is the future leader of the society. The child in this sense is the most 'potential asset' of the society. In majority of the advanced countries childcare has been accorded the highest priority and only the best is supposed to be good enough for children. Therefore, every child whether slow learner, average and gifted must be allowed to grow in its own settings. Proper opportunities should be provided to all children, so that their potentials are realised to the fullest extent.

Child psychologists are of opinion that a family is the only place where the physical, emotional and mental needs of a child are sufficiently met, fostering growth and development to the maximum degree. In India, in case of inability of the family to take care of a child in his 2own family, the joint family, the caste system and the village used to provide and take care of children. But with the weakening of these social institutions, some outside agency has to provide the necessary care for children. Though institutional care is helpful to some extent, it is unnecessary and even harmful for others. Services for the care of the working, destitute, disabled, street and delinquent children have to be provided keeping in view their basic needs and rights to family.

PROVISIONS AND POLICIES FOR CARE AND DEVELOPMENT OF YOUNG CHILDREN IN INDIA

Government of India has initiated many provisions and policies for the care and development of young children. These are as follows:

Constitutional Provisions

There are several constitutional provisions for children. These include the following:

Article 14: Provides that the State shall not deny to any person equality before the law or the equal protection of the laws within the territory of India.

Article 15(3): Provides that, "Nothing in this article shall prevent the State for making any special provision for women and children.

Article 21: Provide that no person shall be deprived of his life or personal liberty except according to procedure established by law.

Article 21A: Directs the State shall provide free and compulsory education to all children of the age of six to fourteen years in such manner as the State may, by law, determine.

Article 23: Prohibits trafficking of human beings and forced labour.

Article 24: Prohibits employment of children below the age of fourteen years in factories, mines or any other hazardous occupation.

Article 25-28: Provides freedom of conscience, and free profession, practice and propagation of religion.

Article 39(e) and (f): Provide that the State shall, in particular, direct its policy towards securing to ensure that the health and strength of workers, men and women and the tender age of children are not abused and that the citizens are not forced by economic necessity to enter avocations unsuited to their age or strength and that the children are given opportunities and facilities to develop in a healthy manner and in conditions of freedom and dignity and that the childhood and youth are protected against exploitation and against moral and material abandonment.

Article 45: Envisages that the State shall endeavour to provide early childhood care and education for all children until they complete the age of six years.

Legislative Provisions

There are several Legislations pertaining to children. These include the following:

1. The Child Marriage Restraint Act, 1929.
2. The Child Labour (Prohibition and Regulation) Act, 1986.
3. The Juvenile Justice (Care and Protection of Children) Act, 2000.
4. The Infant Milk Substitutes, Feeding Bottles and Infant Foods (Regulation of Production, Supply and Distribution) Act, 1992.

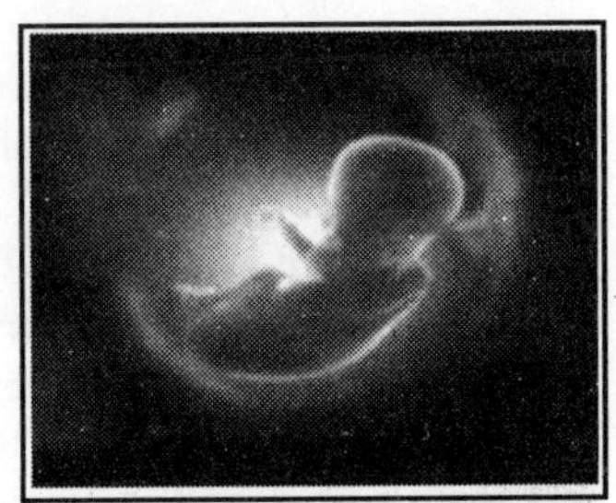

5. The Pre-Conception and Pre-natal Diagnostic Technique (Prohibition of Sex Selection) Act, 1994.
6. The Persons with Disabilities (Equal Opportunities, Protection of Rights and Full Participation) Act, 1995.
7. The Immoral Traffic (Prevention) Act, 1956.
8. The Guardian and Wards Act, 1890.
9. The Young Persons (Harmful Publications) Act, 1956.
10. The Commissions for Protection of Child Rights Act, 2005.

National Policy for Children (2013)

The National Policy for Children has always been a Landmark in the Care of Children in India. India is the home to the largest child population in the world. The Constitution of India guarantees Fundamental Rights to all children in the country and empowers the State to make special provisions for children. The Directive Principles of State Policy specifically guide the State in securing the tender age of children from abuse and ensuring that children are given opportunities and facilities to develop in a healthy manner in conditions of freedom and dignity. The State is responsible for ensuring that childhood is protected from exploitation and moral and material abandonment.

Declaring its Children as the Nation s 'supremely important asset' in the National Policy for Children, 1974, the Government of India reiterated its commitment to secure the rights of its children by ratifying related international conventions and treaties. These include the Declaration of the Rights of the Child, Universal Declaration of Human Rights and its Covenants, the Convention on the Rights of the Child and its two Optional Protocols, the United Nations Convention on the Rights of Persons with Disabilities, the United Nations Convention against Transnational Organized Crime, the Protocol to Prevent, Suppress and Punish Trafficking in Women and Children, the Hague Convention on Protection of Children and Co-operation in respect of Inter-Country Adoption, and the Convention on the Elimination of All Forms of Discrimination against Women.

To affirm the Government's commitment to the rights based approach in addressing the continuing and emerging challenges in the situation of children, the Government of India hereby adopts this Resolution on the National Policy for Children, 2013.

Preamble – Recognising that:

- A child is any person below the age of eighteen years.
- Childhood is an integral part of life with a value of its own.
- Children are not a homogenous group and their different needs need different responses, especially the multi-dimensional vulnerabilities experienced by children in different circumstances; – a long-term, sustainable, multi-sectoral, integrated and inclusive approach is necessary for the overall and harmonious development and protection of children.

Reaffirming that

- Every child is unique and a supremely important national asset.
- Special measures and affirmative action are required to diminish or eliminate conditions that cause discrimination.

- All children have the right to grow in a family environment, in an atmosphere of happiness, love and understanding.
- Families are to be supported by a strong social safety net in caring for and nurturing their children.

The Government of India reiterates its commitment to safeguard, inform, include: support and empower all children within its territory and jurisdiction, both in their individual situation and as a national asset. The State is committed to take affirmative measures – legislative, policy or otherwise – to promote and safeguard the right of all children to live and grow with equity, dignity, security and freedom, especially those marginalised or disadvantaged; to ensure that all children have equal opportunities; and that no custom, tradition, cultural or religious practice is allowed to violate or restrict or prevent children from enjoying their rights. This Policy is to guide and inform all laws, policies, plans and programmes affecting children. All actions and initiatives of the national, state and local government in all sectors must respect and uphold the principles and provisions of this Policy.

Guiding Principles

1. Every child has universal, inalienable and indivisible human rights.
2. The rights of children are interrelated and interdependent, and each one of them is equally important and fundamental to the well-being and dignity of the child.
3. Every child has the right to life, survival, development, education, protection and participation.
4. Right to life, survival and development goes beyond the physical existence of the child and also encompasses the right to identity and nationality.
5. Mental, emotional, cognitive, social and cultural development of the child is to be addressed in totality.
6. All children have equal rights and no child shall be discriminated against on grounds of religion, race, caste, sex, place of birth, class, language, and disability, social, economic or any other status.
7. The best interest of the child is a primary concern in all decisions and actions affecting the child, whether taken by

legislative bodies, courts of law, administrative authorities, public, private, social, religious or cultural institutions.

8. Family or family environment is most conducive for the all-round development of children and they are not to be separated from their parents, except where such separation is necessary in their best interest.
9. Every child has the right to a dignified life, free from exploitation.
10. Safety and security of all children is integral to their well-being and children are to be protected from all forms of harm, abuse, neglect, violence, maltreatment and exploitation in all settings including care institutions, schools, hospitals, crèches, families and communities
11. Children are capable of forming views and must be provided a conducive environment and the opportunity to express their views in any way they are able to communicate, in matters affecting them.
12. Children's views, especially those of girls, children from disadvantaged groups and marginalised communities, are to be heard in all matters affecting them, in particular judicial and administrative proceedings and interactions, and their views given due consideration in accordance with their age, maturity and evolving capacities.

Key Priorities of the Policy: The key priorities of the policy have been briefly summarized as follows:

(a) *Survival, Health and Nutrition:* The right to life, survival, health and nutrition is an inalienable right of every child and will receive the highest priority.
- the state stands committed to ensure equitable access to comprehensive, and essential, preventive, promote, curative and rehabilitative healthcare, of the highest standard, for all children before, during and after birth, and throughout the period of their growth and development;
- every child has a right to adequate nutrition and to be safeguarded against hunger, deprivation and malnutrition;
- the state commits to securing this right for all children through access, provision and promotion of required services and supports for holistic nurturing, well-being with nutritive attainment of all children, keeping in view their individual needs at different stages of life in a life cycle approach;

- provide adolescents access to information, support and services essential for their health and development, including information and support on appropriate life style and healthy choices and awareness on the ill effects of alcohol and substance abuse;
- prevent HIV infections at birth and ensure infected children receive medical treatment, adequate nutrition and after care, and are not discriminated against in accessing their rights;
- ensure that only child safe products and services are available in the country and put in place mechanisms to enforce safety standards for products and services designed for children;
- provide adequate safeguards and measures against false claims relating to growth, development and nutrition.

(b) *Education and Development:* Every child has equal right to learning, knowledge and education. The State recognises its responsibility to secure this right for every child, with due regard for special needs, through access, provision and promotion of required environment, information, infrastructure, services and supports, towards the development.

- the state shall take all necessary measures to: *(i)* Provide universal and equitable access to quality Early Childhood Care and Education (ECCE) for optimal development and active learning capacity of all children below six years of age.
- ensure that every child in the age group of 6-14 years is in school and enjoys the fundamental right to education as enshrined in the Constitution.
- promote affordable and accessible quality education up to the secondary level for all children.
- foster and support inter sectoral networks and linkages to provide vocational training options including comprehensively addressing age specific and gender-specific issues of children s career choices through career counselling and vocational guidance.
- ensure that all out of school children such as: child labourers, migrant children, trafficked children, children of migrant labour, street children, child victims of alcohol and substance abuse, children in areas of civil unrest,

orphans, children with disability (mental and physical), children with chronic ailments, married children, children of manual scavengers, children of sex workers, children of prisoners, etc., are tracked, rescued, rehabilitated and have access to their right to education.

- address discrimination of all forms in schools and foster equal opportunity, treatment and participation irrespective of place of birth, sex, religion, disability, language, region, caste, and health, social, economic or any other status.
- promote engagement of families and communities with schools for all round development of children, with emphasis on good health, hygiene and sanitation practices, including sensitization on ill-effects of alcohol and substance abuse.
- facilitate concerted efforts by local governments, non-governmental organizations/community based organizations to map gaps unavailability of educational services, especially in backward, child labour intensive areas, areas of civil unrest, and in situations of emergency, and efforts for addressing them.
- identify, encourage and assist gifted children, particularly those belonging to the disadvantaged groups, through special programmes.
- provide and promote crèche and day care facilities for children of working mothers, mothers belonging to poor families, ailing mothers and single parents.
- promote appropriate baby feeding facilities in public places and at workplaces for working mothers in public, private and unorganized sector.

(c) *Protection:*A safe, secure and protective environment is a precondition for the realisation of all other rights of children. Children have the right to be protected wherever they are.

- the state shall create a caring, protective and safe environment for all Children, to reduce their vulnerability in all situations and to keep them safe at all places, especially public spaces.
- the state shall protect all children from all forms of violence and abuse, harm, neglect, stigma, discrimination, deprivation, exploitation including economic exploitation and sexual exploitation, abandonment, separation,

abduction, sale or trafficking for any purpose or in any form, pornography, alcohol and substance abuse, or any other activity that takes undue advantage of them, or harms their personhood or affects their development.

- to secure the rights of children temporarily or permanently deprived of parental care, the State shall endeavour to ensure family and community-based care arrangements including sponsorship, kinship, foster care and adoption, with institutionalisation as a measure of last resort, with due regard to the best interests of the child and guaranteeing quality standards of care and protection.
- the state commits to taking special protection measures to secure the rights and entitlements of children in need of special protection, characterised by their specific social, economic and geo-political situations, including their need for rehabilitation and reintegration, in particular but not limited to, children affected by migration, displacement, communal or sectarian violence, civil unrest, disasters and calamities, street children, children of sex workers, children forced into commercial sexual exploitation, abused and exploited children, children forced into begging, children in conflict and contact with the law, children in situations of labour, children of prisoners, children infected/affected by HIV/AIDS, children with disabilities, children affected by alcohol and substance abuse, children of manual scavengers and children from any other socially excluded group, children affected by armed conflict and any other category of children requiring care and protection.
- The State shall promote and strengthen legislative, administrative and institutional redressal mechanisms at the National and State level for the protection of child rights. For local grievances, effective and accessible grievance redressal mechanisms shall be developed at the programme level.

(d) Participation

- the state has the primary responsibility to ensure that children are made aware of their rights, and provided with an enabling environment, opportunities and support to develop skills, to form aspirations and express their views in accordance with their age, level of maturity and evolving capacities, so as to enable them to be actively involved in their own development and in all matters concerning and affecting them.

- the state shall promote and strengthen respect for the views of the child, especially those of the girl child, children with disabilities and of children from minority groups or marginalised communities, within the family; community; schools and institutions; different levels of governance; as well as in judicial and administrative proceedings that concern them.
- the state shall engage all stakeholders in developing mechanisms for children to share their grievances without fear in all settings; monitor effective implementation of children's participation through monitor able indicators; develop different models of child participation; and undertake research and documentation of best practices.

The Ministry of Women and Child Development (MWCD) is the nodal Ministry for overseeing and coordinating the implementation of this Policy. A National Coordination and Action Group (NCAG) for Children under the Minister in charge of the Ministry of Women and Child Development will monitor the progress with other concerned Ministries as its members. Similar Co-ordination and Actions Groups will be formed at the State and District level. The Ministry of Women and Child Development, in consultation with all related Ministries and Departments, will formulate a National Plan of Action for Children. Similar Plans at the State, District and local level will be formulated to ensure action on the provisions of this Policy. The National, State and District Coordination and Action Groups will monitor the progress of implementation under these Plans. The National Commission for Protection of Child Rights and State Commissions for Protection of Child Rights will ensure that the principles of this Policy are respected in all sectors at all levels in formulating laws, policies and programmes affecting children.

EXISTING CHILD WELFARE SERVICES AND PROGRAMMES IN INDIA

Although child welfare has been given a prominent place in the welfare services of a country since ages, yet child welfare in India got real impetus when the Government focussed special attention on child development as a part of the Five-year developmental plans. In context to the present welfare programmes, in the country, child welfare services have been classified into institutional and non-institutional services, applicable to both normal and abnormal children.

Institutional Services

The Institutional services for the welfare of children in India are as follows:

- Foundling Homes.
- Homes for destitute children.
- Shorts stay homes for children of needy families *e.g.*, healthy children of leprosy and TB patients, children of women prisoners, children of mothers having prolonged illness or hospitalised treatment etc.
- Institutions for care of mentally retarded and dependent children.
- Home and placement services for children of unmarried mothers.
- Home and residential schools with or without sheltered workshops for delinquent children.
- Home or night shelters for the care of vagrant children.
- Residential treatment centres for emotionally disturbed children.

Non-Institutional Services for Normal Children

Apart from the above mentioned institutional services available for children, there are non-institutional services available for the normal children of this country. These are as follows:

- Crèches, Day centres and pre-primary schools.
- Recreational and Hobby clubs.
- Library facilities.
- Holidays Camp.
- School Health Services.
- School Social Work Services.
- Nutrition Services.
- Foster Care and adoption Services.
- Services for Children of migrants and those affected by riots.

Children in Need of Special Care

The number of children in need of special care in India is quite substantial. In order to provide them with special care and assistance, Government of India has made provisions for them as follows:

- School for mentally retarded children.
- Nurseries, schools and training for handicapped children, the blind, the deaf etc.
- Audiology Centres and hearing and classes.
- Allowances to children of destitute women, who are maintained in their own homes.
- Adoption services for destitute children.
- Sponsorship of poor and neglected children.
- Institutions and services for the juvenile delinquents, children of unwed mothers and handicapped children.

Integrated Child Development Services (ICDS)

Child development is central to the National strategies for Human resource development in India. The range of our interest concerns from the pre-natal stage to the full development of the child as a healthy person. It has received great attention in recent years and a National plan of Action has been prepared for a holistic approach to realise the objectives against set time schedules. Among the various child-oriented programmes in the country, Integrated Child Development Services (ICDS) is a unique, comprehensive and the largest child care intervention programme reaching out to more than 21 million children, and expectant and nursing mothers through 3,945 projects. It has become the largest child care programme encompassing integrated services for survival, protection and development of children, as well as taking care of the pregnant and nursing mothers living in the most backward, rural, urban tribal areas. It has emerged from a mere experiment in school development to a rewarding experience of social change.

ICDS is a means of empowering community and creating an environment for child survival, protection and development so that children are able to live securely and realise their full potential to life. The programme aims to meet the time-bound challenge of achieving the set targets of the National Plan of Action for Children which provides the framework for making child's rights a reality.

Source: Universal Children's day (14th Nov. 1995): 20 years of ICDS Department of HRD, Government of India, New Delhi.

India's commitment to children enshrined in the directive principles of the constitution and envisioned in the National Policy for Children gave birth to Integrated Child Development Services (ICDS). ICDS scheme was evolved on the basis of experience in sectorial programmes for children during the first four five year plans. In

1972, the Planning Commission to work out a scheme for integrated childcare services constituted eight inter-ministerial study teams. On the basis of recommendations made by them, a proposal for integrated childcare services was made. The steering group set-up by the planning commission to advice on the Fifth Five-year Plan suggested adaptation of an integrated approach to early childhood services. Thus, the plan scheme was included in the plan in the social welfare section. The ICDS programme was launched on an experimental basis on 2nd October 1975 with only 33 projects. After one-year, the impact and reach of ICDS was assessed. Based on the evaluation report submitted by the planning commission in august 1977, 67 additional projects were sanctioned during 1978-79. During the next two years, 100 additional projects were added raising the total number of ICDS projects in the country to 200. Since then, there has been spatial expansion of the programme and enrichment of its contents. Objectives of ICDS are as follows:

- Improve the nutritional and health status of children below the age of six years.
- Lay the foundation for the proper psychological, physical and social development of the child.
- Reduce the incidence of mortality, morbidity, malnutrition and school dropouts.
- Achieve effective co-ordination of policy and implementation among various departments to promote child development.
- Enhance the capability of the mother to look after the normal health and nutritional needs of the child, through proper health and nutrition education.

Key Features of ICDS in Mission Mode

- ➢ Programmatic, Management and Institutional reforms.
- ➢ Anganwadi as 'vibrant ECD centre' through revised package of services.
- ➢ Greater focus on under three years children.
- ➢ Strengthening early childhood education.
- ➢ Care and counselling of mothers and family.
- ➢ More than 2 lakh Anganwadis to be constructed.
- ➢ More than 2700 new technical human resource.
- ➢ More than 4.5 lakh additional Anganwadi workers/ nutrition counsellors/link workers.

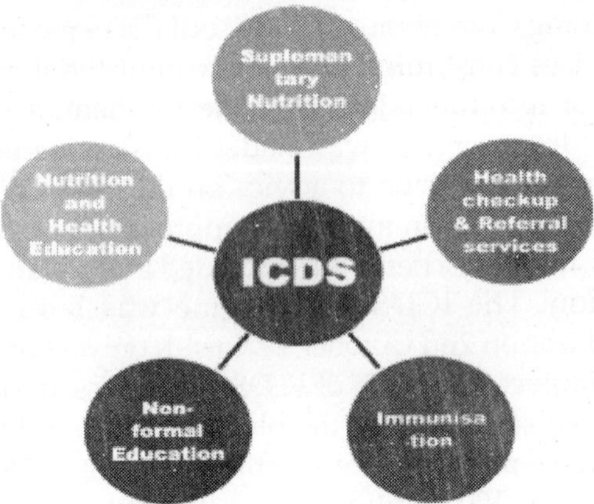

Fig. 5.1: Role of ICDS (Services) in Child Development

- Improved Supplementary nutrition.
- 70,000 Anganwadi cum crèches.
- Intensive monitoring, training, and capacity building.
- Greater convergence and linkages with other sectors as: Health, PRIs, and Rural Development.
- Flexibility to States and flexibility in programme implementation.

- *Services and Beneficiaries:* ICDS takes care of children below six years, expectant and nursing mothers, adolescent girls and women between the age group 15-45 years. It takes a holistic view of the development of the child and provides a package of integrated services based on consideration of multi-dimensional needs of children, synergetic relationship between the services, costs and administrative feasibility.

The Packages of Services Included in ICDS Programme are:

- *Supplementary Nutrition:* It is given to children below six years of age and to those nursing mother who come from low income families and in accordance with the guidelines issued from time to time for the purpose of solution of beneficiaries.
- *Immunisation*: Immunisation is given to all children below six years of age against diseases like: small pox, diphtheria, tetanus, whooping cough, typhoid and tuberculosis.
- *Non-Formal Pre-school Education*: Children between 3 to 5 years have the benefit of non-formal, pre-school education in their villages under the set-up called 'Anganwadies'.

- *Nutrition and Health Education*: All women in the age group of 15-45 years are given nutrition and health education. Priority is given to nourishing and expectant mothers.
- *Health Check-up and Referral Services*: This includes anti-natal care of pregnant lady, post-natal care of nourishing mother and care of children under six years.

The concept of providing a package of services is based primarily on the consideration that the overall impact will be much larger if the different services develop in an integrated manner as the efficacy of a particular service depends upon the support it receives from related services.

Table 5.1: Packages of Services Provided by the ICDS Programme and the Target Beneficiaries

Services	Target Group	Service Provided by
Supplementary Nutrition	Children below 6 years: Pregnant and Lactating Mother (P&LM)	Anganwadi Worker and Anganwadi Helper
Immunization	Children below 6 years: Pregnant and Lactating Mother (P&LM)	ANM/MO
Health Check-up	Children below 6 years: Pregnant and Lactating Mother (P&LM)	ANM/MO/AWW
Referral Services	Children below six years: Pregnant and Lactating Mother (P&LM)	AWW/ANM/MO
Pre-School Education	Children 3-6 years	AWW
Nutrition and Health Education	Women (15-45 years)	AWWANM/MO

*AWW assists ANM in identifying the target group.

Source: www.wcd.gov.in

ICDS provides increased learning opportunities in early childhood resulting in improved school retention and reduction in the number of school dropouts. It also contributes towards prevention, early detection and community based management of childhood disabilities. ICDS serves the community through a network of Anganwadis. An Anganwadi is the focal point for delivery of ICDS package of services. It is run by an Anganwadi

Worker (AWW) who is supported by a Helper in the delivery of services, and they build-up linkages with the health system, empower mothers with knowledge related to issues concerning child survival and development. Thus, it build-up the capacity of the communities to renew and renovate themselves through the development of children.

ICDS, the community based Child-Oriented development programme rededicates itself for the cause of children on its 20th anniversary (1995) and aims to meet the challenges of bringing about desirable social change through the development in Children.

Source: Universal Children's day (14th Nov. 1995): 20 years of ICDS Department of HRD, Government of India, New Delhi.

- *ICDS Frontline Workers:* The ICDS functionaries comprise the Anganwadi worker, the Supervisor and the Child Development Project Officer (CDPO). Medical Officer, lady Health Visitor and Female Health Worker for facilitating the delivery of services for improved child care and development, supports the team.
- *Monitoring and Evaluation:* ICDS Management Information System (NIS) helps in assessing the reach of the programme, analysing the field situation in terms of objectives of the programme and introducing corrective measures at the various levels of ICDS project implementation, as and when required.
- *The Impact:* ICDS has been subjected to intensive research since the beginning. The impact of the programme is evident from the remarkable improvements made in child survival and development indicators, such as:
  - decrease in prevalence of Malnutrition among pre-school children;
  - improved Immunisation coverage in ICDS areas;
  - decrease in Infant Mortality Rate (IMR) in ICDS areas;
  - improvement in School enrolment and reduction in school dropout rate in ICDS areas.
- *New Thrust in ICDS Programme*: The new thrust areas in ICDS programme includes:
  1. *Gender Equality*: It addresses gender in equalities at different stages of the life cycle through development and learning opportunities.
  2. *Scheme for Adolescent Girls:* For the first time in India, a special intervention has been devised for adolescent girls using

the ICDS infrastructure. The scheme of adolescent girls focuses on school dropout girls in the age group of 11 and 18 years and attempts to meet the special needs of nutrition, education, literacy, recreation and skill development of the adolescent girls. It attempts to make the adolescent girls a better future mother and tap her potential as a social animator. The scheme for adolescent girls has been operationalised, would benefit about 4.50 lakh girls in India.

3. *Community Empowerment*: Through the following comprehensive community based intervention programmes, ICDS addresses the issue of community empowerment.
   - Women's Income Generation Activities;
   - Women's Integrated Learning for Life (WILL);
   - Services for Adolescent Girls;
   - Strengthened Health Component;
   - Experimentation with Nutritional Rehabilitation Centre and therapeutic food;
   - Communication;
   - Intensive Training.

- *Foreign Assistance under ICDS:* Various internal funding agencies have come forward to assist ICDS programme in different ways, such as:
  1. *UNICEF:* It assists the ICDS programme in the sphere of consultancy services, training, certain initial supplies and equipment and in monitoring and research.
  2. *NORAD:* The Norwegian Agency for Development assists includes expenditure on nutrition and for construction of Anganwadis.
  3. *USAID*: It has assisted 11 ICDS projects in Gujurat and 10 in Maharastra.
  4. *SIDA*: The Swedish International Development Agency is assisting 8 ICDS projects in Tamil Nadu.
  5. *WFP:* World Food Programme supplies food to a number of projects.
  6. *CARE:* Co-ordination of Co-operative American Relief Everywhere provides food to several projects.
  7. *World Bank:* The centrally sponsored World Bank assisted project was started in tribal areas of Andhra Pradesh in 1990-91 and still continuing.

Early Childhood Education (ECE) Initiatives

The provision of centre based early childhood education in India is available through three distinct channels – *(i)* public; *(ii)* private; and *(iii)* non-governmental.

1. *Public Initiatives:* Public, government sponsored programmes are largely directed towards the disadvantaged community, particularly those residing in rural and marginalised areas. Though a number of programmes are being implemented by various departments and ministries, the more important, on which the attention is required to be focussed in XI Five-year Plan are as under.
2. *Voluntary and Corporate Initiatives:* The ECE services, being provided by voluntary or non-governmental organizations with financial assistance of national and international aid agencies, trusts, denominational and parochial groups, also play a marginal role especially in socially and economic backward areas, special communities in difficult circumstances like: tribal people, migrant labourers and for children affected by natural calamities of specific contexts like: flood, earthquake etc. The various integrated services under these NGOs run initiatives are either being provided in the name of crèches or in the name of ECE centres. Some NGO s also run mobile crèches, which move along with the construction labour from one site to another. In addition to these, some Universities also have Laboratory Nursery Schools attached to them, particularly to Departments of Child Development like in M.S. University, Vadodara in Gujarat state of India.

NATIONAL AND INTERNATIONAL AGENCIES AND FUNCTIONARIES OF CHILD WELFARE AND DEVELOPMENT IN INDIA

There are national and international agencies and functionaries working for the child welfare and development in India, whose works are very encouraging and praise worthy. They are being discussed as follows:

National Agencies and Functionaries

Today all the programmes adopted by the Government of India and non-Governmental agencies have centred around child survival, development and welfare reflecting the ideas as stated in the UN convention on the right of the child, which further lead to the formulation of National Children's Policy and the National Plan of action for child development, 1992. The emphasis on child development by the government of India lead to the development of two ministries – *(i)* Ministry of Human Resource Development (with Department of Women and Child Development) and *(ii)* Ministry of Welfare – who are responsible for the implementation of the several policies on children. These two ministries with the support of several other ministries or department are working to bring about overall development of children. The matters regarding child survival, protection, growth, development and welfare are distributed among various ministries/departments/autonomous bodies. These functionaries are indicated below:

1. *National Children's Board*: As a result of National Policy for Children (1974), National Children Board was constituted to provide focus on the implementation of various programmes for the health, nutrition, education and welfare services for the children. It also aim to ensure at different level continuous planning, review and co-ordination of all the essential services, concerning children. The Prime Minster of India is the Chairman of the Board. Similar State boards are also constituted in all the state of India.
2. *Ministry of Human Resource Development*: Under this ministry, Department of Women and Child Development is responsible for all the welfare and developmental programmes concerning children, with its auxiliary organizations:
   (a) National Children Policy;
   (b) Care of Pre-school Child – which is mostly carried out by the following programmes – Integrated child Development Services (ICDS); Balwadies, Crèches, early childhood education's, Nutrition of mother and children, training of child care functionaries;
   (c) Child Welfare and Care funding;
   (d) Food and Nutrition Board;
   (e) United Nations International Children Emergency Fund (UNICEF), Council of Social Welfare Board, (CSWB), National Institute for Public Co-operation and Child development (NIPCCD);
3. *Ministry of Welfare:* This ministry is responsible for all welfare services for children such as: orphans, destitute and those

children in difficult circumstances, street children, physically and mentally handicapped children, juvenile delinquents, children of scheduled caste and tribes and other backward class.

4. *Ministry of Education:* This ministry is responsible for the primary and elementary school education, Bal Bhawans, National Book Trusts, United Nations Educational and Scientific Co-operation (UNESCO) and National Council of Educational Research and Training (NCERT).
5. *Ministry of Health and Family Welfare*: This ministry is responsible for family welfare programmes, maternal and child health (MCH) programmes, rural health services, health and population policy along with the work of world health organization (WHO) and National Institute of Health and Family Welfare (NIHFW).
6. *Ministry of Rural Development:* This ministry looks after the work of Rural sanitation and water supply; Development of Women and Children in Rural Areas (DWACRA); Anti-poverty and rural employment programmes, TRYSEM along with the investigation of the work of National Institute of Rural Development (NIRI), which are all directly or indirectly responsible for child development and welfare.
7. *Ministry of Home Affairs*: If not directly, this minister is indirectly responsible for the welfare of the children through non-institutional financial assistance to children of families affected by communal riots and national foundation for communal harmony.
8. *Ministry of Information and Board Casting*: This ministry also plays a very significant role in the development and welfare of our children through:
   (a) *All India Radio*: Children's Programmes, Yuva Vani, Educational Programmes, Family Welfare, Farm and Home etc;
   (b) *Door Darshan (Television)*: Educational Programmes, Sports, Information etc;
   (c) Films and Children Film Society of India;
9. *Autonomous Bodies/Institute:* The following autonomous (semi-government) organization handle certain aspects of child welfare and development. These are:

- *Central Social Welfare Board (CSWB):* CSWB established in 1953 continues to promote voluntary action in child welfare. It provides assistance to existing and working voluntary organizations for carrying on a variety of services and programmes for children such as: orphanages, crèches, short-stay homes, cultural/recreational centres and libraries, infant health centres, and child guidance clinic, Balwadis etc.
- *National Institute of Social Defence (NISD)*: This institute is engaged in collection, compilation, dissemination and analysis of social defence information including institutions set-up under the juvenile justice Act, 1986, Under the Ministry of Welfare, Government of India.
- *National Council for Educational Research and Training (NCERT):* The National Council of Educational Research and Training, Sri Aurobindo Marg, New Delhi - 16 is an autonomous organization under the Ministry of Human Resource Development, Government of India. It was established in September 1st, 1961. It is fully financed by the Government of India. NCERT functions as an academic adviser to the Ministry of Education. It formulates the policies and programmes in school education and undertakes the following programmes and actions such as:
  - *(i)* It conducts, aids, promotes and co-ordinates research in all branches of school education.
  - *(ii)* It organizes pre-service and in-service training mainly at an advance level.
  - *(iii)* It develops, improves educational techniques, practices and innovations.
  - *(iv)* It collects, complies and disseminates educational information.
  - *(v)* It collaborates with international organizations like: UNESCO, UNICEF etc.
  - *(vi)* It assists the state level educational institutions and organizations.

NCERT in the Field of Pre-School Education – The NCERT undertakes various programmes in the area of pre-school education. Following are the important programmes in this area:

1. *Children s Media Laboratory (CML):* This Laboratory has been set up with the UNICEF assistance. It undertakes the following activities.
   (*a*) It discovers and develops inexpensive and effective aids of educational value for children in the age group 3 to 8 years;
   (*b*) It gives assistance to State Governments, Departments of Education to set up Early Childhood Education Units;
   (*c*) It develops learning and play materials for pre-school children;
   (*d*) It conducts National and State level toy making competitions;
   (*e*) It has developed many picture books, graphic materials, song books, audio and slide tape programmes on a variety of themes.
2. *Training Courses for Pre-school Teachers:* Many training courses are organized from time to time for pre-school teachers. A great deal of stress is laid on creative drama, puppet play and creative art. The course also aims at acquainting the participants with the trends in child development and their application to early childhood education.
3. *State Level Course for Pre-school Education Supervisors*: Similar courses are conducted for headmasters, supervisors and teacher education educators.
4. *National Seminars on Child Development and Early Childhood*: National level seminars and workshops on the various aspects of Child Development and Early Childhood years are being organized time to time. Educationists, researchers, policy makers, administrators and people interested in child developments participate in it.
5. *Developmental Activities in Community Education and Participation*: Development and testing of educational programmes to meet the minimum educational needs of learners in the age group 3-6, 6-14 and 15-35 years have been taken up in 18 States and Union Territories.
6. *Publications*: NCERT has brought out three publications on pre-school education namely: Early Childhood Care and Education Programme, Stimulation Activities for the Young Child, and Child to Child.

7. *Training Film*: A training film (still video) on the training of Anganwadi Workers in ECCE has been developed.
8. *Early Childhood Education Programme in Nursery Schools of Delhi*: The NCERT had been engaged in the implementation of the Early Childhood Education (ECE) programme in some of the schools with nursery/pre-primary sections run by the Municipal Corporation of Delhi.
9. *Home-based programme in Child Development*: A home-based instructional package was developed to promote awareness among parents about their role as potential educators and to develop the necessary skill in them. The instructional package covered the areas of health, nutrition and education of children.
10. *Early Childhood Education (ECE) Project*: The NCERT has strengthened the early childhood education units under the UNICEF assisted project of ECE, operating in 10 States.
11. *Evaluation Studies*: NCERT has undertaken a number of studies on pre-primary education, its enrolment and retention in primary grades in relation to pre-school experience in the sate participating in the ECE project.

- *National Institute of Public Co-operation and Child Development (NIPCCD)*: The National Institute of Public Co-operation and Child Development is an autonomous organization under the administrative charge of the Department of Women and Child Development, Ministry of Human Resource Development, Government of India. It functions in its own building at 5, Siri Institutional Area, Hauz Khas, New Delhi. The institute has three regional Centres at Bangalore, Guwahati and Lucknow. The main functions of the Institute are:
  - *(i)* Research and evaluation studies in public co-operation and child development.
  - *(ii)* Training of Government and voluntary sector personnel engaged in social development, child development and allied activities.
  - *(iii)* Dissemination of information pertaining to child development and public co-operation through documentation and publications.
  - *(iv)* Technical advice, consultancy to Central and State Governments and other agencies in promotion and

implementation of policies and programmes for child development and voluntary action.

(v) Liaison with international and regional agencies, research institutions, Universities and technical bodies engaged in activities similar to those of the institute.

The Institution functions under the overall executive control of the director. He is the head of both academic programmes as well as administration. The activities of the Institute are divided in five broad divisions; each headed by a Deputy Director:

1. Public Co-operation Division.
2. Child Development Division.
3. Training Division.
4. Monitoring and Evaluation Division.
5. Common Services Division.

The Institute has three Regional Centres located at Guwahati, Bangalore and Lucknow. The primary responsibility of each of the centre is to provide training, research, documentation and consultancy services to State Governments and voluntary organizations in areas falling within its specified jurisdiction.

- *Bal Bhawan Society:* Bal Bhawan aims at providing a number of recreational and cultural activities for normal children, in a single through composite and comprehensive organizations. Bombay was the first state to set up a Bal Bhawan.

Digboi, Rajkot, Chandigarh and Delhi followed. A Bal Bhawan is a centre, where there is an atmosphere of freedom, cultural-rooted set up and understanding teachers that support our children to help themselves to grow to their full structure. Where a child can utilise his leisure time in a purposeful and constructive manner, so as to help the development of a harmonious personality. Bal Bhawan also has some nursery school during the daytime and a child guidance clinic to help those children having maladjustment and behavioural problems. Bal Bhawan to some extent fulfils the needs unfulfilled by the family and the school.

- *Rehabilitation Council of India*: Rehabilitation council of India was set up in 1986. It is responsible for:
  - ➢ providing training and developing policies and programmes for the disabled persons;
  - ➢ to standardise the training courses for professionals dealing with disabled persons;

- to grant recognition to the institutions running the training courses for the disabled children and individuals;
- to maintain a central rehabilitation register of the rehabilitation professionals;

- *Save our Soul (SOS) Children's Village of India, New Delhi*: The SOS village movement began in India in 1963 when Prof. Gmeiner visited the then Prime Minister Pt. Jawaharlal Nehru. In 1964, SOS Children s village Association was formed and in 1967, the first village Greenfield was founded near Faridabad, Haryana. It has registered societies in 13 states. It is concerned with long-term care and rehabilitation of orphan and destitute children. It is housed in Children s village complexes in family type homes or single unit family homes. SOS has now constructed 21 children's villages. The pilot project at Greenfield has started a family helper programme for disadvantaged children in nearby villages. It has started Balwadis, Medical services centre and education for 250 quarry worker's children. The SOS also runs a foundling home, Udayan in New Delhi. The construction of the SOS Children's village was started in March 1967. Twenty family cottages have been constructed at Greenfield. The 21 Children's Villages in India look after 5,700 Indian Children. Pedagogical Principles behind SOS Children's Village:

1. In Children's village mother takes the role of real mother.
2. The child grows up with 'brothers' and 'sisters' as real brothers and sister.
3. An atmosphere full of warmth is created in the village.
4. Children attend community schools. They grow up under normal family conditions.
5. Children learn to work and play together. They follow rules in playing games and make new friends.
6. It has all the things found in conventional kindergarten schools – Photograph records, educational toys, puzzles, puppets, filmstrips, bulletin boards and blackboards.
7. Mothers are provided with materials to be used by the child every week.
8. In this programme, one teacher can cover as much population as is covered by seven in traditional teaching.
9. About one lakh youngsters are being benefited by this programme.

- *Indian Council for Child Welfare (ICCW)*: It was founded in 1952 and has branches in every state. It has been a major organization for policy planning, child welfare, and training. The primary responsibility of each of the centre is to provide training, research, documentation and consultancy services to State Governments and voluntary organizations in areas falling within its specified jurisdiction. It covers Balsevikas, Work related to adaptations, integration camps, national awards to children for courage. The state councils undertake various activities relating to child welfare. This is affiliated to the International Union for Child Welfare, Geneva. The main aims of the ICCW are to:
  - ➢ Initiate, undertake or aid directly or through its branches or affiliated bodies schemes for furtherance of child welfare in India.
  - ➢ Promote dissemination of knowledge and information and to educate public opinion for child welfare programmes on scientific basis.
  - ➢ Establish a Central Bureau for the study and collection of data and statistics in respect of child welfare work;
  - ➢ Co-operate with National and International Organizations having similar objectives and to depute or receive representatives to and from such organization;
  - ➢ Publish studies, treatise, books, periodicals, reports and other literature relating to Child Welfare.
- *National Trust for Mentally Retarded*: This institute is an apex level organizations in the field of education, training, vocational guidance, counselling, research, rehabilitation and develop suitable service modules for the mentally retarded children. This institute also solves as premier documentation and information centres. It also provides opportunities for skill development and loan assistance on easy terms to the disabled persons to set up self-employment ventures.
- *National Institute of Health and Family Welfare (NIHFW)*: The National Family Welfare Programme was launched in India in 1951 with the objective of reducing the birth rate to the extent necessary to stabilise the population at a level consistent with the requirement of the National Economy (First Five-year Plan). This implemented through the state

Governments with hundred per cent central assistance. In rural areas services are provided through the network of sub-centres, primary health centres, community health services. Both directly and indirectly, these services are for the welfare of the children of this country.

- *National Centre of Films for Children and Young People*: The National Centre of Films for Children and Young People (N CYP), formally known as the Children s Film Society, India (CFSI) was established in May 1955. The prime objectives were – production, acquisition, distribution, exhibition of films, especially made for children and the promotion of Children's Film Movement. Since April 1992, the scope of the activities of the organization has been widened to include 'young people' along with children, leading to a change in the name of the organization. Since its inception, N CYP has produced and acquired more than 249 feature, short animation and puppet films. The organization continues to distribute and exhibit its films through normal theatre programmes and through National T.V. Network. To overcome the difficulties in theatre exhibition and to carry children cinema to the mofussli area, N CYP has over the years, been organizing festivals (District-wise capsule programmes) of its films at district levels, each consisting of 8 to 10 films lasting about a week, in collaboration with local authorities and welfare organizations.
- *Indian Association for Pre-school Education (IAPE)*: In 1964 small group of people interested in Pre-school education formed the IAPE. This association started gaining momentum by including all those were interested in pre-school education in different parts of the country to take its membership. Objectives of IAPE are as follows:
  - The prime aim of IAPE is to bring together all the workers who are involved in promoting pre-school education.
  - To disseminate the new concept and innovation in child development and pre-school education.
  - To undertake projects related to pre-school education and child development.
  - To be a forum for discussing and debating on the different issues in pre-school education.

- ➤ To organize seminars, workshops and conferences on different themes of pre-school education, care and development for the teachers, experts in the field, educators and for the public.

IAPE as well as state branches throughout the country carry out these activities. Thus, association of IAPE is mainly focussing on the education of growing children so as to promote human development.

- *National Children's Fund (NCF)*: The Government if India, Ministry of Social Welfare in the International Year of the Child created the national Children s Fund, vide notification no, S.O. 120 (E) dated 2nd March 1979. The main aim is to augment resources from the community and utilising the interest thereof for assistance to voluntary organization. These agencies engaged in the child welfare/development for undertaking innovative projects specially designed to meet the needs of the children of poor families in backward areas, particularly in SC and ST sections. The objectives of assistance from the National Children's Fund are:
  - ➤ Ensure flexibility, experimentation and innovation in child welfare/development programmes of direct benefits to the children.
  - ➤ Priority to be given to the projects for the welfare of children belonging to schedule cast and schedule tribe and other backward classes.
  - ➤ Avoid duplication of efforts in the same area.
  - ➤ Priority should be given to the programme for the children of pre-schoolage, rehabilitation of destitute and working children.
  - ➤ Raise funds for welfare of children from the community and non-governmental sources.

Role of International Agencies in Child Welfare and Development in India

Realising the importance of human race in development, a large number of International agencies are engaged to bring about social development throughout the globe by doing child welfare and developmental programmes.

- *United Nations*: The United Nations adopted the Declaration of the Rights of the Child on 20th November 1959. The declaration on state that all children should have certain rights including the right to have affection, love and understanding and free education. Moreover, UN agencies encourage governments to include programmes for children in their countries to exchange ideas, train specialities and set up community services for children.
- *United Nations Educational, Scientific and Cultural Organization (UNESCO)*: It is concerned more with better education for children. Moreover, it aims at promoting peace and security in the world through collaboration among nations with regards to education, science and culture. It provides assistance to develop text-books and teaching of national languages to the children of migrant workers, training of staff for pre-school children and assists projects to set up production of children's books and libraries. A National Commission for Co-operation with UNESCO is working as a part of Ministry of Human Resource Development, Government of India.
- *United Nations Children's Fund (UNICEF)*: India has been associated with UNICEF since 1949. India has also progressively increased its contribution to UNICEF. There is a UNICEF Regional Office at New Delhi and branch offices in different states. UNICEF has been assisting India in programmes like Integrated Child Development Services (ICDS), Urban Basic Services, nutrition etc. UNICEF has helped India in the setting up of Children's Media Laboratory (CML) in NCERT. Following are the important projects implemented in India with UNICEF assistance:
  1. Nutrition, Health Education and Environmental Sanitation (NHEES).
  2. Primary Education Curriculum Renewal (PECR).
  3. Developmental Activities in Community Education and Participation (DACEP).
  4. Children's Media Laboratory (CML).
  5. Early Childhood Education (CEC).
  6. Comprehensive Access to Primary Education (CAPE).
  7. Integrated Child Development Services (ICDS).

8. Assistance to Child Development Wing of the National Institute of Public Co-operation and Child Development.

- *Food and Agricultural Organization (FAO)*: It aimed at developing rural families with particular reference to women and children by helping people to fight against hunger and malnutrition through programmes as for CAPART and World Food Programme. FAO's prime function is to increase production of foods to keep pace with the ever-growing world population. The most important aspects of FAO's work is towards ensuring that the food is consumed who need it in sufficient quantity and right proportion to develop and to maintain a better state of nutrition throughout the world. In this context the FAO has organized a World Freedom from Hunger Campaign in 1960. The main goals are to combat malnutrition and to disseminate education and information.

The FAO is also collaborating with other international agencies in the applied nutritional programmes. The joint FAO and WHO Committee provide the basis for many co-operative activities such as: nutritional surveys, seminars, training camps, and co-ordination of research programmes on certain diseases.

- *World Health Organization (WHO)*: It has its main target 'Health for all by 2000'. It aims to improve the health of children, particularly through Primary Health Care. WHO has assisted India in establishing Primary Health Centre and sub-centres in rural areas.
- *International Labour Organization (ILO)*: It has been concerned with questions relating to Children and youth since 1919. It assists states for prevention, treatment and rehabilitation of working children through child welfare programmes, social security measures and anti-child labour measures.
- *Co-operative for American Relief Everywhere (CARE)*: It is important Programme which provides the following services:
  - supplementary Feeding Programmes, especially to the weaker sections of the students in the schools. As a part of this activity in India, it provides daily food to about 55 lakhs pre-school children and pregnant women. It also provides daily food to about one-crore school children in the pre-schools in 15 states under special nutrition and mid-day meal programmes of Government of India;

- assists in the construction of Balwadis;
- it supplies classroom kits;
- it assists in ICDS projects in few states.

There are other international agencies contributing to child development in India. However, the efforts of the International bodies are only supplementary to the National effort.

FUTURE ROAD MAP FOR DEVELOPING YOUNG CHILDREN IN INDIA

The National ECCE Policy visualizes achieving holistic development and active learning capacity of all children below six years of age by promoting free, universal, inclusive, equitable, joyful and contextualised opportunities for laying foundation and attaining full potential. On a similar vein 'The vision of Indian Child' reflects our beliefs about children and childhood and what is possible and desirable for human life at the individual and societal levels. This curriculum \ framework supports the creation of a shared image of the Indian child that can guide our efforts to promote early learning at the Local, State and National levels.

"It views children as happy, healthy and confident; as persons with unique identity, grounded in their individual strengths and capacities; and with respect for their unique social, linguistic, and cultural heritage and diversity".

As children grow and learn, they explore, enquire, make discoveries and apply their understanding to become self-regulated lifelong learners. Furthermore they are sensitive to diversity, are communicative, caring and creative in their relationship with people and environment. The Ministry of Women and Child Development (MWCD) is the nodal Ministry for overseeing and co-ordinating the implementation of Child Policy in India. A National Coordination and Action Group (NCAG) for Children under the Minister in charge of the Ministry of Women and Child Development will monitor the progress with the concerned Ministries as its members. Similar Coordination and Actions Groups will be formed at the State and District level. The Ministry of Women and Child Development, in consultation with all related Ministries and Departments, is formulating a National Plan of Action for Children. Similar Plans at the State, District and local level will be formulated to ensure action on the provisions of this Policy. The National, State and District Co-ordination and Action Groups will monitor the progress of implementation under these Plans. The National Commission for Protection of Child Rights and State Commissions for Protection of Child Rights will ensure that the principles of this Policy are respected in all sectors at all levels in formulating laws, policies and programmes affecting children.

SUMMARY OF CHAPTER

Meaning of Child Welfare

- Children are the most vulnerable and valuable resources of a country that have the right to demand for care, protection, support and development.
- Child welfare covers the entire spectrum of services for children in need of help and care.
- Child welfare programmes thus seek to provide direct care and supportive services to the families of these children because one of the important responsibilities of the community and state is to assist the family in its natural obligations for the welfare of the children.
- Child welfare services are provided in various facets as direct care giving, nurturance, supportive, preventive, and rehabilitative in nature.

History of Child Welfare and Development Programmes in India

- Earlier, Care of the child was the responsibility of the extended family in its own 'socio-cultural niche'.
- In the pre-independence period, child welfare services were in the nature of providing institutional services to the orphans, destitute, poor and the disable children.
- It was only after independence when the constitution was enacted that the responsibility of social welfare was taken over by the government.
- The constitution of India proclaimed that the state shall in particular, direct its policy towards ensuring that children of tender age are not abused, childhood and youth are protected against moral and material abandonment.
- Child welfare received its major focus, as an integral part of the development process in India from the Fourth Five-year Plan.
- During the Fifth Five-year Plan, along with the launching of Integrated Child Development Service (ICDS), several other services related to child welfare began.

Concept of Early Child Care and Development (ECCD) in India

- "Early Childhood Care and Education (ECCE) is an indispensable foundation for life-long learning and development, and have critical impact on the success at the primary stage of education.
- Early Childhood Care and Development refers not only to what is happening within the child, but also to the care the child requires in order to thrive, grow and develop to its maximum extent in normal as well as in difficult circumstances of life.
- ECCD is seen as a lifetime programme of continuous learning and experience from birth through adolescence for children.

Need for Child Welfare Programmes and Policies

- Need for child welfare programmes and policies in India are great.
- Influence of modernisation and industrialisation, has resulted in degeneration of family systems.
- Social and economic changes have eroded the quality of childcare leading to the increase of social problems like: destitution, delinquency and vagrancy.

Provisions and Policies for Child Care and Development in India

- Constitutional Provisions and Legislation has been the first step in taking Care of Children by the State and the Country.
- The National Policy for Children 1974 and subsequently 2013 is intended to serve as a guide to the official and non-official agencies alike with regard to the direction in which they should move for achieving full and integrated development of our children, which constitute the most valuable assets for our country.

Existing Child Welfare Services and Programmes

- Seventh Five-year Plan laid stress on expansion of schemes such as: services for children in need of care and protection; and crèches for the children of working/ailing mothers.
- Development through programmes in different sectors, important among these being ICDS, universal immunisation, maternal and child care services, nutrition, pre-school education, protected drinking water, environmental

sanitation and hygiene, and family planning.

- Pre-school education centres were supported in the educationally backward states through grant to voluntary organizations and then both NGOs and Government organizations and agencies started working together for the welfare of these young children.
- Integrated Child Development Services (ICDS) is a unique, comprehensive and largest childcare intervention programme in India to improve the nutritional health status of children below six years of age.

National and International Agencies and Functionaries of Child Welfare and Development in India

- The emphasis of child development by the Government of India leads to the development of two ministries such as: Ministry of Human Resource Development with the Department of Women and Child Development and Ministry of Welfare.
- Apart from these, other government departments, ministries and autonomous bodies are also involved in the matters regarding child survival, protection, growth, development and welfare of the children in our country.
- These functionaries are – National Children s Board, Food and Nutrition Board, National Council of Educational Research and Training (NCERT), Central Social Welfare Board, National Institute of Social Defence, National Institute of Public Co-operation and Child Development (NIPCCD), Save our Soul (SOS) children's village, Indian Council for Child Welfare (ICCW), United Nations, UNICEF, WHO, FAO, ILO, and CARE.

Future Road Map for Development and Welfare of Young Children in India

- Every child is taken care of in its own 'socio-cultural niche', but the settings have changed now due to the impact of globalization.
- The National ECCE Policy has been visualized as the Future Road Map for bringing Development among young Children in India in more sustainable meaner.
- The Ministry of Women and Child Development (MWCD) is the nodal Ministry for overseeing and coordinating the implementation of Child Policy in India.

References

Aggarwal, J.C., (2000), History and Philosophy of Pre-Primary and Nursery Education, Doaba House: Delhi.

Arya, S.C. (1972), Infant and Childcare. Vikas Publishing House Pvt. Ltd., New Delhi.

Begum, R. (1995). A Text-book of Food, Nutrition, Dietetics. Sterling Publishers Pvt. New Delhi.

Bhalla, M.M. (1985), Studies in Child Care, National Institute of Public Co-operation and Child Development: New Delhi.

Bronfenbrenner, V. (1979), The Ecology of Human Development, Cambridge M.A. Harvard University Press.

Brookman, B. (1998), Parent to Parent: A Model for Parent Support and Information. Topics in Early Childhood Special Education, 8(2): 88-93.

Brophy, J. (1997), Child Development and Socialization. Science Research Associates, Inc: Chicago.

Brubaker, T. (Ed.) (1993), Family Relations: Challenges for the Future, Newbury Park, CA: Sage.

Cataldo, C. (1987), Parent Education for Early Childhood. College Press: New York.

Central Technical Committee (CTC), ICDS (1994), Monitoring, Motivation, Continuing Education Evaluation Research and Training in ICDS, Department of Women and Child Development, Ministry of Human Resource Development, Government of India: New Delhi.

Cochran, M. (1988), Parental Empowerment in Family Matters: Lessons Learned from a Research Programme. In D. Powell (Ed.), Parent Education as Early Childhood Intervention, Norwood, NJ: Alex.

Cochran, M., and Dean, C. (1991), Home-school Relations and the Empowerment Process. *Elementary School Journal*, 91(3): 261-270.

Cohen, D. J. (1975), Serving Pre-school Children. U.S. Department of Health, Education and Welfare of office of Human Development.

Daccy, J.S. (1996), Human Development – Across Life Span. Brown and Benchmark: London.

Dasgupta, M.A. (1999), Low Cost, No Cost Teaching Aids. National Book Trust of India: New Delhi.

Davis, D. (1976), Schools where Parents make a Difference. Boston: Institute of Responsive Education.

Devdas, R.P., Jaya, N. and Kamala, S. (1979), Low Cost Equipment for Pre-school Children. Publication of Sri Avinashilingam Home Science College for Women: Coimbatore.

Dunset, C., Trivette, C., and Deal, A. (1988), Enabling and Empowering Families – Principles and Guidelines for Practice. Lexington, M.A: Lexington Books.

Early Childhood Focus Series (2013-14), Published by Bernard van Leer Foundation, The Netherlands.

Early Childhood Matters Series (2013-14). Published by Bernard van Leer Foundation, The Netherlands.

Educational Planning Group (1995), The Future School. Strategies in the Classroom. Exploring Some Strategies and Techniques – Module I, II, III: New Delhi.

Gordeon, I. (1977), Building Effective Home-School Relationships, Boston: Allyn and Bacon.

Grave, M. E. and Walsh, D.J (1998), Studying Children in Context: Theories, Methods and Ethics, Sage Publications: New Delhi.

Hymes, J. (1981), Teaching the Child under six, Columbus, OH: Merrill.

Islam, S.K.U. and Rao, V.K. (Ed.) (1997), Early Childhood Care and Education. Commonwealth Publisher: New Delhi.

Kaul, B. (1991), Early Childhood Education Programme, NCERT: New Delhi.

Kusum, A. (1997), Child Rearing Practices in Tribals. Discovery Publishing House Pvt. Ltd., New Delhi.

Kusum, A. (1997), Creativity and Cognitive Styles in Children. Discovery Publishing House Pvt. Ltd., New Delhi.

Marker, W. (1987), Early Childhood Care and Education: The Challenges. Occasional Paper Number 1, Vernard van Leer Foundation: The Netherlands.

Maslow, A. (1959), New Knowledge in Human Values. New York: Harper and Row.

Meisels, S.J. and Shonkoff, J.P. (Ed.) (1990), Handbook of Early Childhood Interventions. Cambridge University Press: New York.

Ministry of Women and Child Development Government of India. (2013), Early Childhood Care and Education Curriculum Framework: New Delhi.

Ministry of Women and Child Development Government of India (2013), Early Childhood Education in the Eleventh Five-year Plan (2007-12) Working Group on Development of Children – A Report: New Delhi.

Mohanty, J. and Mohanty, B. (1994), Early Childhood Care and Education (ECCE). Deep and Deep Publications: New Delhi.

Muralidharan, R. (1987), Let Preschools Play. CEF Instructional Material Series – 2, NCERT: New Delhi.

Naidu, U.S. and Nakhate, V.S. (1985), Child Development Studies in India. Tata Institute of Social Sciences: TISS Series – 56: Bombay.

National Curriculum Framework: Early Childhood Care and Education. (2013), Ministry of Women and Child Development. Government of India.

National Institute of Public Co-operation and Child Development (1979), Facts of Child Development: New Delhi.

National Institute of Public Co-operation and Child Development (2006), Strong Foundations: Early Childhood Care and Education. Background paper prepared for the Education for All Global Monitoring Report 2007, Select issues concerning ECCE India.

Osborn, K. (1991), Early Childhood Education in Historical Perspective. Attens, GA: Educaton Association.

Paz, R. (1990), Paths to Empowerment – Ten Years of Early Childhood Work in Israel. Bernard van Leer Foundation: The Netherlands.

Rao, D.B. (Ed.) (1997), Care the Child, Vol. (I and II), Discovery Publishing House Pvt. Ltd., New Delhi.

Siddiqui, N., Bhatta, S. and Biswas, S. (2000), Early Childhood Care and Education (ECCE), Doaba House: Delhi.

Singh, B. (1997), Preschool Education, APH Publishing Corporation: New Delhi.

Singh, D. (1995), Child Development: Issues, Policies and Programmes, Vol. - I, II, III, Kanishka Publishers and Distributers: Delhi.

Singh, U. K. and Sudarsan, K.N. (1996), Child Education, Discovery Publishing House: Delhi.

Sreelaxmi, B. (2010), Dietetics, New Age International (P) Ltd Publisher: New Delhi.

Swaminathan, I. (1986), Developing Creativity in Young Children, ECE Instructional Material Series – 7, NCERT: New Delhi.

Swaminathan, M. (1985), Who Cares? A Study of Child Care Facilities for Low Income Working Women in India. Centre for Women's Development Series: New Delhi.

Swaminathan, M. (1991), Play Activities for Young Children. UNICEF Publication: New Delhi.

Swick, K., and Graves, S. (1993), Empowering at-risk Families during the Early Childhood Years. National Education Association: Washington DC.

Swick, K.J. (1993), Strengthening Parents and Families during Early Childhood Years. Stipes Publishing: Illinois.

Thakkar, A. (1987), Significance of Early Childhood Education. ECE Instructional Material Series – 4, NCERT: New Delhi.

UNESCO Principal Regional Office for Asia and the Pacific (1988), The Learning Environments of Early Childhood in Asia. Research Perspectives and Changing Programmes: Bangkok.

UNICEF (1994), The Child and the Law. New Delhi.

UNICEF (1997), The State of the World's Children: New Delhi.

Woodhead, M. (1996), In Search of the Rainbow Pathway to Quality in Large Scale Programmes for Young Disadvantaged Children. Bernard van Leer Foundation: The Netherlands.

Suggested Reading

- Social Welfare.
- Childhood Matters.
- Navantika.
- Childhood Focus.
- ICCW Journals.
- Bernard van Leer Foundation, the Netherlands Study Materials.
- NCERT Study materials.

Index

F

G

❑❑❑